The Cottonwood Tree

The Cottonwood Tree

An American Champion

Kathleen Cain

Johnson Books
BOULDER

Published by Johnson Books, a Big Earth Publishing company,
3005 Center Green Drive, Suite 220, Boulder, Colorado 80301.
E-mail: books@bigearthpublishing.com
www.bigearthpublishing.com
1-800-258-5830

Cover design by Polly Christensen
Cover photo by Cheryl Rankin
Text design and layout by Constance Bollen, cb graphics

9   8   7   6   5   4   3   2   1

Library of Congress Cataloging-in-Publication Data
Cain, Kathleen.
  The cottonwood tree: an American champion / By Kathleen Cain.
    p. cm.
Includes bibliographical references and index.
ISBN 1-55566-370-2

QK495.S16C35 2006
583'.65—dc22

                    2006035455

Printed in the United States of America

This book is dedicated to my father,

Jerome A. Cain,

who first picked up a cottonwood twig

and showed me the "hidden star"

CONTENTS

ACKNOWLEDGMENTS

While a book is ultimately the result of one author's writing, *The Cottonwood Tree* would never have been possible without so many teachers, mentors, and guides through the world of cottonwoods. If I have forgotten anyone, please know it's not intentional.

As always, I offer special thanks to Kim Long of *The American Forecaster* for continued support with writing projects as well as a steady supply of common sense, skepticism, humor, and friendship.

My family and close friends have listened to me blather on about cottonwoods for quite a while now. Many have posed good questions and sent along articles and ideas, and have understood when I couldn't go out and play because I was working: Jerome and Helen Cain (Dad first put me on the "star path"); Dan and Kathy Cain, and family (Dan's persistence in getting a photo of the cottonwood star paid off); Keenan and Peggy Cain, and family; Sean and Dot Cain, and family; Kelly Cain; Marilyn Auer (who helped arm-wrestle chapter 5 to the ground); Sandy Cabana; Marcia Earlenbaugh; John Hodges; Linda Hogan; Eileen Niehouse (with thanks for the back cover shot); Mark Shaw; Karen Shoemaker; Dale White (interlibrary loan librarian extraordinaire); and Lola Wilcox. My neighbors Bill and Jean Mekelburg came to the rescue with their digital camera to take shots of the Blue Corn Woman at the eleventh hour. My neighbor Fran Armstrong always knew when I was working too hard and it was time to go to Starbucks or Dairy Queen.

There is not enough time left in the world to thank Ray Daugherty, chair of the Horticulture and Landscape Technologies Department at Front Range Community College, Westminster Campus, for generously sharing his knowledge and love of cottonwood trees, as well as patience, humor, and all-around good nature; for keeping my science accurate (any mistakes are mine); and for showing me my first cottonwood seedling in the wild!

My friend John Vaske and his daughter Liz let me invade their house on several occasions so I could have a quiet place to write—their dog Jessie offered unconditional love. John scouted out the "Hi Trees," contributed photographs, and contacted people who know and appreciate several important Nebraska cottonwoods. Lorie and Scott Helvie, and Marilyn Giles (Denton Community Historical Society) in Denton, Nebraska, arranged for me to see several trees in their area and shared the stories.

Greg McNamee has always offered encouragement of this and other projects, and has generously shared the use of his excellent cottonwood photos. To see Greg's full cottonwood gallery, visit: http://www.flickr.com/photos/gregorymc namee.

David Martin Perkins (a.k.a. Martin Dickinson) provided technical and moral support during times of crashing computers, missing disks (what "Cottonwood from Floppies" file?), as well as rapier wit, persistent good humor, and an endless supply of friendship.

Christine Meyer, Big Tree Coordinator for the State of Nebraska, answered many questions and helped arrange a visit to the Big Tree Champion Eastern Cottonwood. Susan Hackbart graciously guided me to that tree on two occasions. Other Big Tree coordinators who helped include Suzanne Probart (New Mexico), Pete Smith (Texas), and Neil Bamesberger (Colorado).

Jim McMahon and Jeff Bradybaugh promptly and generously shared information about the Virgin River restoration project in Zion National Park.

Keith Wood, urban and community forester for Colorado State University, taught me how to officially measure a cottonwood tree, and answered many questions and provided referrals to other references and hard-working "tree people," including the Colorado Tree Coalition.

Craig Hillegass, my own city forester (Arvada, Colorado) took time to find and arrange for measuring a Plains Cottonwood and directed me to a fascinating tree I'd have missed otherwise. Mrs. Schaaf kindly allowed us to come and measure her tree.

Pascale Fried, Education and Outreach Coordinator for Boulder County Parks and Open Space, provided a personal tour and history of the Plains Cottonwood Big Tree champion in Boulder County, Colorado.

Kirk Johnson, Chief Curator of the Denver Museum of Nature and Science, helped me understand the ancient history of cottonwoods.

Tim Buchanan, city forester for the City of Fort Collins, Colorado, gave me a firsthand look at a Black Cottonwood champ and a guided tour that taught me how important cottonwoods are to his city.

Suzanne Probart of Tree New Mexico answered many questions and provided resources about cottonwoods in New Mexico. Matthew Schmader, Superintendent of Open Space for the City of Albuquerque, offered his time and expertise, and showed me one of the most beautiful Rio Grande Cottonwoods on the planet.

Nurserywoman Sally Koppenberg gave me a firsthand account of the importance of the Black Cottonwood as a native tree of Alaska.

Oscar Mestas (Texas Forest Service) shared the photograph of the champion Ft. Davis Rio Grande Cottonwood and answered other questions. Pete Smith helped track down the elusive Palmer Cottonwood.

Mike Jeronimus took time out of his busy schedule to teach me about the 'Jeronimus' cultivar at his Box Elder Creek nursery in Lochbuie, Colorado.

Thanks to the many courteous and professional people who answered and forwarded queries about photos, permissions, and all the other logistics of putting a book together.

The poem *What This Means, Being Cottonwood* was first published in *City Kite on a Wire/38 Denver Poets* edited by Ray Gonzalez (Mesilla Press, 1986). It has since been performed as a dramatic reading, a modern dance, and often been reprinted, most recently in *Times of Sorrow, Times of Grace: Writing by Women of the Great Plains/High Plains* edited by Marjorie Saiser, Linda Sandlin, and Greg Kosmicki (Backwaters Press, 2002).

Thanks to Mira Perrizo and Johnson Books/Big Earth Publishing, for the opportunity to write!

What This Means, Being Cottonwood

Stand near the river with your feet
slightly apart. Push your toes down
beyond the mud, below the water.
Stretch arms and head back
deliberately, until straight lines
no longer matter—until the sky
from any angle is your desire.
Let the skin go gray and split open.
If you die a little somewhere
the wind will carve the branches back
      into an alphabet
someone will try to remember
how to read. Stay this way
half a century or more, turning leaves
in the half-note tides of the air.
Inside, with that blood so slow
no one hears it, set buds for spring
by each late October. November,
December, dream what it means
being owl . . . or star.

INTRODUCTION

"Why cottonwoods?"

I stopped counting how many times I heard this question while I worked on *The Cottonwood Tree: An American Champion*. Last summer one of my aunts, an Ursuline nun in Brazil, asked via e-mail how the work was going. My goal at that point was to write three pages a day. She couldn't imagine, she replied, writing more than three pages total about "that old tree."

A friend I have known since second grade—a connection of more than fifty years—whispered with some concern when he got me off to one side at a party: "*But who's going to read a book about cottonwood trees?!*"

After considering whether I should ask him to write a jacket blurb, I said I hoped the same people who bought and read my first book, *Luna: Myth and Mystery*, a book about the moon, would consider one about a tree that could stand as a symbol for American history. My readers would be curious about nature and history. They would love stories filled with amazing detail *and* big-picture patterns. They would be systems-thinkers: people who, while not forgetting the "O" ring if they were designing a new space shuttle, could also visualize the whole ship in a single blink of imagination. They would be daydreamers, people unafraid of quiet and who sometimes prefer the company of trees, who cherish trees. More specifically, people who love cottonwoods, though they may not know there are different *kinds* of cottonwoods. People who love the country in which cotton-woods grow. Two of the better-known species travel through more than two dozen latitudes and nearly as many longitudes. Cottonwoods follow waterways. They march along the open plains, climb hills and mountains, and walk through valleys. Readers most likely to enjoy this book would also be likely to know or be curious about the riparian side of the natural world, the watercourse habitats over which cottonwoods reign. These are readers whose hearts flutter at the sound of cottonwoods rustling, shaking, talking, whispering, or translating some wind-borne secret of nature.

I grew up near cottonwood trees. Their voices were as ordinary as any in my childhood. You might think that means I took them for granted. I didn't. I *expected* them.

I never tire of their voices, whether mimicking the cool sound of water or urging one to just hush and listen. Trees have always been an important part of the prairie landscape; Nebraska is, after all, the place where Arbor Day was born. My hometown, Lincoln, has long prided itself on being an American "Tree City." Residents still grieve about the loss of trees during an ice storm in October 1997. The storm caused millions of dollars in property damage, but I am not sure how you measure the loss to people's hearts and memories. Even on casual drives around the city, someone still points out an amputated cottonwood or a cedar tree cleaved in two, or whole bare blocks where trees once stood.

The favorite local historian can tell you where an old lover's lane was, the same place where the notorious "Officer Louie" (on his bicycle, yet) used to hide behind the trees and trap speeders. Formerly a dirt road arched with cottonwoods, it's now a four-lane arterial that runs past the Target store. A few of the cottonwoods remain, graceful towers, though a careful eye has to be kept on them. They drop branches and limbs without warning. Not such a problem when they lived in the country, but since the town started absorbing the countryside, the trees have become potential hazards.

One of Nebraska's early historians, Addison Sheldon, recorded that the first plantings in Lincoln—and in Nebraska—were cottonwoods. Some of the oldest stands could be traced, in his time, to Arbor Day celebrations. It was easy enough to go down to the river—or the creek or the stream—and gather wild saplings. This story repeats itself throughout the state and the western United States. That's how "Buffalo Bill's Cottonwoods" got their start outside North Platte, at the Scouts Rest Ranch. Early citizens of Boulder, Colorado, did the same thing with Plains Cottonwoods. The settlers of Fort Collins, Colorado, took advantage of the abundance of native Lanceleaf saplings—plantings that remain today. In Cheyenne, Wyoming, an early resident counted twelve trees in the whole town, so cottonwood stock was sent in from Nebraska and planted along certain streets.

In July 1885, my great-grandfather Daniel Frawley Cain married Alice Jane Hannagan and promptly put himself, Alice, and his prized mules on the train and headed west. He rode in the freight car with the mules to keep them from breaking their legs. His father, an Irish immigrant who signed an "X" for his name on his last will and testament, encouraged Daniel and another son to venture out to the "garden of the West." In addition to wheat, barley, corn, and oats, Daniel planted cottonwoods down along a draw on one side of his farm, a mile above the Republican River.

I always thought Daniel planted those cottonwoods as part of the Timber Claim Act of 1873, a government incentive to gain another section of land—640 acres—and a way to "prove up" homestead pre-emptions like the one Daniel bought. But my father says no, the timber claim trees were elsewhere on the farm, though in general cottonwood trees were planted for that reason. Then as now, they grew like weeds, easily four to five feet a year. They kept the soil of creek banks in place and prevented erosion. In a largely treeless area, they provided shade and shelter for livestock as well as humans.

My father grew up under Daniel's cottonwoods. He chopped the wood for fuel. Although it didn't make the best firewood, when you didn't have much some was better than none. And chopping wood was more enjoyable than picking up cow pies, even dried ones. My father liked chopping that wood. It split easily and required less muscle than pine or cedar.

When I was old enough, my father took me to the draw where Daniel had planted those cottonwoods. Their descendants still grow there today. Though there was nothing remarkable about that particular stand of trees, it was the second step I took on the path of the hidden star. This is a path of continuity and connection, not just one of family, though certainly that—after all, a hand like mine first planted the trees that are still there more than a hundred years later. That hand planted hope and the future. I, as much as the trees, was part of that hope, part of that future. What could I plant that would possibly last as long?

I have now lived longer in Colorado than I did in my native state. It's given me plenty of time to get to know the local cottonwoods. There's a chatty one in my neighbor's yard that I've gotten well acquainted with during the last fifteen years— I know the tree better than I know the neighbor. Front Range Community College, where I worked for nearly thirty years in Westminster, Colorado, borders an open space where I watched the cottonwoods long enough to see a generation of them grow tall, fall, and rise again. I have learned to keep my "cottonwood eyes" open wide enough to find and follow aging battalions of old venerables marching single-file through the neighborhoods of my town, marking the path of old streams and creek beds.

Trees are the oldest living creatures on earth. Within that group, cottonwoods rank as elders. They have a lot to teach. They are ancient libraries of natural history. Who wouldn't want to know more about them? Why *not* cottonwoods? On another level, I know the comfort they bring in a vast, open space, as they did to Native Americans and European immigrants alike who made their way along trails often marked only by a single tree. And I can understand how the cottonwood tree became not just the convenient center pole for the Sun Dance of many northern Plains tribes but the symbol of an entire cosmology.

During a reading in Denver many years ago, the poet Robert Bly told the audience how ancient Chinese poets encouraged students who wanted to learn about pine trees to go to the trees and ask. I have been going to cottonwood trees all my life, though I only learned to ask within the last few years.

"Have you ever seen the cottonwood star?" my father asked, as we were out walking one day.

The question took me by surprise. No, I told him, I hadn't.

"Here." He stopped and picked up a twig from the ground. He turned it over. He was looking for something. "You have to find one with a sturdy knuckle on it."

That's what the joints that mark each growth spurt on a cottonwood twig look like: the folded, loopy skin of knuckles.

He pulled a tiny silver knife from his pocket. "You have to cut cleanly," he instructed. "No hacking. Not jagged. One cut is best."

He sliced through the center of the most promising wooden knuckle, his physician's hand steady from long years of practice and patience.

"There, now. Look." He turned the twig so I could gaze directly into its center. The cut, running crosswise through the middle of the small piece of wood, revealed a reddish-brown and nearly perfect five-pointed star.

The rest is history, too. I have spent the last couple of years learning as much about the life and times of the cottonwood tree—cottonwood trees, to be exact—as I can. It's an ongoing lesson. I am lucky to have met so many guides along the way, people you will meet throughout the book. The path of the hidden star stretches out into the future of every cottonwood branch. It is pure hope, as each tree pushes itself forward, through the life-giving pith in the shape of a star. Nature has a great sense of irony as well as a highly developed sense of interior design. And even though the star has its practical purpose, it has its magic, too. Through it we can relate, as Native Americans did, to the lesson of "as above, so below": star inside the tree, star in the sky. Nature's way teaches us the connections and how to find them. For if the star stretches toward the future, it also directs us back to the places we have come from, through our own history, and back beyond that to the geological time that is so hard to imagine, but where the trees, cottonwoods early among them, were already standing up and talking, waiting for us to arrive. I invite you to join me on the star path.

So, why cottonwoods? Well, lean in a little closer and let me tell you. And, by the way, do *you* know about the cottonwood star?

1

MEETING THE COTTONWOODS

Have you ever attended a family reunion, thinking ahead of time that you'd probably know most of the people there, only to find aunts, uncles, and cousins galore, some you've never heard of? And while faces and voices seemed familiar, you had no idea there were so many? You recognized your grandmother's dark eyes and quiet smile on more than a few faces, but where did that sudden shock of red hair come from? And how is it that cousins in different branches of the family have that same chatty way about them?

When it comes to understanding family connections among cottonwoods, we think of trees we've known: the cottonwood that sheltered our grandparents' farmhouse; one that lined the banks of a creek where we fished or played; these days maybe a tree in a park or open space; or one that follows a river, a swamp, or a mountain valley—even in the desert—somewhere in the vast spaces of our country. We don't make many distinctions. We think, "oh, cottonwood," whether we're in Vermont, Arizona, or Alaska. We often assume we're all talking about the same tree.

Cottonwood Genealogy

Cottonwood genealogy is more complicated—and since it dates at least to the Miocene Epoch, about 24 million years ago (mya), more distinguished. The system that describes plant genealogy reveals a masterpiece of heritage and descent. No wonder Carolus von Linnaeus, the Swedish botanist who in the 1700s developed the system of names (nomenclature) we still use today, went mad toward the end of his life! His system of classification, just counting flower parts, was replaced by the "kingdom system" about 150 years after he died.

Here's the current pedigree for the Plains Cottonwood, as described by the
United States Department of Agriculture (USDA), from the largest division,
Kingdom, to the smallest, Subspecies:

Kingdom	Plantae =	Plants
Subkingdom	Tracheobiota =	Vascular Plants
Superdivision	Spermatophyta =	Seed Plants
Division	Magnoliophyta =	Flowering Plants
Class	Dilleniidae =	Unique tissue
Order	Salicales =	Willow
Family	Salicaceae =	Willow
Genus	*Populus* L.(innaeus) =	Cottonwood
Species	*Populus deltoides*	
	Bart. ex Marsh. =	Eastern Cottonwood
Subspecies	*Populus deltoides*	
	Bart. ex Marsh. subsp.	
	monilifera (Ait.)	
	Eckenwalder =	Plains Cottonwood

(abbreviated, non-italicized surnames represent botanists)

In other words, the Plains Cottonwood is not just a plant but a vascular plant (it has
plumbing). It also has seeds, flowers, and is dicotyledonous—when the seed
germinates it produces two seed leaves before the root and shoot develop.

The Dilleniidae are a group of plants within the dicots that share certain anatom-
ical traits. If they were animals, the Dilleniidae would have vertebrae, or backbones.

Our Plains Cottonwood belongs to a larger—and some think more distinguished—group, the order and family of willows, that also includes aspens,
cottonwoods, and poplars. Cottonwoods follow the family line into the genus of the
poplars. *All cottonwoods are poplars, though not all poplars are cottonwoods*—
as all bugs are insects but not all insects are bugs. Current botanical practice, following a standard established by the USDA, says the Eastern Cottonwood is the species to
which the Plains Cottonwood belongs. The Plains is a subspecies; not exactly standing
alone at the family reunion, but certainly unique enough to be picked out of a crowd!

Like human families, plant families share certain traits that make them a
family, even though the individuals can be distinctive. For example, all members
of the big Salicaceae (sal-uh-KAY-see-ay or sal-uh-KAY-shee-ay), or willow,
family love water. Since they first appeared on earth many millions of years ago,

they have favored streamsides and waterways. They shed their leaves each fall and grow new ones each spring, which places them in the ranks of deciduous trees. They can also be described as dioecious; this deliciously long word means "two houses," a way of saying each tree is either male or female. Each gender bears distinct flowers early in the spring before the leaves unfurl (more modern plants have male and female flowers on the same tree). Reflecting their venerable Miocene and Eocene origins, cottonwoods rely on the wind to carry pollen from male trees to the sticky flowers of female trees—the source of all those cottony seeds. This wind-riding habit marks them as an ancient tree, even older than the oaks.

The genus name that identifies all poplars and cottonwoods is *Populus*, the Latin word for poplar. The word "people" comes from this root, and some have suggested that the prolific genus was once common enough to be considered the "people's" tree by the Romans. Poplars share certain characteristics, too; no red hair or green eyes, but they are all well known for being chatty—a sound caused by the way their leaves move in the wind. That's because their petioles (leaf stalks) are vertically flattened, which allows the leaves to move back and forth independently, in a way that's matchless among trees. This movement creates the familiar chattering sound in the wind. They're fast growers: the fastest-growing hardwood tree in North America. Trunks and branches spread upward. Some species develop into graceful, thin columns or pillars. Others look more like vases at the bottom and big inverted triangles up top. Some species grow round and full above elaborate multiple trunks. Shallow roots travel two or three times beyond the spread of the canopy, persistently searching for water and nutrients. The roots balance the tree and keep it from tipping over, trying to center the weight like Tai Chi masters.

While plants in the same genus share many physical characteristics and habits, ultimately what makes a species distinct is sex—members of a species have the ability to reproduce among themselves. Most experts agree that poplars number about thirty-five species, eight of which are native to North America. "Native" describes plants that were growing here before Columbus arrived. Worldwide, eight of these species can be described as cottonwoods: Black, Eastern, Fremont, Lanceleaf, Narrowleaf, Plains, Rio Grande, and Swamp. All are indigenous to North America. These are the characters you will meet in this book.

The common names reflect a well-known characteristic of the species. Botanically speaking, though, cottonwood naming is tricky. Using Linnaeus's methodical approach, as botanists continue to study and propagate different species, the names change. As anyone who works with trees for a living will tell you, botanical naming is as much an art as a science. Former historical names are called synonyms. Though the USDA has established a current naming protocol for all plants, many other references are still popular, and they often use different names for the same trees. Historical names linger. Local practice dictates the names of cottonwoods in a given area. Many arborists and horticulturists in Colorado refer to the Plains Cottonwood as "Sargent's Cottonwood" or "the Western Cottonwood." Charles S. Sargent (1841–1927) is the noted botanist who first described the species. "Western" identifies the geographic region where the Plains Cottonwood prevails. Plus, it's a whole lot easier than saying the official name, *Populus deltoides* Bart(ram) ex Marsh(all) subsp. *monilifera* (Aiton) Eckenwalder, although some botanists and foresters still call it *Populus sargentii*, an old synonym and the Latin version of "Sargent's Cottonwood." See what I mean? And though *Populus* describes the entire genus, it's used interchangeably for cottonwood. In the section that follows, you'll get to meet each cottonwood individually. I've followed current USDA naming practices but listed the common names most of us are likely to use.

Cottonwood Controversy

When it comes to naming and identification, controversy lingers in the air above cottonwoods. The disagreement, still active though more subdued these days, centers on two of the best known of the bunch. The Eastern Cottonwood started off in life as *Populus deltoides* L.(innaeus) and is currently described by the USDA as *Populus deltoides* Bart.(ram) ex Marsh.(all)—scientists use a shorthand to abbreviate the surnames of botanists who described the species. The Plains Cottonwood, formerly *Populus sargentii*, is now that big mouthful, *Populus deltoides* Bartram ex Marshall subsp. *monilifera* (Aiton) Eckenwalder. Notice that "deltoides" appears in both names and that the abbreviation subsp. (subspecies) appears in the second description.

The use of "deltoides" is a scientific way of saying that the Eastern and the Plains Cottonwood are a single species; that the Plains variety shows differences determined only by geography, making it a subspecies rather than a separate species. And though a standard official source (USDA) says so, that doesn't mean that all those involved with trees agree. So, how can ordinary observers learn to tell the difference between an Eastern and a Plains Cottonwood?

Geography does help. Eastern Cottonwoods are native trees east of the Missouri River, Plains Cottonwoods to the west—generally speaking. Different geographies create different growing conditions. More rainfall east of the

Missouri allows cottonwoods to grow taller. Many sources record average heights of 50–75 feet. Others say 75–100 feet, though this upper limit is often surpassed. In upstate Vermont, for instance, three Eastern Cottonwoods of more than 120 feet have recently been reported. According to the National Register of Big Trees, the national champion Eastern Cottonwood in Nebraska (and west of the Missouri) stands 93 feet tall. Plains Cottonwoods are frequently described— and the description is proven in the field—as stockier, sturdier trees, a physical response to a harsher climate, more direct exposure to wind, and less moisture. They, too, often average 50–75 feet. At its most recent measurement in 2005, though, the national champion Plains Cottonwood in Colorado stood at 95 feet— slightly taller than its Eastern counterpart. Plains Cottonwoods usually prefer elevations between 3,500–6,500 feet. But for every champion standing that tall, thousands more along the waterways top out at 40–60 feet.

What's in a name, Shakespeare asked? Easy for him to say—he didn't have to try and identify cottonwoods! If it's any comfort, even the USDA has documented at least nine different botanical names for the Plains Cottonwood in the last two hundred years. One early lesson about cottonwoods: expect the unexpected when it comes to naming.

However you define them, cottonwoods are native to North America. The poplar genus is found on all continents. The existence of poplars as native species throughout the world provides evidence for the breakup of the single land mass known as Pangaea and evidence that the big willow family has been around longer than most. When the earth's tectonic plates began to shift (as they do still), Pangaea divided, about 200 mya. The land masses drifted apart, creating what we recognize today as the seven continents: Africa, Antarctica, Asia, Australia, Europe, North America, and South America. As the lands split apart, the trees moved with them. Continents drifted. Climates changed. And the trees, respond- ing to the changes, evolved into new species.

Intergradation: Shall We Dance?

In their natural patterns of movement over time, cottonwoods have found their way across the North American continent, overlapping in a process called intergradation. Though that's the technical name for it, think of it as a dance, as elaborate as a tango and ordinary as a waltz. Old native range maps of the U.S. Forest Service and current distribution maps for cottonwoods developed by the USDA make it easy to see how and where intergradation occurs. Space does not exist to reprint the maps here (though you can easily find them online for each species listed in the PLANTS database at: http://plants.usda.gov). But let me draw a word map for you.

Imagine the shape of the continental United States for a moment.

Let your mind's eye wander from the northern coast of Maine (go ahead, venture a little into Canada) to the southern tip of Florida.

Go west. Stop at the Mississippi River.

Now divide the eastern United States in half, along the imaginary line that separates Kentucky from Tennessee and Virginia from North Carolina (OK, go get the atlas...).

In the northern portion of this map, the Eastern Cottonwood (*P. deltoides* Bartr. ex Marsh.) flourishes. In the southern portion, it has traveled all the way west to the Mississippi. It has moved north into Canada and south into Mexico. But below that line marking the northern borders of Kentucky and North Carolina, the Eastern meets and dances—intergrades—with another close relative commonly known as the Swamp Cottonwood, Black Cottonwood, or Swamp Poplar (*P. heterophylla* Linnaeus). The tree thrives in the swamps and marshes from which it takes its common names.

By turning west and traveling to the Mississippi River, we can follow the trail of the Eastern Cottonwood right up to the river bank, go across, and travel until we reach Kansas or Nebraska, or any of the Great Plains states. Somewhere between the 98th and 100th meridians, another change occurs in the cotton-woods, along with geography and altitude. We've crossed the rain line, right about at Salina, Kansas—where the amount of annual rainfall decreases dramatically to less than twenty inches a year. Moisture in a given geography determines what vegetation grows there—or not—and how tall or straight or full it grows. Many species adapt by staying near the ground where they can keep out of the wind and closer to water. They grow sturdier, better able to use whatever moisture comes their way. Eastern cottonwoods prevail east of the rain line. Plains Cottonwoods prefer the west. Yet still the two dance together in the same space. They all doggedly pursue the riparian life along paths of rivers, creeks, streams, even waterholes—as they have done since time out of mind. The Plains even dances closely enough with another species prevalent in the western United States to produce a unique offspring (but more about that later).

Lumpers and Splitters

But back to the one-species-or-two question for a moment. How did it come about? As Colorado horticulturist Ray Daugherty explains, "in botany there are lumpers and splitters." The argument comes down to perspective: lumpers tend to lump everything in the natural world together. They view cottonwoods as part of a continuum stretching across the trees' native range, changing form and habit as geography dictates, ever changing, ever evolving . . . even now. Splitters, on the other hand, after the fashion of Linnaeus, want to understand every species to the utmost detail possible. Now that a genetic evaluation has been made of the Black Cottonwood (*P. trichocarpa*), the day is not far off when every single species can be compared with others and deciphered through its own history. Until then, lumpers and splitters have to rely on the established methods of science: observing, comparing, and testing in order to understand the features of plants and how they behave in their surroundings. For those of us out here on the sidelines who just want to know more about and appreciate cottonwood trees, the debate can get as confusing as it is invigorating.

Let's return to the map and dance of intergradation again, this time passing through the Rocky Mountains and on to the area known as the Great Basin, that region of the United States encompassing parts of Nevada, Utah, California, Oregon, and Idaho where no rivers drain into an ocean, A distinct species has been identified in this area, the Narrowleaf Cottonwood (*P. angustifolia* James). Here, as it does elsewhere, intergradation results in the natural hybridization

---

How to read a botanical name

Here's the botanical name for what's commonly called the Plains Cottonwood:
Populus deltoides Bart. ex Marsh. subsp. *monilifera* (Ait.) Eckenwalder

Populus = genus

deltoides = specific epithet

Bart. ex Marsh. = botanists who described the species; Bartram originally described the species and Marshall sanctioned or validated it.

subsp. (also ssp.) = abbreviation for subspecies

monilifera = subspecies designation

(Ait.) Eckenwalder = Aiton, Eckenwalder, botanists who described the subspecies; Aiton provided the name, Eckenwalder published it.

between species. The Plains Cottonwood—or whatever name you want to give it—and the Narrowleaf Cottonwood hybridize naturally to create the Lanceleaf Cottonwood. Reports exist that the Plains Cottonwood has also crossed with the balsam poplar (*P. balsamifera* L.) and perhaps even a slightly more distant relative, the quaking aspen (*P. tremuloides*). Even more complex hybridization has been reported (Lanceleaf with Lanceleaf, for example), but it's far too detailed to explore here. Suffice it to say that where two species of cottonwood grow together, integration and hybridizations occur. The Fremont Cottonwood (*P. fremontii* S. Wats.) also follows the waterside paths of the Great Basin—in fact, it's *the* cottonwood of Arizona and California, as natural historian Donald Culross Peattie first called it.

The final zone for cottonwoods on this map extends along the West Coast, roughly from the Baja Peninsula to southern Alaska. This is home territory for the Black Cottonwood (*P. trichocarpa*) (not to be confused with *P. heterophylla*, also called Black Cottonwood). *P. trichocarpa*'s river is the Columbia.

So, with some general knowledge of the cottonwood family history behind us, let's meet the cottonwoods individually. Moving from east to west, let's drop in and say hello to the Eastern Cottonwood.

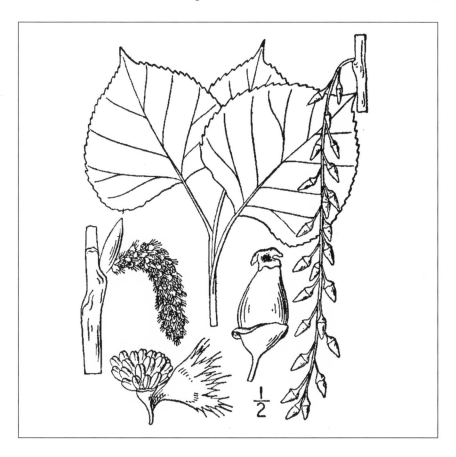

— **Eastern Cottonwood** —

CURRENT BOTANICAL NAME (USDA)
Populus deltoides Bartr. ex Marsh.
Populus deltoides Bartr. ex Marsh. subsp. *deltoides*

(LISTED FOR SUBSP. DELTOIDES)
Populus angulata Ait.
Populus angulata Ait. var. *missouriensis* A. Henry
Populus balsamifera L. var. *missouriensis* (A. Henry) Rehd.

Source: USDA-NRCS PLANTS Database / Britton, N.L., and A. Brown. 1913.
Illustrated flora of the northern states and Canada. Vol. 1: 590.

Populus balsamifera L. var. *pilosa* Sarg.

Populus balsamifera L. var. *virginiana* (Foug.) Sarg.

Populus canadensis Moench var. *virginiana* (Foug.) Fiori

Populus deltoides Bartr. ex Marsh. var. *angulata* (Ait.) Sarg.

Populus deltoides Bartr. ex Marsh. var. *missouriensis* (A. Henry) A. Henry

Populus deltoides Bartr. ex Marsh. var. *pilosa* (Sarg.) Sudworth

Populus deltoides Bartr. ex Marsh. var. *virginiana* (Foug.) Sudworth

Populus nigra L. var. *virginiana* (Foug.) Castigl.

Populus palmeri Sarg.

Populus virginiana Foug.

Populus virginiana Foug. var. *pilosa* (Sarg.) F.C. Gates

IMPORTANT CULTIVARS
'Siouxland' (probably *P. nigra* x *P. angulata*)

P. robusta: selections include "Noreaster, Mighty Mo, Platte, Ohio Red, Lydick, Schictel"

ELEVATION
sea level—6,500 ft.

COMMON NAMES

Álamo (Sp.)	Aspen Cottonwood	Big Cottonwood
Carolina Poplar	Common Cottonwood	Cottontree
Eastern Poplar	Missourian Poplar	Necklace Poplar
Southern Cottonwood	Tennessee Poplar	Vermont Poplar
Virginia Poplar	Water Poplar	Whitewood
Yellow Cottonwood		

Native range maps created by the U.S. Forest Service during the first half of the twentieth century (http://www.na.fs.fed.us/spfo/pubs/silvics_manual/volume_2/vol2_Table_of_contents.htm) show that Eastern Cottonwoods extended south from Quebec and west through the Dakotas, Nebraska, Kansas, Oklahoma, and eastern Texas. Eastward, the range pushes through Ohio, and in its southern portions, through Georgia and the Carolinas. From the lower Great Lakes region, the range moved south through the Ohio, Mississippi, and Missouri river basins. Keep in mind, though, that's the native range.

The current distribution map from the USDA differs slightly from these first native range maps. Indicating a presence, every state is color-coded green except California, Nevada, Idaho, Oregon, and Washington—indicating the tree's natural presence now from Maine to Montana. The new map doesn't show the waterways Eastern Cottonwoods have followed through this part of North America. We don't get to see how the trees have flowed in their own migration, like the waterways themselves, through the Connecticut River Valley up into Vermont, for example. There's no marking on the map to indicate the Ohio River Valley, or those of the Mississippi and Missouri. There's no indication of the way Eastern Cottonwoods have stood along the shores of the Great Lakes, moving north to Lake Ontario and the St. Lawrence River—or of the path of escape from landscape plantings.

This tree was part of the great eastern forests, long familiar to the woodland nations of Native Americans, yet strange to the French and English immigrants who had become more accustomed to gardens than to forests in their own native lands. And though they knew poplars, the new strangers did not know cotton-woods. One species among so many in a view that closed out the sky, the Eastern Cottonwood was just another tree among so many unless it distinguished itself, as the Balmville Tree in New York state did, as we shall learn later. As many social and natural historians have recorded, white European settlers began to pay more attention to the Eastern Cottonwood as travelers pushed out across the conti-nent—passing through what they called "oak openings," which they thought at first were temporary spaces between trees, not realizing the landscape had been transformed from closed-in woodland to wide-open prairie. The open spaces frightened many travelers at first, as they still sometimes do. But explorers, trap-pers, traders, and finally settlers followed the paths of the cottonwoods—water trails. As other trees diminished, the cottonwoods became even more visible, more recognizable as individuals. Those trees described by early settlers were straight-up forest dwellers, often rising 150 feet or more. Today's champion Eastern Cottonwood measures 93 feet. Out on the open prairies the cotton-woods, alone or in stands, became beacon, shelter, mileage sign, emergency lumber yard, social club, cooling-off spot, campground, mailbox, meeting place, and bulletin board. Travelers felt safe and welcome beneath them, at least temporarily, and delighted in the sounds that ranged from once-familiar running water to friendly chatter. The wood was used to build everything from starter cabins to coffins. It made workable fence posts and storage sheds. People made do with what they could find and use. Merchants could even box cigars with the wood and use it to protect a piano being shipped out to Kansas. Cottonwood was put to use in making household items such as trunks, ironing boards, barrel staves, and support poles. There's a chicken coop in east-central Nebraska whose owner complains of the "horrible old wood" it's made from—yet the cottonwood structure is one hundred years old! The wood served light duty, too.

Split, shaved, or ground up, it could be used to make packing crates and excelsior, a primary use even today.

As the eastern forests were left behind, the Eastern Cottonwood became easier to recognize. Settlers dug in and discovered what a fast-growing tree it was, easily gaining four to five feet a year. They couldn't help but notice how, with its massive split trunks and branches, it kept the wind away. With its feet rooted— not so deeply as other trees, but more widely—they saw how it kept the soil on the banks of a creek from eroding. It provided shade and cooled not only humans but water and wildlife. It had its own aesthetic. The branches and limbs spread out into mighty sculptures, giving each tree a special character and personality: craggy and massive to awe-inspiring and stately, the list of adjectives used to describe it is endlessly inventive. The green leaves glistened and waved in the sunlight, chattering both welcome and warning. It changed as the year changed, and signaled each season by turn. Its budding catkins gleamed red or yellow in the early springtime, then green, depending on the tree. As the air warmed and the buds relaxed and opened, it cast a slight aroma through the air—slightly bitter, slightly sweet, as fresh as a new stalk of asparagus. The females let their downy seeds loose in the air, and as early as 1859 housewives were already cursing the "cotton" for the way it clogged window screens. The leaves waxed to a fine sheen in spring and summer, when the tree provided welcome shade and shelter. In the alchemy of fall, the broad, heart-shaped leaves that measure nearly as wide as they do long turned gold little by little, until the whole tree became a shimmering mass of miniature suns. The leaves, often gone by September, dropped earlier than usual if drought conditions grew too severe; twigs, too. By October the tree was bare, a skeleton in which imaginary alphabets could be traced and read all winter long.

On closer examination, those settlers new to the prairies could see, as we can still, how the bark of the Eastern Cottonwood, as it ages, changes from greenish-gray or yellow to the color of wood ash—and like many of the cottonwoods, the Eastern develops deep furrows, ridges, and ruts as it grows from the smooth-skinned texture of youth into middle and old age. The twigs are stout and you wouldn't be wrong if you described them as yellowish-green or gray green. In the summer, when they put on new growth for the following year, the green is unmistakable. Lenticels—little "mouths" that help the tree breathe—appear like whitish-gray polka dots all over the surface of the twigs. The twigs change shape within only a year, becoming less stout and more pointed. Winter buds have been described as plain brown, chestnut brown, or even olive and reddish-brown. They shine with a protective coat of red-dotted resin that makes them look like they've been varnished. Crush them between your fingers and you can detect the slight but unmistakable odor which has sometimes caused the Eastern Cottonwood to be mistaken for balsam poplar (the Balmville Tree caused such confusion). The leaves of the Eastern Cottonwood are usually the largest among any of the cottonwoods, averaging 2–3 inches long and from 3–7 inches wide— though it's not unusual to find leaves double this size. Many sources remark that Eastern leaves are frequently as wide as they are long—or wider. Counting the pointed "teeth" that grow along the edges of the thick, coarse-veined leaves is a good way for amateur naturalists to separate the Eastern from other cottonwoods in regions where different species of the tree grow. Count ten or more, and it's probably an Eastern! Though seldom seen (or even noticed) by nonprofessionals, flowers appear in catkins in early spring (March–April) and can be differentiated by their color. Dangling male catkins show off a deep reddish-purple best described as maroon or carmine. Once fertilized, females light up the still sparse winter sky with a yellowish-green halo, cast by the color of their seed pods, which resemble delicate strings of green beads containing the tufted white seeds, not even as big as this parenthesis:) .

Though technically categorized as a hard wood, the wood is soft and weak. It's not durable, it's hard to season, and it's prone to warp, crack, and split unevenly. It dulls even the sharpest blade, doesn't burn well, and smells like a combination of mildew and vinegar when it's tossed on the fire. For all these reasons it is currently relegated, for commercial purposes, to lesser (but no less essential) needs: boxes, crates, pallets, matches, plywood, lath, pulp, and to line the interiors of furniture. To meet these needs, cottonwood is farmed commercially. In some states, like Nebraska, it is the most manufactured tree. Artisans use it for raw material, since the soft wood is easy to carve. It is still planted as a windbreak and used to control soil erosion. It grows best in soils that are moist and well drained—sandy loams or silt loams. It won't last long in coarse sands or heavy clays. Yet because of its ability to draw certain elements out of the soil, it's currently being planted successfully on land that has been strip-mined and polluted. It helps control erosion, and the same wood can later be used commercially. In its own natural state, dead or alive, it provides habitat for high percentages of insects, birds, and mammals, which also use it for food and shelter. And though the western pioneers have gone, the Eastern Cottonwood remains (it's even considered invasive in some areas of the northeastern United States), as the increased spread of its range on those USDA maps shows.

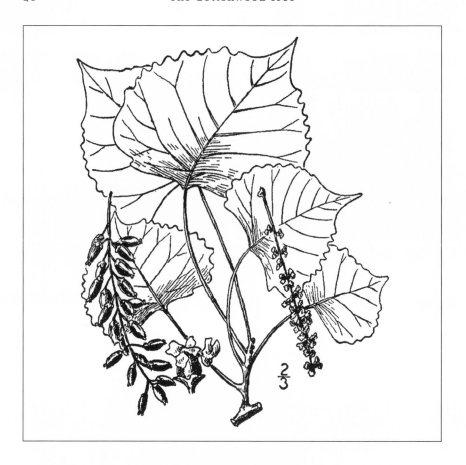

— **Plains Cottonwood** —

CURRENT BOTANICAL NAME (USDA)
Populus deltoides Bartr. ex Marsh. subsp. monilifera (Aiton) Eckenwalder

SYNONYMS
Monilistus monilifera (Ait.) Raf. ex B.D. Jackson
Populus besseyana Dode
Populus deltoides Bartr. ex Marsh. var. occidentalis Rydb.
Populus monilifera Ait.

Source: USDA-NRCS PLANTS Database / Britton, N.L., and A. Brown. 1913.
Illustrated flora of the northern states and Canada. Vol. 1: 591.

Populus occidentalis (Rydb.) Britt. ex Rydb.
Populus sargentii Dode
Populus sargentii Dode var. *texana* (Sarg.) Correll
Populus texana Sarg.

NATURAL HYBRIDS
Populus xacuminata, Populus xandrewsii = *P. acuminate* x *P. sargentii*

IMPORTANT CULTIVARS
'Jeronimus'

ELEVATION
1,000–6,500/7,000 ft.

COMMON NAMES

Fremont Cottonwood	Great Plains Cottonwood	Northern Fremont Cottonwood
Palmer Cottonwood	Plains Poplar	River Cottonwood
River Poplar	Sargent/Sargent's Cottonwood	Sargent/Sargent's Poplar
Sweet Cottonwood	Texas Cottonwood	Western Cottonwood

As we have seen, some "tree people" still argue over whether the Plains Cottonwood is really a separate species. The current protocol followed by the USDA recognizes it as a subspecies of the Eastern. A specialized encyclopedia of trees assigns three geographical subspecies to the Plains Cottonwood. And, as the wise and witty Gary Naughton (in one of the best articles about cottonwood trees you'll ever read) dares to ask: Who cares?! Well, of course those in the thick of the argument care, but for our purposes maybe it's enough to know that there's ongoing discussion. Ironically, the Plains Cottonwood was not recognized as different from other cottonwoods that grow in the Great Plains for many years, but as Ray Daugherty points out, not more than a dozen botanists visited the western United States during most of the eighteenth and nineteenth centuries. Ordinary people who travel or live in the western United States are quick to recognize the craggy, erratic—and unique—Plains Cottonwood.

Though it's not always easy at first glance to distinguish the young Plains Cottonwood from the Eastern, comparing leaves is one way to begin to learn the difference. Both are triangular, as the name "deltoides" implies, a definition we can trace to the Greek letter *delta* (Δ)— although the more romantic among us can easily see a heart shape in the leaf. As you should expect with cottonwoods, sources vary in describing the leaves. They're usually smaller than those of the Eastern. About three inches long and almost as wide, says one. Another stretches leaf length by half an inch and the width half an inch beyond that to 3.5–4 inches. P. A. Rydberg, a botanist whose name is affiliated with the Narrowleaf Cottonwood, offers this point of comparison: the length of the Plains petiole (leaf stalk) is about one-third that of the leaf. Still, environment and moisture can determine size. Tim Buchanan, city forester for Fort Collins, Colorado, talks about the "bell curve" of variation in leaf size and shape on any cottonwood. He searches for the predominant look of each. And, if you want to count teeth on the edges of the leaves, ten or fewer should indicate a Plains Cottonwood. Plains teeth are also more jagged than those of the Eastern, and the bottom edge of a Plains leaf is often so straight you could use it as a ruler if you had to. The Eastern leaf has just that little bit of curve along the bottom. You can easily conduct these three field tests, and use the illustrations above as a guide.

On average, Plains Cottonwoods stand from fifty to seventy-five feet tall—their Eastern relatives tend to stretch a little higher, from seventy-five to one hundred feet. As for looks, think of the Plains Cottonwood as a wrestler—more squat and square—and the Eastern Cottonwood as a pole vaulter—a little leaner, a little taller, and a little straighter. Shape and form can also be determined by whether trees stand alone or in groves. As solitaries, cottonwoods often divide into multiple trunks that spread out as well as up. The Plains variety leans, bends, and stretches into angles that defy verticality in every imaginable way. In groves, trees are forced to stand up straighter among their companions, whether growing among like species or more diverse neighbors in their riparian community: elms, sycamores, and hackberries, to name a few. The western boundary for the Eastern Cottonwood is imprecise because of intergradation, that big tango of species. Nature doesn't maintain a border patrol and create precise boundaries. It's never that simple.

Old native range maps and current distribution maps for the Plains Cottonwood prove the complexity. The native range map illustrates how the indigenous territory of the Plains Cottonwood—from southern Alberta in Canada—widens until it reaches the Missouri River on the east; then the range narrows westward like an arrow pointed at central Texas—after it's crossed through Kansas and Oklahoma. Kansans like to point out the place where Plains Cottonwoods begin to replace Easterns on the landscape, where you can draw a north–south line through Salina. Another way to consider this range is to know that it lies between the 98th and 100th meridians, where the amount of annual rainfall dramatically decreases to less than twenty inches a year. As the species moves west, and from north to south, the Plains Cottonwood follows the river lines on the native range map, particularly throughout Canada, western Montana, and the Dakotas. The current USDA distribution map shows how the Plains subspecies has moved east beyond its native range, crossed the Missouri River, and spread across the upper and central Midwest, moving as far east as Pennsylvania. Things change. Species grow in and out of their native ranges—and are transported and cultivated as well. Cottonwoods now grow in all fifty states. Plains Cottonwoods grow in nineteen of them.

However detailed, though, maps can't replace firsthand physical observation. In addition to differences in shape, height, and the size of leaves, Plains bark is distinguished by its deeply furrowed ridges. Even in a young tree, these ridges can stretch three to four inches across, with furrows big enough to slip your hand into. Seen either from a distance or close up, the bark has a distinct color, more gray than brown (with Easterns more brown than gray). Like the tree itself, Plains Cottonwood twigs are generally stouter. In good designer fashion, Nature gives a slightly orange cast to brown winter buds. In early spring, the male catkins stretch to nearly three inches long and dangle in a profusion of maroonish-brownish-black haze around the tree. One volunteer naturalist describes the catkins' texture as like that of chenille. I see beautiful dark red lanterns hanging on the tree, waiting for spring to light them. The females set out first their pale white flowers that, once fertilized by male pollen, stretch into long strings of green beads (that's what *monilifera* means). These are really seed pods, sometimes measuring up to one half inch long, though I have seen them much smaller, about the size of BBs. Strung together, they stretch from four to eight inches. Although one North Dakota resident writing to a local cottonwood expert described them as "ugly green pouches," the dangling seed pods create a haze of shimmering green air around the trees that sends out an early signal for spring and lets you know that the tree is female.

The Plains Cottonwood is *the* tree of the Great Plains, past and present. For Plains Indians nations and tribes such as the Sioux, Cheyenne, Kiowa, Omaha, Pawnee, Apache, Shoshone, and Arapaho, the tree held a practical as well as a spiritual value. Native Americans often described it (and still do) as one of the "standing peoples" or "talking peoples." You needn't be long upon the Great Plains, whether alone or traveling in a group, to recognize and realize the value of even a single tree. So to find a grove of them, and then another to point the way along a watercourse, was not only a landmark worth treasuring, but for native people a haven and refuge, a place for the band or the tribe to camp. Even today, standing alone in what's left of the prairie sea of grass (long or short), bounded only by horizon and sky, you can still lose your bearings. A lone tree or a grove, presided over by the Plains Cottonwood, provides as welcome a relief as it ever did, offering certain knowledge that you are no longer alone, and the surety that water is nearby—even if you're viewing the trees from a distance, in the safe metal nest of your car as you speed along the interstate.

Native Americans made every practical use of the Plains Cottonwood imaginable, from cradleboards and toys to tipi poles. The cottonwood was—and is still—the sacred tree used in the Sun Dance ceremony. The Sacred Pole of the Omaha people was carved from cottonwood. The wood served as fuel. Leaf buds made a fine yellow dye. Children fashioned make-believe tipis from the leaves. Native Americans taught the early French trappers and traders the use of Plains Cottonwoods, from the medicinal to the everyday. The wooden "pirogues" used by French explorers—and later by Lewis and Clark—were made from hollowed-out cottonwood logs. Early immigrant guides, like the one Josiah Gregg wrote, instructed travelers that they could feed the sweet inner bark of the wood to their horses if need be—one of the early lessons General George Armstrong Custer also learned. European settlers who moved across the western United States in wave after wave used the Plains Cottonwood as they had to, from a temporary fix on a broken wagon wheel to finding simple shade and shelter from the elements out in such unprotected open spaces. The cattleman Charles Goodnight, for whom the Goodnight Trail was named, offered the recipe to cure the ill effects of drinking water contaminated with alkali—a sturdy tea made of cottonwood bark.

What's in a Synonym? The Palmer Cottonwood

One of the common names for the Plains Cottonwood is the Palmer Cottonwood, and the story of its naming offers a good example of why "cottonwood talk" gets confusing. Science doesn't stand still when it comes to naming plants. Names change!

Different cottonwood species share many common names that reflect their history. In his landmark study of western trees of the United States, Donald Culross Peattie described the Palmer Cottonwood in a subsection on the Rio Grande Cottonwood. Yet he lists the Palmer's botanical name as *Populus Palmeri* Sargent, which would seem to indicate a connection to the Plains, still called a "Sargent Cottonwood" or just "the Sargent." Peattie describes a particular geographical region for the Palmer, limited to the Chisos Mountains and to two counties in Texas that are miles apart, Uvalde and Palo Pinto. To Peattie, the distinguishing characteristics of the Palmer are described as glands near the intersection of leaf stalks; fine slender leaves and stalks; narrowly ridged furrows; and droopy branches.

The Palmer Cottonwood was first described as a new species in the 1919 *Botanical Gazette* (probably Peattie's source), even though—shame, shame—the flowers weren't examined. Pete Smith of the Texas Forest Service picks up the story from there. The Palmer was accepted as a new species in the plant checklists for 1927 and 1953, but by 1961 further study resulted in its being relegated to synonym status for the Eastern Cottonwood, where it remains today, firmly (for the moment, anyway) ensconced in the USDA PLANTS database.

— Narrowleaf Cottonwood —

CURRENT BOTANICAL NAME (USDA)
Populus angustifolia James

SYNONYMS
Populus balsamifera L. var. *angustifolia* (James) S. Wats.
Populus canadensis Moench var. *angustifolia* (James) Wesmael
Populus fortissima A. Nels. & J.F. Macbr.
Populus salicifolia Raf.

Source: USDA-NRCS PLANTS Database / Britton, N.L., and A. Brown. 1913.
Illustrated flora of the northern states and Canada. Vol. 1: 588.

Populus xsennii Boivin
Populus tweedyi Britt.

NATURAL HYBRIDS

Balsam poplar (*P. balsamifera*) = *P.* x *brayshawii* Boivin (Brayshaw's poplar)
Eastern Cottonwood (*P. deltoides*) = *P.* x *acuminata* Rydb. (Lanceleaf poplar)
Fremont Cottonwood (*P. fremontii*) = *P.* x *hinckleyana* Correll
Lanceleaf Cottonwood (*P.* x *andrewsii* Sarg.) = *P. angustifolia* x *P. deltoides*

IMPORTANT CULTIVARS
None

ELEVATION
5,000–10,000 ft.
4,000–8,000 ft. (southern part of range)

COMMON NAMES

Balsam	Balsam Cottonwood	Bitter Cottonwood
Black Cottonwood	Mountain Cottonwood	Mountain Willow
Narrowleaf Balsam Poplar	Narrow-leaved Cottonwood	Narrow-leaved Poplar
Rydberg Cottonwood	Smooth-Bark Cottonwood	Willow Cottonwood
Willow-Leaf Cottonwood	Willow-Leaved Cottonwood	

All the references to willows in the common names for the Narrowleaf offer clues to the look of its leaves. The Narrowleaf is often mistaken for a willow—and though cottonwoods and willows are cousins, they're still different. One sure way to tell the difference is to follow your nose. When spring arrives (and even into summer) you can detect the Narrowleaf's balsam incense as resin on the buds and leaves warms up and spreads through the air. You can use all your senses to identify the Narrowleaf. Smooth to the touch, the branches of new growth are serpentine and slender. Their color matches that of the husks that protect the sticky new leaves— about the same shade as the flesh of a fine smoked trout or a tobacco leaf. Slender is the keyword for this species, from the look of the long vertical buds that alternate on either side of the thin branches to the more columnar look of the whole tree as it matures. Its graceful, tapered leaves, about four inches long, look nothing like the familiar broad triangle—or heart shape—of the Eastern and Plains Cottonwoods. Don't let the leaves fool you, though. The bark provides another mark of distinction. Mottled is the word that describes this tree's skin, especially on the lower trunk. Slightly waxy to the touch, the unmistakable patterns of the young white bark

on some trees look more like cracks in dry earth than the deep furrows of the Plains
cousin; pieces of a jigsaw puzzle more than armored plating. Narrowleaf cultivars
are sometimes used as residential plantings in western regions of the United States,
in spite of their rampant suckering—the trade-off is shade and shelter at higher
elevations. In the wild, suckering proves valuable, especially in efforts to restore or
preserve habitat. A single, quick-growing Narrowleaf can create its own stand of
trees within a few years. Narrowleafs are at home in canyons and along mountain
streams and waterways—even as high as 9,000 feet. The trees manage to find their
way downstream to lower elevations as well, moving along unimpeded creeks and
waterways still able to scour their own banks and create the right conditions for
germination. The Chatfield Arboretum of the Denver Botanic Gardens offers such
a setting. Deer Creek flows freely from the foothills through the arboretum
property, nourishing a gallery of cottonwoods where all three species native to
Colorado—the Plains, the Lanceleaf, and the Narrowleaf—flourish and regenerate. The drawback of having no dams on the creek is that in a drought year like the
current one (2006, and year number seven of the cycle), by June no water had
arrived to carry the cottony parachutes downstream.

One of the most perspicacious observers of his time, Meriwether Lewis,
recognized the Narrowleaf as a cottonwood and could distinguish it from its
broader leaved relatives. It was, he wrote, "a species of cottonwood with a leaf like
that of the wild cherry." That's a distinction we take for granted, but Lewis recorded
it for the first time in his journals in June 1805 as the Corps of Discovery traveled
along the upper Missouri River. Lewis and Clark also noticed that horses would not
eat the leaves or bark of the Narrowleaf, as they had those of the Plains
Cottonwood at lower elevations, thus verifying another of its common names (in
spite of its lovely if pungent smell): the Bitter Cottonwood. Lewis also noticed how
the Narrowleaf flourished at higher altitudes than other cottonwoods and that like
all its cousins it kept close company with water. Though he may have suspected a
wider range throughout the western United States, he couldn't have known that
this species extended from southern Alberta in Canada all the way south into
Chihuahua and the Sierra Madre Mountains of Mexico. Using USDA distribution
maps, you can draw a line, roughly, at the Missouri River and let that be the general
eastern limit of the Narrowleaf—with the exception (there are always exceptions)
of North Dakota, Kansas, and Oklahoma. The exception in the far west seems to
be the state of Washington. The Narrowleaf follows streams in mountainous areas
through all these states, growing beside them as the waterways pass through high,
dry, elevations, desert shrub lands, prairie grasslands, and pine forests. In undis-
turbed locations the Narrowleaf grows in communities with Douglas fir,

blue spruce, ponderosa pine, Rocky Mountain juniper, maple, birch, alder, other cottonwoods, and aspen. The USDA reports the maximum height of the Narrowleaf at twenty years of age as sixty feet, though it easily keeps pace as it grows tall and lean beside its mountain companions. Its overall look tends to resemble a slender pyramid more than the full, more round appearance of the Plains or Eastern Cottonwoods. And though a slight oval sometimes appears in the overall shape, this is a tree that's bound to grow taller if not necessarily wider than its relatives. Observers have noted that damage can cause the trunk to sprout in ways that make it look more like a shrub than a tree. Like other poplars—and cottonwoods—it cannot tolerate shade but provides both shade and habitat for many other species of insects, birds, and mammals. On the day I visited Chatfield Arboretum, box elder bugs swarmed a female Narrowleaf "in cotton" the way bees hover around their favorite flowers. Box elder bugs eat cottonwood seeds, as it turns out, but do not harm the tree. Because of its habit of growing a thick, matted root system, the Narrowleaf is more helpful in restoring wild areas than residential ones, although in high, mountain towns that run long on sun and short on trees, the Narrowleaf takes its place as an ornamental. It grows quickly and brings the welcome relief of shade—a natural air conditioner. It begins to flower at about fifteen years of age. Microscopic blossoms appear in May, during or a little before leaf break. The seed pods, about the size of a grain of barley, are even smaller than those of the Plains Cottonwood. The pods develop from May to July, and seeds float through the air in May and June, making tiny, fuzzy sticks of the stems upon which they grow. The Narrowleaf hybridizes naturally with several other cotton-wood species. The best known natural hybrid is the Lanceleaf.

In spite of being a favorite of box elder bugs, the Narrowleaf has a high graz-ing value but a medium browsing value for animals and is low on the list for fuel use. Overgrazing from domestic livestock and wildlife such as elk quickly destroys the trees, a loss increasingly experienced throughout the western United States. From top to bottom, many animals use the Narrowleaf for food and shelter. Quail and grouse feast on the catkins and buds. Rabbits, deer, and moose browse leaves and twigs. Beavers make use of all sizes of Narrowleaf branches for dams and lodges, but too much activity on their part quickly threatens the tree's ability to regenerate. The Narrowleaf provides accommodation for squirrels, bears, white-tailed deer, and numerous bird species, from songbirds to raptors. The young trees, like other cottonwood species, cannot tolerate fire, although as the Narrowleaf matures the bark develops more resistance.

Though Native Americans once found a remedy for scurvy in the inner bark and used small branches for basketmaking, current commercial use of the

Narrowleaf is more limited than with some other species of cottonwood. Several artisans make soap, massage oil, and incense from the early season buds. The wood decays and warps easily. And although it's still used as nursery stock and to make fence posts and wood pulp, it's employed less often for manufacturing than other cottonwood species. The USDA attributes this to the tree's "relative scarcity" as well as its less desirable qualities. What caused the "relative scarcity" is unclear; possibly the overgrazing and some of the other indignities the tree suffers in its natural range. Shavings can be used for bedding, insulation, and, even though its nutritional value is low, the Narrowleaf can serve as a food supplement for animals if need be.

Discerning the characteristics of the Narrowleaf proves how minute the points of comparison between different species of cottonwood are. It's not always a matter of just looking at a tree and deciding. Comparing leaf shape and size, the look of the bark and the overall shape of the tree, the length, width, and look of the buds and flowers—these are all essential ways to go "cottonwooding." It's the standard field guide approach. Unfortunately, not all field guides include all the cottonwoods. Oh, and one more distinctive mark of the Narrowleaf. Montana tree hunter Martin Flanagan reports that his favorite Narrowleafs have a gorgeous red petiole (leaf stalk), distinct from the deep gold or pale yellow colors found elsewhere among its relatives—beauty marks worth searching for.

— Lanceleaf Cottonwood —

CURRENT BOTANICAL NAME (USDA)
Populus x *acuminata* Rydb. (pro sp.) [*angustifolia* x *deltoides*]

SYNONYMS (USDA):
Populus acuminata Rydb. var. *reheri* sargent

IMPORTANT CULTIVARS
'Highlands'

Source: USDA-NRCS PLANTS Database / Britton, N.L., and A. Brown. 1913.
Illustrated flora of the northern states and Canada. Vol. 1: 589.

ELEVATION
4,500–8,500 ft.

COMMON NAMES
Mountain Cottonwood   Smoothbark Cottonwood   Smoothbark Poplar

This member of the cottonwood family claims a special heritage. The Lanceleaf is the natural offspring, or hybrid, of two distinguished parents: the Plains Cottonwood and the Narrowleaf Cottonwood. As do many trees in the poplar genus, these two cottonwood species are compatible and hybridize naturally. That's one of the marks of a species: its members are similar enough that they can reproduce. You'll find Lanceleaf Cottonwoods in the wild throughout the western U.S.: namely, Idaho, Montana, North and South Dakota, Nebraska, Wyoming, Colorado, New Mexico, Arizona, and Texas. And although like the Narrowleaf parent they can travel up or downstream, or whichever way the wind blows, Lanceleafs prefer altitudes of 4,500 to 8,500 feet, also the range of elevations their parents prefer. The Plains Cottonwood ranges from 3,500 to 5,000 feet, and the Narrowleaf climbs a little higher, generally from 5,000 to 8,000 feet and sometimes even higher than that.

Donald Culross Peattie, the eloquent natural historian, is curiously silent on the topic of Lanceleaf Cottonwoods. Likewise, though the Natural Resources Conservation Services (NRCS) branch of the USDA provides a PLANTS Profile for the Lanceleaf, it's terse. A Google search for *Lanceleaf cottonwoods research* retrieved 356 hits. So while you can't say there isn't *any* Lanceleaf research out there, you also can't say there's *a lot* (certainly not by Google standards). Limiting the search to the .gov domain narrowed the results to 57; the .edu domain to 83; and .org to 62. Not bad, in terms of useful information (and yes, I know, I used only the tree's common name instead of its botanical one). Much of the research on Lanceleafs usually involves research on other species of cottonwood as well.

By contrast, a similar search for Fremont Cottonwoods netted a minimum of 400 results in each domain. At more than 20,000 in each domain category, the Rio Grande took the prize. The Easterns brought up from 13,000 to 16,000 hits. Plains Cottonwoods hits ranged from 1,000 to 10,000+ and the Narrowleaf 400 or fewer in each domain.

Yet there is plenty to say about this unique, natural cross–species.

As it has been since 1893, the Lanceleaf is well named, as the illustration above shows. The "acuminata" of its botanical name comes from the Latin word for sharp point: *acumen*. The leaves measure about two inches by four inches and

develop on a leaf stalk (petiole) about a third the length of the blade. In the frac-
tal geometry common to cottonwoods (and to many members of the plant world),
when you look at this tree from a distance you can see the slender, slightly curved
lance shape of the leaves repeat itself in the overall form of the tree—though, like
most of us, it will round out with age. If you step closer and look up you'll notice
that Lanceleaf bark is almost white, a striking feature during the winter months
and a trait inherited from its Narrowleaf parentage. Where the bark on the Plains
Cottonwood quickly grows furrowed as a new-plowed field, new Lanceleaf bark
is smoother and waxy to the touch. It looks more like poplar bark that's been
etched with triangular patches, at least along the trunk. The farther up the tree
you look, the more white you'll see. The light color serves a purpose; nothing has
been lost on cottonwoods during their millennia of evolution. Especially at higher
altitudes, white reflects winter sunlight and keeps the tree from heating up too
quickly in the spring. Though the buds of the Narrowleaf parent, even when shed
and lying dry beneath the tree, are unmistakably aromatic, Lanceleaf buds are
not. While not as profusely as the Narrowleaf, the Lanceleaf suckers badly
enough that many cities prohibit its planting in public rights of way. The roots
of even young trees can slither through lawns and invade pipes, sewers, and
drains. On average this species measures 40–60 feet tall with a crown spread of
30–40 feet, taller than its Narrowleaf parent but shorter on average than its
Plains relative.

One city where Lanceleaf cottonwoods are at home, however, is Fort Collins,
Colorado. As city forester Tim Buchanan points out, Lanceleafs define the floral
character of the town. On the job for nearly thirty years, Buchanan knows every
cottonwood—individuals as well as stands of trees—in and around the city.
Residents have told him stories about how their relatives planted trees throughout
the town during the early twentieth century. One stately avenue still hosts a
promenade sheltered by hundred-year-old Lanceleafs. The street was once a
county road, along which the trees were planted at the turn of the century. With
their spear-headed leaves, they show off a certain finer texture as they toss their
branches in the wind, offering both shade and grace. Size and maturity gives them,
and the city, a relaxed and self-assured feel. Though the university town is modern
in every way, the Lanceleafs lend it an air of old-fashioned dignity.

One behemoth of the tribe that lives in City Park gets rented out regularly by a
professional tree climber who tosses his ropes over the hefty limbs and leads
novices into the upper stories of the woody mansion. And though Buchanan has
not been able to thoroughly document them, he has found thirty to forty plantings
of Lanceleaf Cottonwoods throughout surrounding Larimer County. The plantings

are deliberate. The trees stand twenty feet apart—an obvious sign of planning, and at a distance that works better in the wild than it does in town, incidentally.

The Lanceleafs of Fort Collins keep company with their parent trees, the Plains and Narrowleafs. With an eye for detail and his training, Buchanan can still read the landscape a century after enormous changes have occurred. He describes how Fort Collins was built on bluffs above the Poudre River. He can still see the bluffs, even from the vantage point of a modern apartment complex parking lot. As for all those Lanceleafs, he conjectures that early founders like Frank Avery, who loved cottonwood trees, may have gone down to the river and gathered wild saplings, and planted them throughout the ever-expanding city and county. Gathering cottonwoods from riverbanks was a common practice throughout the West and Midwest as a way to bring the green world to town. And if there's a dearth of research about Lanceleafs, there's no shortage of questions. Buchanan mentions a man, unnamed, who has wondered whether Lanceleafs propagate on their own; whether the seed they produce is viable. The man became curious when he discovered Lanceleafs growing on their own in a place where no parent trees— no Plains or Narrowleaf varieties—were within possible range. Lanceleafs (*P. acuminata*) are known to backcross with the Plains Cottonwood (*P. sargentii*). So why not with each other? As a distinct species, they should able to reproduce. Is their seed viable? Buchanan repeats the man's question and wonders whether maybe someone will do more research, or has already.

— Fremont Cottonwood —

CURRENT BOTANICAL NAME (USDA)
Populus fremontii S. Wats.
Populus fremontii S. Wats. Subsp. fremontii
Populus fremontii S. Wats. Subsp. mesetae Eckenwalder

SYNONYMS (USDA)
for *Populus fremontii* S. Wats. Subsp. *fremontii*
Populus arizonica Sarg.
Populus arizonica Sarg. var. *jonesii* Sarg.

Source: United States Department of Agriculture Forest Service Collection. Hunt Institute for Botanical Documentation.
Carnegie Mellon University, Pittsburgh, PA.

Populus canadensis Moench var. *fremontii* (S. Wats.) Kuntze
Populus fremontii S. Wats. var. *arizonica* (Sarg.) Jepson
Populus fremontii S. Wats. var. *macdougalii* (Rose) Jepson
Populus fremontii S. Wats. var. *macrodisca* Sarg.
Populus fremontii S. Wats. var. *pubescens* Sarg.
Populus fremontii S. Wats. var. *thornberi* Sarg.
Populus fremontii S. Wats. var. *toumeyi* Sarg.
Populus macdougalii Rose

for *Populus fremontii* S. Wats. Subsp. *mesetae* Eckenwalder
Populus fremontii S. Wats. var. *mesetae* (Eckenwalder) Little
Populus mexicana auct. non Wesmael [misapplied]

ELEVATION
sea level – 6,500 ft.

COMMON NAMES

Álamo	Arizona Cottonwood	Fremont Poplar
Fremont's Cottonwood	Guerigo	Meseta Cottonwood
Poplar	Valley Cottonwood	White Cottonwood

Writer after writer describes the Fremont Cottonwood as the tree of Arizona and of the Great Southwest. And, indeed, as the current USDA distribution maps show, this tree and its subspecies can be found there—as well as in Texas, New Mexico, Colorado, Utah, Nevada, and California. The maps don't show its existence in northern Mexico, although it grows there, too. Stretch along the Pecos River and you will find it. Stare down into the Grand Canyon and this is the tree you will see, following the Colorado River in its descent through time. Fremont Cottonwoods are the trees of Zion National Park, struggling to survive in places where the Virgin River has been restrained. From their roots Hopi carvers once exclusively selected the Fremont's wood to create the sacred *tithu* and the more commercial figures we have come to call Kachina dolls. American artist Maynard Dixon memorialized them in painting after painting, even adopting the tree as a personal symbol. In frequent and local use, these trees still bear the name of the man who first described them, John Charles Fremont (1813–90). Though Fremont's reputation was challenged (he endured a court-martial), he remains a nineteenth-century "Renaissance man." He served as an explorer, a military officer, and a politician. He studied cartography, geology, linguistics, mathematics, and botany. He was as attentive to his note-taking as Meriwether Lewis had been eighty years earlier. In January 1884, while camped near Pyramid Lake in current-day Nevada, Fremont first described the tree that would come to bear his name. He noted the sweetness of the bark, which, like that of the Plains Cottonwood, horses sometimes preferred to grass. Later that same year, while in the San Joaquin Valley in California, Fremont again described a good camping spot with a fine stream flowing through it and large cottonwoods standing beside it. The Fremont Cottonwood currently has two subspecies listings: the *fremontii* and a tree known as the Meseta Cottonwood, common to two counties in Texas near Big Bend National Park.

The presence of nearby water distinguishes cottonwoods from other trees. The Fremont further distinguishes itself from other cottonwoods by this need. It simply will not endure without water—and some is not enough. The supply must be steady and reliable. That's why, in the low-lying desert areas of the southwestern United States, it is the prominent tree of streams, rivers, and water holes, an indicator of permanent water sources. And while it seems like a large tree in such an otherwise treeless landscape, it's smaller than other cottonwood species; usually reaching 60 feet and ranging from 40 to 80 feet. Young trees show a smooth, grayish-brown bark. As they age, the bark transforms into the rutted, ragged gray furrows typical especially of Plains Cottonwoods. Stout twigs change color, from pale yellow to yellow-gray. Terminal buds measure from one-third to one-half inch. As you might expect in desert country, the leaves of the Fremont are smaller than those of other cottonwoods, ranging from two to three inches and often grow more broad than long. Catkins are smaller when compared with other species: 2–3.5 inches long. The fruit containing the seeds is a mere one-third to one-half inch long and reveals a tiny triptych when it opens. Seeds are even smaller, an eighth of an inch long. The heartwood of the Fremont is light brown, the surrounding sapwood white. Like many other cottonwoods, the Fremont's commercial use is primarily limited to crate and box construction. It has been used for firewood, and its habit of self-pruning leaves kindling scattered around for desert travelers. Although certain projects require it, foresters, arborists, and wildlife managers don't routinely reproduce cottonwood from seed. They let the regeneration occur naturally wherever it can and lend a hand with other means of reproduction. The Los Lunas, New Mexico, Plant Materials Center, working with several other government agencies, has developed a "pole" method for establishing (and re-establishing) Fremont Cottonwoods, which will be discussed in a later chapter. The Los Lunas project is just one of several ongoing efforts to compensate for the incursion that our own species has made into cottonwood habitat.

Depending on where we live, we don't all have the opportunity to see each of these magnificent species of cottonwoods up close. So before we leave the introduction to the Fremont Cottonwood, let me give you a little homework assignment. Go to your nearest library or bookstore. See whether you can find James Balog's extraordinary *Tree: A New Vision of the American Forest.* You might need help carrying the book home—it's nearly a foot and a half long (be sure to open the cover completely for a true surprise). Browse until you find the Fremont Cottonwood, described as *Populus fremontii* var. *fremontii*. Balog has photographed national and state Big Tree Champions, as determined by nominations and official measurements submitted to the citizen conservation group, American Forests. Both pilgrim and photographer, Balog has documented these champion trees in portraits that capture the power of the trees and yet remain quite intimate. He pays tribute to the Fremont Cottonwood champion, near Patagonia, Arizona, with a brief essay and five pages of photographs. Though it's not the same as visiting the tree and standing beneath it, as Balog has been able to do, a visit to the tree through his photography is like embarking on a minor pilgrimage nevertheless. He has captured the primal spirit of the tree, with its knots of memory that living so long in this dry place have solidified; mighty and capricious all at once, this tree. Sit beside it for a while in the comfort of your own space and see what else you might learn about the Fremont Cottonwood.

— Rio Grande Cottonwood —

CURRENT BOTANICAL NAME (USDA)
Populus deltoides Bart. ex Marsh. subsp. wislizeni (S. Wats.) Eckenwalder

SYNONYMS (USDA)
Populus deltoides Bartr. ex Marsh. var. wislizeni (S. Wats.) Dorn
Populus fremontii S. Wats. Var. wislizeni S. Wats.
Populus wislizeni (S. Wats.) Sargent

Source: Wislizeni's Cottonwood (*Populus Wislizeni*), Burton O. Longyear. 1927.
Trees and Shrubs of the Rocky Mountain Region.

ELEVATION
4,000-1,000 ft.

COMMON NAMES

Álamo, Álamillas, Álamillo	Common Cottonwood	Fremont Cottonwood
Marsh Cottonwood	Rio Grande Cottonwood	Valley Cottonwood
Water Tree	Wislizenus Cottonwood	

The Rio Grande Cottonwood is a well-loved tree, and deservedly so. Georgia O'Keeffe captured the luxuriant beauty of this tree in a series of paintings. In one view a sculpted snag with a hole through its center stares back at the viewer like a cosmic eye. In another, the tree becomes an overlarge ruffle of gold, caught in time as an autumn wind shuffles the leaves. In an aesthetic that cannot be missed if you travel to New Mexico, long the "Land of Enchantment," the Rio Grande Cottonwood provides green relief in the landscape of junipers and piñon pines that dot the rough hills erupting from desert plains. Descending the central mountains of Colorado and moving into southeastern Utah, this cottonwood has also traveled south along the Rio Grande, from which it takes its name, through New Mexico all the way to Texas and into Mexico. One of the best places to see the Rio Grande Cottonwood is to take the back road from Taos to Santa Fe. Take your time. Pull off if you have to and let the tailgaters go on by. Let the river be your guide, as it is for these graceful trees. They shoulder along its banks after descending the hills, following any stream into the river. Depending on the time of year, the Rio Grandes provide a variable visual treat. Among cottonwoods, they could win a prize for best of show. Their lovely, bushy forms soften the landscape of gorges the river has carved through the dark and somber land. If their stouter Plains cousins can be thought of as the Martha Grahams of their kind, bending a branch or a limb at right angles like an arm or a leg, then the Rio Grandes are the ballroom dancers of the genus. In springtime, just after the trees have set their leaves, the color from a distance challenges description: not quite chartreuse; maybe more like a lime Popsicle or the deep heart of an artichoke. Yet that description fails to honor their grace and majesty. Wallace Stegner's warning to forget about green in the western landscape is lost on me, at least temporarily, as I follow the Rio Grande into the valley west of Albuquerque, where my eye takes in all the sudden green it can. I wonder whether the vista of cool cottonwood green, mixed with the silver of Russian olives and the hunter's green of junipers and scrub oak can lower the human body temperature just by looking. Why not? Cottonwoods lower water and land temperatures—a boon to vegetation, fish, birds, and other wildlife.

The sight of the Rio Grande Cottonwoods is such a relief that it's hard, as Matt Schmader, superintendent for the City of Albuquerque Open Space says, to try and imagine what the valley—or New Mexico—would be like without them. To him, they "transcend planthood." If you could ever "accuse a plant of having a soul," Schmader begins . . . but he leaves the sentence unfinished. His colleague Suzanne Probart, executive director of Tree New Mexico, agrees, and stresses the intrinsic cultural value of the Rio Grandes. They were used for the roofs of pit houses by Native Americans. Fossil leaves that date to 1.2 mya have been found near the Albuquerque Airport. Matt gets calls from Kachina carvers in search of roots after reports of Rio Grandes struck by lightning. A Rio Grande Cottonwood named Naomi stood at the center of a recent cultural battle in Albuquerque—we will learn more about her in a later chapter, "Trouble in Cottonwood Country."

If you understand the word *bosque*, you understand the Rio Grande Cottonwood. The Spanish word describes the groves of trees that line New Mexico's river valleys. There's the Bosque Redondo, for example—the "round grove" of cottonwoods that once caught the eye of a U.S. Army major now remembered for the cottonwood groves he destroyed and his cruel treatment of Navajo and Apache people in what became known as "the Long Walk." The bosques are groves of natural beauty yet, though some, like the Bosque Redondo, have had to be restored. The Rio Grande cottonwoods that dominate them are so well loved that people over the centuries have carried them by hand and transplanted them to the plazas of the pueblos, to the Navajo hogans, or to the farms and towns like Taos and Santa Fe, built by the Spanish and other European immigrants as they moved into the southwest. Travelers found their way along the Santa Fe Trail tree by tree, grove by grove.

The Rio Grande Cottonwood bears in its scientific name the surname of the man who first discovered and recorded the species, Frederick Augustus Wislizenus. A naturalist as well as a physician, Wislizenus made several trips to the southwest from St. Louis. In 1846 he traveled the Santa Fe Trail and ventured on to Mexico, watching for cottonwoods along the way. What he saw and described is similar to many other species, although he could tell the differences. The thick trunk of the Rio Grande turns a pale gray–brown, becoming more furrowed as it ages. The twigs have learned to grow stout in the land of diminished rain. Twig colors differ from other cottonwoods in some ways, and are the same in some ways: from faint orange–brown they turn gray and grow rough because of the way the leaf scars lift as they age. Winter buds are a third to three-fifths of an inch long, distinguished by a lack of fragrance, though they glisten brown and shiny with resin like other cottonwoods. At 2–2.5 inches long, the leaves are smaller than some other cottonwood species, though they can stretch more broadly, to 3 inches, a familiar ratio in these trees. The leaves wear waxy coats, a protection against loss of moisture in a place where 14 percent humidity is not unusual, giving the leaves a leathery feel. Leaf tops shine yellowish-green, the bottoms even paler. The always-flattened leafstalks, a distinct family trait of cottonwoods, measure 1.5–2 inches long. Elongated and without blemishes or a rough surface, they lack the glands found in some other species. Flowers droop in catkins that stretch 2–4 inches long. The females in this species appear pale red. Seed pods develop thick walls, and when compared with those of the Plains Cottonwood, it's like comparing BB pellets to grapes. The seed capsules divide into three or four parts when they open to release light brown seeds, as many as 25 million of them. The trees stand from 50 to 100 feet high, with about 60 feet being average, and appear larger in a landscape that stretches across great open distances (think how big a full moon looks when it first appears above the horizon). As always, the quality of the wood must bear the same adjectives as other species of cottonwood: light, brittle. It warps. It cracks. It seasons badly. Yet the poles, with little treatment, have been used for hundreds of years as fence posts and thousands of years as ceiling beams. In the Pueblo plazas the cottonwood poles also make good drying racks and frames for shelter from the sun, as well as ladders to descend into the kivas. Drums made to celebrate the rituals of the turning year are still built from cottonwood. After the Spanish arrived, their woodcarvers, the santeros, preferred this cottonwood to carve the santos, the sacred figures of Christ and the saints.

In spite of the shortcomings of its overall quality as timber, the Rio Grande cottonwood provides blessed relief in its shade—step out of the sun into the shadow of one in Taos or Santa Fe in the summer, and you'll know the feeling, like instant air conditioning! The Rio Grandes offer shelter to southwestern bird species, including blue herons and two species of orioles. Cavity nesters, in this case Gila woodpeckers and red-shafted flickers, find ready-made homes in the upper limbs. Owls remodel once cavity nesters have vacated the premises (though their work wounds an already wounded tree). Nuthatches, finches, bluebirds, and even swallows can find a cozy home in an old Rio Grande. Like so many species of cottonwood, this one offers a food source (and sometime habitat) for beaver, deer, rabbits—even field mice. Perhaps more than other cottonwood species throughout the West and Southwest (maybe that's why there's so much research) the Rio Grande suffers from the ill effects of human intervention—urban development of riparian areas, damming, streamflow diversion, diminishing water tables, pollution from mining and the introduction of harmful elements like salt into the soil. In New Mexico alone, 95 percent of the riparian habitat is gone—no wonder people working to protect the Fremont Cottonwoods have taken to giving them individual names! Invasive species like Russian olives and tamarisks crowd out the native cottonwoods and alter the soil chemistry. Yet this tough survivor hangs on, even in places that seem unlikely to support it: White Sands National Monument, for example. In spite of heat, wind, little rain, and sand, the cottonwoods have sustained themselves by tapping into an ancient water table, a shallow lake left over from the geological past known as the Permian. The roots of the Rio Grande Cottonwood were also once a primary source for Pueblo, Navajo, and Hopi carvers who sculpt the sacred tithu, figures of the Katsina deities used in religious practice (more about them later). Some of the figures carved from the root of the tree, the part that finds and draws up life–sustaining water, represent the very deities who bring water to the pueblos. These days, however, the sculptors must go farther afield to buy their root–wood, paying the price for scarcity in more ways than one. In New Mexico, the Rio Grande is more than just another tree on the landscape. It has come to represent the culture of the state, past and present. If groves of Rio Grandes once marked the way to Santa Fe, in more recent times individual trees came to represent the struggle between past and present, a story that's still unfolding, and one about which we'll learn more later.

— Swamp Cottonwood —

CURRENT BOTANICAL NAME (USDA)
Populus heterophylla Linnaeus

SYNONYMS (USDA)
Populus argentea Michx. f.

ELEVATION
Sea level—80 ft.

Source: Britton, N.L., and A. Brown. 1913. *Illustrated flora of the northern states and Canada.* Vol. 1: 589.
Courtesy of Kentucky Native Plant Society.

COMMON NAMES

Bigleaf Cottonwood	Black Cottonwood	Black Poplar
Cottontree	Cottonwood	Downy Cottonwood
Downy Poplar	River Cottonwood	Swamp Cottonwood
Swamp Poplar		

When he wrote his classic on the natural history of trees of North America more than fifty years ago, Donald Culross Peattie expressed the hope that the Swamp Cottonwood, a quick starter, would be able to outgrow the commercial demand then beginning to make its wood scarce. His hope has not come true. The United States Fish and Wildlife Service has declared the Swamp Cottonwood a rare species. The USDA currently shows the tree's status as endangered in Connecticut, Massachusetts, and Michigan; threatened in New York; potentially threatened in Ohio; and "extirpated"—extinct—in Pennsylvania. Yet the Swamp Cottonwood continues to surprise botanists and conservationists. Individuals like Jim Bissell at the Cleveland Museum of Natural History, as well as conservancy groups, have been delighted to find stands of Swamp Cottonwood in the United States and Canada. As the tree becomes protected, perhaps it will resume its place in its own forest home—helping Peattie's wish come true.

The Swamp Cottonwood is the poor relation among cottonwood trees. In Peattie's time (the 1950s) it was the source of 50 percent of all the excelsior manufactured in the United States. Current assessments dismiss its value as a commercial lumber product; one even states that it lacks a specific market because such a small amount is harvested. Catch-22: it's not valuable because there's not much of it, yet there's not much of it because so much was harvested all those years ago. Go figure. In addition to being scarce, it's not an easy tree to grow from cuttings, which limits its interest to commercial growers. And our consumer culture doesn't respect any creature that can't make itself useful. Beauty might make up for what utility lacks, but the Swamp Cottonwood is seldom described as beautiful. Researchers pay such little attention to it that no races or hybrids have been reported (a fact that might challenge some eager young graduate student out there). Peattie remarked that sometimes only people who live in the same area where it grows recognize it as a distinct cottonwood. Is the Swamp Cottonwood your rare native?

Those areas include the eastern and southeastern United States, with some exceptions. A lover of swampy bottomlands, sloughs, and low-lying areas near tidewater, the tree has staked out its home territory along the eastern coastal plain from southern Georgia through Connecticut. From northwestern Florida the range moves as far east as Louisiana. It follows the Mississippi Valley and can be found in patches throughout Missouri, Tennessee, Kentucky, Illinois, Indiana, Ohio, and southern Michigan. In this humid range, rainfall is more extensive than the stingy twenty-inches-per-annum-or-less that the Plains Cottonwood and its western relatives anticipate: from thirty-five to fifty-nine inches a year. The Swamp Cottonwood likes the heavy clay soils along the edges of swamps. And though it won't be found growing waist-high there, it can tolerate having its feet in more water than its Eastern cousin. Its Plains relative wouldn't know what to do with so much water. Though sparse even in its native range, where it's not thought of as a primary species, it shares the forest with different willow species as well as water hickory, sycamore, sugarberry, red maple, and American elm. Understory trees and shrubs include water elm, buttonbrush, swamp-privet, and possumhaw.

Physical descriptions of the tree vary. One source describes the trunk as smooth, sleek, and gray-green, while another calls it dirty brown dashed with red on coarse, furrowed bark. Though contradictory, these descriptions probably fit the bark at different ages. At twenty years old, a maximum of fifty feet is not unusual. Straight trunks of fifty to sixty feet have been described (it's the straight trunk that caught the excelsior maker's eye so long ago). An old tree may top out at around 100 feet, an ordinary stretch for mature cottonwoods, though the tallest of the Swamp Cottonwoods actually measure 115–130 feet. Stout twigs show pale lenticels and have a downy, orange look to them in the spring (the origin of one of their common names). The orange turns dark brown or ashy-gray as the season advances. Resinous winter buds emit the familiar poplar fragrance. The thin leaves shine dark green on top and pale green on the undersides. A pale yellow midrib divides each leaf. Usually 4–7 inches long, leaves measure about 3–6 inches wide. A net of veins decorates the leaf edges. Male catkins hang from 2–4 inches and females about 2–6 inches. Unlike other cottonwoods with their green dangling seed pods, these are dark reddish-brown (to match the bark, perhaps) and not as thick-walled. It takes about 150,000 of the tiny white seeds to make a pound. Trees can produce seeds at about ten years. The light wood weighs in at only twenty-five pounds per cubic foot (easy to understand why they were once coveted for excelsior). Even the heartwood of this less-loved cotton-wood is characterized as dull, and the surrounding band of sapwood as thin and pale. Seedling development is like that of other cottonwoods. Once released from the tree, traveling a few hundred feet in the kind of dense cover you'd expect in a swamp, the seedlings take a water taxi in search of the open ground they prefer for germination. Like all cottonwoods, they remain viable for only a week or two and require full sunlight in order to survive. With their survival in question due to their scarcity, we'll see in a later chapter just how well they're doing.

— **Black Cottonwood** —

CURRENT BOTANICAL NAME (USDA)
Populus balsamifera L. subsp. *trichocarpa* (Torrey & Gray ex Hook.) Brayshaw

SYNONYMS (USDA)
Populus balsamifera L. var. *californica* S. Wats.
Populus hastata Dode p.p.
Populus trichocarpa Torr. & Gray ex Hook.
Populus trichocarpa Torr. & Gray ex Hook. subsp. *hastata* (Dode) Dode p.p.
Populus trichocarpa Torr. & Gray ex Hook. var. *cupulata* S. Wats.

Source: United States Department of Agriculture Forest Service Collection.

Hunt Institute for Botanical Documentation. Carnegie Mellon University, Pittsburgh, PA.

Populus trichocarpa Torr. & Gray ex Hook. var. *hastata* (Dode) A. Henry p.p.
Populus trichocarpa Torr. & Gray ex Hook. var *ingrata* (Jepson) Jepson
Populus trichocarpa Torrey and Gray

ELEVATION
Sea level—5,000 ft.

COMMON NAMES

Balm	Balm Cottonwood	Balm of Gilead
Balsam Cottonwood	California Poplar	Common Black Cottonwood
Western Balsam Poplar		

In one sense, the Black Cottonwood is to the Pacific coastal region what the Eastern Cottonwood is to the Atlantic, even though the tree can be found in Nevada (around Tahoe) and the northern mountains of the Baja Peninsula, as well as northern and western portions of Idaho, Montana, and western Wyoming. The range extends from the Sierra Nevada Mountains up through northern California, Oregon, Washington, and Vancouver Island. Like any good coastal traveler, it's found along the Kenai Peninsula in Alaska through the south Yukon Territory—an answer to the often-asked question: Are there cottonwoods in Alaska?

At this point, I have a concession to make. As I mentioned earlier, all cotton-woods are poplars though not all poplars are cottonwoods. Botanically, the Black Cottonwood is described as a subspecies of the Balsam Poplar (*Populus balsam-ifera* L.—Linnaeus again). But the Balsam Poplar and its attendant species have been cottonwoods for so long in most people's minds and hearts, why spoil it now? The Black Cottonwood exhibits many of the same characteristics other cottonwoods do—and some differences. The bark of young trees or new growth runs green and smooth, for example, though the lower trunk develops into the thick, gray, somewhat furrowed ridges so common to cottonwoods. You can see this difference on a single tree if you stand back and compare the lower bark from the new branches, at even a slight distance. The whitish-gray upper limbs and branches are patterned with checks and triangular patches beautiful enough to be considered artwork. The twigs are sleeker than those of most other cottonwoods (except the Narrowleaf), distinguished by narrow ridges that change from reddish-brown to dark gray as they age. The lenticels on the Black Cottonwoods, those little "mouths" that look like polka-dots or freckles on the twigs, are orange, another feature as distinct as a beauty mark—or, these days, I suppose, as a tattoo. It's these minute distinctions that botanists search for, especially among species that look alike even under the microscope. Leaf scars, the place where last year's leaf grew, give the twig a rough feel and appearance. Orange winter buds are slightly less than an inch long and are sealed in the aromatic balsam resin that gives the tree some of its common names. In the summer, you can find amber-colored patches of the gummy resin on the underside of the leaves. More rounded leaves grow three to six inches long and half as broad. Thick and leathery, they sport a dark green topcoat, but turn them over and they reveal silvery white undersides, giving the tree a beautiful two-toned look when the wind blows. The veins of the Black Cottonwood are easy to see, like miniature rivers running out to the leaf's edge. It's the dark green leaves that give this tree its name. As Tim Buchanan, city forester in Fort Collins, Colorado, points out, when you stand back and get the "long view" of this tree you can see the distinct texture, a softer, rounder look that sets it apart it from other cottonwoods. (Though Black Cottonwoods are not native to Colorado, the state's Big Tree Champion Black Cottonwood, a residential planting of some fifty years ago, grows in Fort Collins.) Buchanan also mentions that the petioles of this species are recognizably flat, but in a different way than on other cottonwoods. The smaller petioles (about one-third the length of the leaf) wave vertically, as opposed to the more horizontal motion of the Plains or Eastern trees.

The number of flowers is different in this species, one of the fine points botanists and arborists use to tell species apart. Male flowers bloom in elaborate, weighty catkins that have a distinct purple hue (from the stamens). Female catkins are a bit more open and looser. In residential areas, the large catkins are messy and often cause as much complaint as "cotton" does in other areas where these trees are natives. The fruit is the usual thick-walled, green capsule, only a third of an inch long, which dangles like a necklace and opens three valves to release the tiny cottony seeds—0.078 740157 of an inch long. And while male and female trees are separate in this species, rare reports of small numbers of male flowers found on female trees exist.

In commercial terms, Black Cottonwood is lighter yet than the Swamp Cottonwood, about twenty-three pounds per cubic foot (dry weight). Other ways to describe the wood are words we've heard before: soft, weak, the heartwood dull brown, the sapwood thin and white. Yet the straight towers these lofty giants can create kept the Oregon lumbermen busy. In the mid-twentieth century, one report says that 7,000,000 board-feet of Black Cottonwood were cut there to make crates, barrels and wooden implements. Though the viewpoint varies from state to state, the trees are still considered commercially valuable. Unlike other cottonwood species, this one takes a nail easily. What doesn't get nailed can be used to make particle board, veneer, pallets, and boxes. Short, fine fibers make good wood pulp, which makes high-quality paper for books and magazines. Even that next tissue you pick up to catch a sneeze might contain pulp from the Black Cottonwood. And chances are good that you could be sitting in a Black Cottonwood tree—a likely choice for the inner wood used in the construction of furniture.

The Black Cottonwood has other bragging rights too. Distinguishing itself as the largest poplar as well as the largest hardwood tree in North America, it can easily stand 80-125 feet tall. An Alaska nursery owner says that 120-foot trees around Palmer, in the south central part of the state, are normal. Descriptions of the tree in the pre-logging, pre-clear-cut days mention trees that reached 200 feet, with trunks that stretched 7-8 feet across. Such specimens were found on the Black Cottonwood's favorite terrain. Like its counterparts, the Black Cottonwood finds a river and follows it. As the Eastern Cottonwood has its Mississippi and Ohio river valleys, the Black Cottonwood has the Columbia. In the dry areas of eastern Washington it seeks low-lying valleys and canyon bottoms where it finds protection and moisture. Wherever it climbs the mountains, it always seeks moist areas. A thick matted root system makes it helpful in habitat restoration, where it prevents erosion and holds disturbed soil in place. And though such a root system makes it a nuisance near houses and buildings, it is being used increasingly in ornamental plantings. It also serves as a shelterbelt and windbreak.

Like all of its cottonwood and poplar relatives, the Black Cottonwood provides food, habitat, and shelter for wildlife. Deer, elk, and beaver are among the species that benefit most. In Alaska, small brown bats make their homes in the trees. Two species of butterflies feed on this tree, and one species uses it to winter over. The open crown provides nesting sites and perches for large birds. Smaller birds and mammals take up residence in the tree cavities, a result of the heart rot common to all cottonwoods. Like its relatives, in wild areas Black Cottonwoods keep stream temperatures cool, a benefit it extends to all other species in the habitat.

Tim Buchanan mentions that the "Balm of Gilead," a tree with healing properties described in the Bible, is thought to refer to this species. Native Americans found plenty of practical uses for Black Cottonwood. Its resin made an early disinfectant in treating sore throats and other respiratory ailments. Some natural health remedies still contain this ingredient. Ground up, the early buds and inner bark make a sweet-scented, skin-softening soap, and the wood works well as part of a fire-starting kit.

While the Swamp Cottonwood is ignored by researchers, a Black Cottonwood hybrid, *Populus trichocarpa* x *P. deltoides* (a cross between the Eastern and Black

Cottonwood) has become to plant genetics research what the Human Genome Project is for humans. We'll learn more about this scientific breakthrough in the last chapter, "Good News." In the meantime, Black Cottonwoods regenerate the old way, as other cottonwood species do: wind-pollinated, with the short-lived seeds set adrift and usually carried by water to open ground recently given a good stir by flooding. Viable for only a week or two, seeds germinate in the usual alluvial settings, riparian sites, and wherever moisture can be found on mountain slopes. And though like all green and growing things the Black Cottonwood loves water, it needs sun and little interference from other vegetation to make a first stand, which it usually does, growing in groups that march along the waterways of the West and Northwest. We'll learn more about the real-life story of the Black Cottonwood in south-central Alaska in a later chapter as well.

Now that you've met the family, you can tell that just talking about "a cottonwood" is a misnomer. Yet we talk about trees and lots of other creatures this way all the time—a pine, an oak, an elm—without distinguishing species or genus. Wherever we live, from Connecticut to Georgia, from Kansas to Arizona, or all the way to Alaska, we probably each know "a cottonwood" that fits one of these descriptions. Now that we've had the chance to get acquainted, let's explore just how they got here, and try to answer the question: What is a tree, anyway?

Sources

In describing the legal names of plants, I have followed primarily the USDA PLANTS Database. I have also used the International Code of Botanical Nomenclature/St. Louis Code where appropriate. http://www.bgbm.org/iapt/nomenclature/code/SaintLouis/0000St.Luistitle.htm

Extensive information on cottonwood species appears in *Silvics of North America. Volume 2. Hardwoods.* USDA Forest Service. Agriculture Handbook 654. http://www.na.fs.fed.us/spfo/pubs/silvics_manual/table_of_contents.htm

The Plains Cottonwood is described in "*Populus deltoides* Bartr. ex Marsh. subsp. *monilifera* (Ait.) Eckenwalder plains cottonwood." PLANTS Profile. Natural Resources Conservation Service. USDA.

"Cottonwood Hollow. Concord Township, Lake County. 77.65 acres." The Cleveland Museum of Natural History. http://www.cmnh.org/naturalareas/cottonwood-hollow.html

Daugherty, Ray. "*Populus sargentii* Dode/Plains Cottonwood." Handout to students. 2002–2005. "*Populus angustifolia* E. James/Narrowleaf Cottonwood." Handout to students. 2002–2005. "*Populus deltoides* Bartram ex Marshall (including P. Canadensis Moench)/Eastern Cottonwood/Carolina Cottonwood. 2002–2005.

Charles Fergus reports the heights of three Eastern cottonwoods in *Trees of New England: A Natural History*. Falcon Guide. Guildford, Conn., and Helena, Mont. 2005. p.101

USDA species distribution maps can be found at: http://www.usda.gov

The Lewis and Clark Journals/The Abridgment of the Definitive Nebraska Edition. Ed. Gary E. Moulton. University of Nebraska Press: Lincoln and London. 2003. p. 139

Little, Elbert L., Jr. *Checklist of the United States Trees (native and naturalized)*. U.S. Department of Agriculture, Agriculture Handbook 541. Washington, D.C. 1979. Cited in Van Haverbeke, David F. "*P. deltoides* var. *occidentalis* Rydb." http://forestry.about.com/library/silvics/blsilpopdel.htm

Peattie, Donald Culross. *A Natural History of Western Trees*. Bonanza Books. New York. 1950.

Measurements for the big tree champions are posted at American Forests, National Register of Big Trees Web site: http://www.americanforests.org/resources/bigtrees

USDA, NRCS. 2005. *The PLANTS Database*, Version 3.5 (http://plants.usda.gov). Data compiled from various sources by Mark W. Skinner. National Plant Data Center, Baton Rouge, LA 70874–4490

Walter E. Rogers describes the flowers of the Eastern cottonwood in *Tree Flowers of Forest, Park, and Street*. Dover Publications, Inc. New York. 1965. p. 94

"Eastern Cottonwood/*Populus deltoides* Bartr. ex Marsh.." USDA. National Resources Conservation Center. Plant Fact Sheet. February 2002.

Encyclopedia of North American Trees. Ed. Sam Benvie. Firefly Books. Buffalo, N.Y. 2000. p. 193.

Naughton, Gary. "The Cottonwood: Prairie Pioneer." *Wildlife and Parks*. 53 (3): 3–7. May–June 1996.

The article by David F. Van Haverbeke, "*P. deltoides* var. occidentalis Rydb. Plains Cottonwood," at http://forestry.about.com/library/silvics/blsilpopdel.htm includes a native range map for the Plains Cottonwood.

Gregg, Josiah. *Commerce of the Prairies.* J.W. Moore. Philadelphia. 1881.

Charles Goodnight describes the cottonwood concoction for stomach ailments in *Charles Goodnight, Cowman and Plainsman* by J. Evetts Haley. University of Oklahoma Press. 1949.

Information about the Chatfield Arboretum of the Denver Botanic Gardens comes from a visit there in June 2006 and from e-mail correspondence with Larry Vickerman, director at Chatfield.

"*Populus × acuminata* Rydb. (pro sp.) [*angustifolia × deltoides*] lanceleaf cottonwood. PLANTS Profile. Natural Resources Conservation Service. USDA. http://plants.usda.gov/

Jacobson, Arthur Lee. *North American Landscape Trees.* Ten Speed Press. Berkeley, Cal. 1996. Jacobson provides one of the most exhaustive accounts of the *Populus* genus available, including natural and artificial hybrids. pp. 467–483.

Donald Culross Peattie quotes Fremont's description of cottonwood in *A Natural History of Western Trees.* Bonanza Books. New York. 195. p. 332.

General characteristics about the Fremont Cottonwood have been drawn from several sources, including Peattie above, as well as the USDA PLANTS database: http://plants.usda.gov and the description of "Fremont Cottonwood/*populus fremontii* available from the National Wildlife Federation's eNature at: http://www.eNature.com.

These magnificent pictures of the Arizona champion Fremont cottonwood can be found in James Balog's *Tree: A New Vision of the American Forest.* Barnes and Noble Publications. New York. 2004. pp. 26–31.

Jay W. Street, in *Rio Grande Cottonwood Tree*, discusses some of the environmental concerns about this species. http://www.desertusa.com/mag01/jan/papr/cwood.html

Donald Culross Peattie discusses the Swamp Cottonwood in an article by the same name in *A Natural History of Trees of Eastern and Central North America.* No publisher listed. 1950. pp. 96–98.

Current information about the Swamp Cottonwood appears in "*Populus heterophylla L.*/Swamp Cottonwood." R. L. Johnson. http://www.na.fs.fed.us/ spfo/pubs/silvics_manual/volume_2/populus/heterophlla.htm

The USDA PLANTS database has a current Profile and Characteristics sheet for *Populus heterophylla L.* http://plants.usda.gov

Donald Culross Peattie discusses the Black Cottonwood in an article by the same name in *A Natural History of Western Trees.* Bonanza Books. New York. 1950.

Gay Nesom and James Henson. "Black Cottonwood/*Populus balsamifera* subsp. trichocarpa (Torr. & Gray ex Hook.) Brayshaw." USDA. National Resource Conservation Plant Guide. 2003.

In a phone interview, nursery owner Sally Koppenberg provided information about the native Black Cottonwood near Palmer, Alaska.

Tim Buchanan, city forester for Fort Collins, Colorado, provided an on-site visit to the state's big tree champion Black Cottonwood in June 2006.

Fire-resistance information comes from the USDA Forest Service. Fire Effects Information System (FEIS) Index of Species Information. *Populus balsamifera* ssp. *balsamifera.* http://www.fs.fed.us/database/feis/plants/tree/ popbalb/index.html

2

FROM A SEED

Putting the Tree Before the Seed

Before describing how a cottonwood tree grows from a seed, we should answer this question: What is a tree? Maybe it sounds silly, but stop and think about it. Do you really know what a tree is? Can you describe it in twenty-five words or less? I gave it a try. A tree is one of those big woody things with a trunk, bark, and leaves, larger than a bush or a shrub—or is it? Its roots grow down in the ground and its branches spread up in the air. Some trees have leaves. Some don't. Some have flowers. Others don't . . . see what I mean?

Trees grow all over the world except for the Arctic, in the midst of deserts and dry regions (except where they keep to the waterways), and above timberline—an altitude too sparse to support them. In North America, trees grow from the Florida swamps to the Rocky Mountains and from the edges of the Sonoran Desert to the Canadian wilderness. They're the favorite oak or maple growing right outside the window. The sweet gum that scented childhood summers. The hickory that shades the front lawn. The sycamore that seems to drop as many branches as it grows. From bonsai to giant sequoia, we can name and remember trees associated with our own lives. As for the biographies of trees, what do we know?

Trees do have their own lives. Like all creatures in the natural world, they have been studied and described by scientists. Yet even botanists and arborists still struggle with a precise definition. Though some species elude the characterization, as the USDA defines one, a tree must, be a "perennial, woody plant with a single stem (trunk), normally greater than thirteen to sixteen feet in height; under certain environmental conditions, some tree species may develop a multi-stemmed or short growth form (less than thirteen feet in height)." So then, what's the differ-

Populus L. seeds. USDA–NRCS PLANTS Database

---

ence between a tree and the Rose of Sharon bush in the back yard that (untrimmed, I admit), almost touches the power line? Or the pussy willow growing next to it, about which my neighbor has raised both his voice and his eyebrows to muse: "I thought that was supposed to be a shrub?"

If distinctions between shrub and tree are sometimes unclear, there are good reasons why. Some plants respond to their environment by changing the way they grow. The strangler fig, for example, makes its living by wrapping itself around another plant. But remove the plant (it's been squeezed to death anyway) and the strangler can stand up straight—just like a tree. Paper birch and Alaska cedar trees venture only so far into northern climates and then they simply fall down and act like shrubs. They creep along the ground, reducing the amount of plant exposed to the harsh climate. In such cases the definition of *tree* serves merely as a guideline. Plants will always find a way to grow over, under, or around any rule.

Another quality that makes trees different from many other living creatures (chameleons and salamanders excepted) is that they are "modular." Cottonwoods, with their tendency toward constant self-pruning, are perfect examples. If a limb is lost to age, disease, drought, lightning, or insect invasion, while not really able to heal itself, a tree can grow new parts. Under normal conditions, such constant growth is the life of the tree.

Additional personality traits make trees different from other plants. Trees usually grow larger. Taking into account mass, height, and breadth, they're the largest living things on Earth—and the oldest. The mountains of California are home to bristlecone pines thought to be 4600 years old, which dates them to around 2600 BCE. The Great Pyramid at Giza was built about 2900 BCE. Redwoods, among the oldest, at 2200 years of age, also hold the record as the tallest trees in the world. The colossus among them measured 368 feet. A bald cypress is described as the oldest living tree in the eastern United States, claiming a birth date seventy-six years before the American Revolution. Yet an Eastern Cottonwood known as the Balmville Tree in New York state celebrated its three-hundredth official birthday in 1999. But these examples are all exceptions. Most trees live to be about two hundred years old and grow to be about one hundred feet tall. By comparison, cottonwood trees may seem somewhat diminished. Still, they maintain a certain status as venerable elders. Though they have not been around as long as the bristlecone pines, they appeared on earth earlier than the oak trees.

As for current lifetime achievements, Black Cottonwoods recently discovered in British Columbia have proved to be 500 years old. A Plains Cottonwood called "the Vanover Tree" in Golden, Colorado, cored in 1989 and dated at 219 years old, was 236 when it had to be cut down in September 2006. As historical documents and scientific tests have proven, the Balmville Tree is more than 300. The national champion Plains Cottonwood in Colorado is thought to be at least as old as the irrigation ditch that runs beside it. Water rights on the ditch date to about 1866. Its counterpart, an Eastern Cottonwood in Nebraska, is also estimated to be about 200. But the biography of trees began much earlier.

In the history of the Earth, vascular plants evolved by about 400 mya, during the Silurian Period. Trees first appear in the geological record about 300 mya, in the Devonian swamps, as seedless plants that looked like ferns. Seed-bearing ferns, the most likely ancestors of the gymnosperms (trees with "naked seeds," like pines) arrived by about 250 mya but were gone by the time the Jurassic Period ended. During the Carboniferous Period, between 360–290 mya, club mosses and giant horsetails (or equisetum, whose tiny relatives survive today, often in company with cottonwood trees along creeks and streams) appeared. Now extinct, these colossal horsetails and mosses remain as coal deposits. Just under 200 mya, the conifers developed. Angiosperms, plants that produce enclosed seeds, as cottonwoods do, are first detectable in the Mesozoic Period, around 150 mya,. and continued to flourish. By 95 mya the willows (Salicaceae), the family to which cottonwoods belong, finally appeared.

As for the Seed

The biblical parable about the mustard seed teaches how mighty things from small beginnings grow—even if the gospel writer Matthew didn't own a copy of the *Guinness Book of World Records*. If he had, he'd have known that the mustard plant is not the smallest seed on record. But epiphytic orchids, whose seeds are about as big as a speck of dust (it takes more than 28 billion to make an ounce) don't have the same rhetorical ring that mustard seeds do. As close as cottonwoods get to being mentioned in the Bible is the Balm of Gilead—probably a balsam poplar and a cottonwood relative—and since they didn't make it into the *Guinness Book* either, let us examine the cottonwood seed and its role in the earthly realm.

Anyone who has lived near cottonwood trees know when the seeds let loose. They may not know that cottonwoods can begin to flower as early as four to five years of age, or that between five and ten years female trees can begin to "cotton," filling the air with their downy parachutes. As a local cottonwood expert in North Dakota has informed several surprised homeowners, the cottonless male that suddenly started to cotton after many years has not changed sexes; instead, it's a female that slipped into the nursery stock and has just begun her fertility cycle. He also informs readers about a product known as Forel (Ethephon), which lessens cottonwood seed production. The older a tree grows the more seed it produces—to a certain point, anyway, until health falters with age—although I've seen a Rio Grande cottonwood in New Mexico estimated to be eighty to one hundred years old, in full green-pod splendor, preparing to release her seeds. And a female Plains Cottonwood struck by lightning about twenty years ago and left with only half her frame intact was full of seed pods in the spring of 2006. In temperate zones, the release can be in full swing by the end of May and still be going strong in time for an early July picnic. Yet female cottonwoods act independently. Even trees in the same stand may let their seeds go at different times. The "delivery" is unique. Each tree "knows" when her time has come and acts accordingly.

Tim Buchanan, city forester for Fort Collins, Colorado, knows one cottonwood that takes six weeks to set her parachutes loose and another near an apartment building that tends to drop her cotton in a tidy circle on the lawn, causing little or no complaint from residents. Like any good observer, he has noticed that the peak season for release is precisely timed to the peak water flow in the nearby Poudre River. While attending a conference in New Mexico, he was not surprised to learn that cottonwood trees there timed their release to the summer monsoon flow. A tree in my neighborhood released all her fluff in one day. A friend who lives near Evergreen, Colorado, has reported a tree on her property that started to release, then stopped, then started again over a period of several weeks. On average, a single Eastern Cottonwood can release 25–30 million seeds. Estimates on the Fremonts range as high as 48 million. That's a lot of cotton! And it's what all the fuss is about where cottonwoods and humans share living space. Of course, the thing to remember (though it's hard to when you're forced to clean this downy blizzard out of lawns, sidewalks, gutters, screens, and air conditioner filters year after year) is that this is the way the trees reproduce in the wild. You're lucky to still have wild trees. They're part of the natural history of your locale. The trees were probably there before the neighborhood was, patiently sending the tiny seeds along the creek or stream they inevitably followed.

My neighborhood offers a perfect example of such a situation. Lamar Heights, built in the 1960s, was once hill-and-valley farmland stitched by creeks and streams that were channelized into pipes when the housing development went up. A male Plains Cottonwood in my neighbor's yard, here before any of us, overlooks the block. Perched on what was once the bank of an old streambed, the cottonwood relies on the same water we try to keep out of our basements with sump pumps, although the drought here in Colorado for the last several years has kept the pumps pretty quiet. But the cottonwood, true to its species, keeps its roots moving down and mostly out in search of water. Since the neighbor's tree is male, it manufactures pollen, not cotton—which is, incidentally, what you poor allergy sufferers react to. There's nothing allergenic in the cotton except perception: the free-floating seeds release at the same time many other trees and grasses are pushing the pollen count up. Thomas Ogren, creator of the OPALS™ allergy scale, reports that on a scale of 1 (lowest) to 10 (highest), male cottonwood pollen rates a 9 in allergenic properties while the female cotton ranks 1. Consider also that female trees are not sold in nurseries and garden shops, only allergenic males. Seed dispersal, courtesy of the wind, is how cottonwoods have been reproducing since shortly after the dinosaurs disappeared. It's as amazing to contemplate the journey of a single seed as it is to think of how that tiny mustard seed springs up.

The color of cottonwood seed varies with different species, but the tiny, mostly whitish-gray fleck, slightly crescent-shaped (like a Lilliputian parenthesis), is attached to a bit of downy-looking material. Milkweed and dandelion seeds share the same design. Some cottonwood seeds may drift only a few feet from the mother tree. Others, in more open, windy country like the Great Plains (think Kansas or Wyoming) can easily travel a mile or two or three, first on the wind and then by floating along on the waterways the trees frequent.

Set to coincide with the natural rhythms of spring flooding, the seeds drift as far as the water can take them (a problem, as we'll see later, where waterways have been dammed or diverted). The opportune landing spot will be in wet loamy soil, maybe even the sandbar, of a stream or riverbank. Left to do its work, the flood will scour its natural path of other vegetation, preparing the kind of open area cottonwood seedlings prefer. Flooding also stirs up and deposits a rich stew of ingredients to nourish the seedlings. The tiny fluff serves as a landing mat, helping the seed stick to the soil. Chances of survival increase if the seeds can keep moist long enough to germinate. The window of opportunity for cottonwoods ranges from a few hours to a few days. Germination can begin within about forty-eight hours if they land in the right spot.

If you've never seen a cottonwood seedling, it's a thrill. Ray Daugherty and I visited a cottonwood habitat in Coal Creek Canyon, in the foothills near Boulder, Colorado. We had gone to see the native Plains, Lanceleaf, and Narrowleaf species in their natural setting. We made our way down to the creekbed, which had already flooded and was dry enough just then to walk in. The fine sand at the center of the stream squished underfoot. Ray pointed out the seedlings, ranged like tiny rows of baby's tears tucked beneath boulders along the margin of the stream. Not a likely place to build a house, but the risk a wind-pollinated tree must take.

The paratroopers are well prepared for the journey. They wear a sturdy coat (the testa) for protection. Given enough sustained moisture, they're ready to go into action. The embryo produces a tiny root (the radicle) and a shoot (the plumule). That's all it takes to start a cottonwood—a root and a shoot; one to anchor in the soil, the other to reach up toward sunlight. Their germination is described as "epigeal"—meaning that the first pair of leaves to emerge from the seed (cotyledons) rises above ground. Studies of Plains Cottonwoods show that the shoot grows more quickly than the root, in that stretch for light. Cottonwood seedlings have to have light. The tiny, hair-like shoots face mortal danger if they can't get full sunlight for several hours a day. But the seedling Ray and I saw that evening was different. When we pulled it out of the ground I felt guilty, though Ray assured me it wouldn't have survived in the stream. From the tip of the tiny leaves, open as a pair of wings, to the fine, thin root end measuring 1.25 inches long, a full inch was root. What determination—water, water, water! The cotyledons had opened. Two true leaves showed above ground, so small the only thing they might have been able to shelter was a grain of sand.

Unlike some trees (pines and firs) that thrive in the protective shadow of their parents, cottonwood seedlings have to be independent from the start. And though they thrive in the sunlight on well-scoured open ground, weather that's too hot threatens their survival. Like Goldilocks, they have to have things "just right." They need almost a week to get started, and even after nearly two weeks the root is likely to be not quite a tenth of an inch long, although ours from Coal Creek, about the same age by Ray's estimate, was clearly in a hurry. Growth is usually slow going for the first month, and then root growth speeds up. Fortunately, there's an extra food supply packed into either the cotyledons or the tissue around the embryo (endosperm), to be used until the plant can begin photosynthesis and produce its own food. This is when the root requires a steady supply of moisture. Given the favorite location of cottonwoods, water is nearby, but natural dangers still exist.

Our seedling and others like it, lined up beneath the stream's boulders, were going to get washed out in the first serious thunderstorm to send water rushing down the canyon. Drought is an opposite threat to the seedlings, as it has been in the Great Plains and the western U.S. for the last several years. During a historical period of prolonged drought, the Dust Bowl of the 1930s, cottonwood loss was more than 50 percent along some stream paths in the Great Plains. And drought is not just an occasional hazard. It's a way of life in the area most cottonwoods call home. The range of the Plains, Lanceleaf, Narrowleaf, Fremont, and Rio Grande cottonwoods receives annual average rainfall of between ten and twenty inches. Drought can be the norm for one to two months in a row each year. Every ten years, this time period can predictably expand to four months. As I write (2006), the drought in Colorado has entered its seventh year. When local meteorologists give the weather report these days, they often show drought maps as well.

Conversely, as happened with the seedling Ray and I found, spring flooding can wash the future trees into places where they haven't got a chance. Or fungus can threaten them, even at this early stage. Other species, weeds as well as native grasses, can crowd out tender shoots. There's also the wind—it's the matchmaker during pollination and seeding, and the midwife to deliver the seeds, but once those jobs are done, Aeolian currents rise as microbursts, tornadoes and cyclones, a menace to tender saplings. Severe frosts (although as North American natives, cottonwoods have learned to tolerate temperature extremes) can injure male and female trees before either has a chance to flower. Yet in spite of all the hazards, cottonwood trees are notoriously hardy. Tim Buchanan admires the ability of the natives to resist drought, especially when compared with hybrids or most cultivars. Plains Cottonwoods have lived for millennia in areas from central Canada to northern Mexico, where conditions like dry, sub-humid, and semiarid describe a way of life. These same areas endure wild (yet ordinary) swings in temperature, ranging from $-50°F$ in the northern reaches and $0°F$ in the south. At the other end of the thermometer, northern temperatures can sizzle to $100°F$ and southern to $115°F$, temperatures hot enough to blister leaves and stop photosynthesis. In spite of all these natural threats, cottonwood trees persevere. Studies of Plains and Eastern Cottonwoods demonstrate an impressive success rate in germination of between 90 and 100 percent, respectively.

The seeds of many trees require a period of dormancy before they start growing. Dormancy has its own rules, often requiring heat, cold, light, moisture, or some other rough treatment to break the seed case and trigger growth. It's often assumed that all seeds require dormancy, but cottonwoods show no evidence of such a need, other than the winter period. Seeds produced in the spring are ready to develop when they leave the mother tree. They do not need to have a certain kind of light shining on them for a specific period of time. They do not need to be frozen and then thawed like acorns or heated by fire until the seed pods explode like Douglas firs. They don't have to travel through a turkey gizzard or a tortoise gut to have their seed coats broken. In the laboratory, cottonwoods germinate within two days after landing in the right spot—soil moist enough to keep the tiny root wet and growing. In these same conditions Plains Cottonwood seeds have proved to be viable for up to a month. Such scientific reality puts a damper on the story of the origin of the "Statehouse Cottonwood" in Topeka, Kansas. Workers on the nine-teenth–century construction project suspected that the seed of a cottonwood that appeared on the lawn and grew for many years had ridden in—dormant—on the Chase County limestone used for building. It's a tale full of hope and pride, a good example of not letting truth get in the way of a good story. On the other hand, the seeds of the poplar (*Populus*) genus to which cottonwoods belong have been stored artificially at low temperatures, and even vacuum-packed, with good results. Stored at freezing point (32°F), all the seeds in one study were still ready to grow six months later.

Back to seed size for a moment, to the mustard seed. Cottonwood seeds rank right down there with the small fry. Tree researchers often measure seeds by how many cleaned seeds it takes to make a kilogram. In the metric system a "kilo" equals 1,000 grams. In the avoirdupois system, it equals 2.2046 (call it 2.2) pounds. Eastern Cottonwoods produce about 770,000 cleaned seeds per kilo. Plains cottonwoods vary from 500,000–1,000,000 seeds per kilo, or 250,000–500,000 pounds. In contrast, a member of the palm family that grows wild in the Seychelles, known variously as the "double coconut" and "*coco de mer*," holds the record for the largest seed. These monsters can weigh 40–60 pounds each (18–27 kg.). A cottonwood relative, the aspen (*Populus tremuloides*), has to produce 8,000,000 seeds to equal a kilo.

We can tell a lot about a cottonwood's life from the size of its seed. It's typical of such tiny seeds that they're produced by trees that rely on the wind to sow them. More is better: the more seeds that travel through the air, the better the chance of producing new generations. It's all about survival. Since they can't choose their destinations, cottonwoods produce more seeds and increase the chances of land-ing in the right spots. And if producing upwards of a million seeds per tree doesn't guarantee another generation, such an effort goes a long way toward securing it.

As pioneer species, cottonwoods push on ahead, settling on open ground. The fewer neighbors the better, at first anyway. Other vegetation and other tree species often prove a threat, such as invasive Russian olives and tamarisks. The cottonwood root doesn't require much: moist conditions, ideally along a streamside bank. Larger seeds from other types of trees need far more. Some oaks in England have to rely on the local blue jays to distribute their acorns and have even adapted well enough that when a jay rips an acorn out of the ground after it's started to root, the root can start up again elsewhere—a true example of the maxim to "grow where you're planted." If the acorn has the advantage of bulk to help it survive, the cotton-wood seed has the benefit of speed and the ability to travel light and fast. It can quickly rise above the occasion and grow "head-high in a year" as Colorado nurs-eryman Mike Jeronimus likes to say. Once established, both root and shoot grow quickly up out of the threatening shade that nearby neighbors might create. As it matures, the cottonwood can catch even tiny flecks of sunlight from open, swaying branches. Large-seeded trees have found ways to deter animals (toxins, seed coats too tough or bitter to eat, thorns), and they can also attract animals that work as partners in nature, even going so far as to do the planting. The petite cottonwood seed relies on the basic forces of nature—wind, water, and light—to survive.

How Leaves Grow

Without leaves, a cottonwood or any other tree cannot sustain itself. Leaves are the small but essential sugar-making factories. Sugars, the tree's main food source, can be stored in the wood, branches, and roots. Roots of mature trees can form hundreds of miles of underground passageways. I measured the visible roots of a young Plains Cottonwood (about ten years old) that lay exposed along the top of a ditch bank. Forty feet of root traveled west; another thirty feet went east. As a result of the food-making process, minerals and sugars mix to form leaves, fruits, and all the parts of a tree. Like other trees, cottonwoods grow by extending their twigs and buds. As it grows, the new wood turns in a beautiful spiral motion, so slow we can't see it. This slow-motion corkscrew results in phylotaxy, the way buds arrange themselves on the stem—buds that will become branches and leaves. The spiral motion has its own ratio: 1 rotation: 2 buds. To see this, find a cottonwood twig with buds. Turn it once and you'll see the pattern.

This extension of buds each year is like the slow twirling of a magic wand. And what could be more magical—or more practical—than a new branch setting out next year's buds by June? I have not been able to find out how many leaves a cottonwood tree grows, on average. But apple trees can sprout 50,000–100,000; an old oak, 700,000; and an American elm, 5 million. As for protecting their leaves, cottonwoods have learned to live with extremes. A late spring freeze before new leaves develop a resistance to the cold can interrupt the growth cycle, but

Exposed cottonwood roots. Photo by Kathleen Cain

cottonwoods are self-insured. During last year's summer work, they set thousands of potential buds along the new branches. These buds won't bloom unless they have to. Examine any branch or twig, and just below the leaf scar—the indentation left when last year's leaf fell off the tree—you'll see a tiny dot that contains bud-producing tissue. A spring freeze is just one of several triggers that can activate these concealed buds. During multiple millions of springtimes, cottonwoods have learned some simple but sure survival techniques.

To do their part in keeping the tree alive, leaves need sunlight to perform their primary work of photosynthesis. Cottonwood trees are among the original sun catchers. Along with light, they inhale carbon dioxide from the air and mix it with water and nutrients brought up through roots and the vascular tissue of the tree. By combining these elements they create sugars needed to feed, clothe, protect them-selves—and grow. The triangular shape of cottonwood leaves has more than aesthetic value. Because they can move independently and shiver in the slightest breeze, the broad leaves take in more light than many other trees. Leaves on lower branches can even capture patches of sunlight from the spaces between leaves above. There's also a risk, though; with movement the leaves lose moisture.

The activity inside each leaf reveals the beauty of arboreal detail. The sun's energy, transformed into chlorophyll, is stored in hundreds of thousands of tiny (very tiny) compartments called chloroplasts. Even though they need to retain water sent up from the roots, the leaves also need waterproofing on the outside to keep from wilting or drying out. The skin (epidermis) of each leaf "breathes" through thousands of tiny holes called stomata. Typically stomata appear on both sides of the leaf and can open or close as needed to prevent moisture loss. One Kansas author says this is not true of cottonwoods, wisdom passed on to him by a former professor. And though I have not found anyone else who mentions this, I find his point worth considering. Because they are such an ancient tree, he writes—and thus less developed in some ways—they do not have the ability to close their stomata. Persistent moisture loss like that endured in a drought causes the leaves to dry and drop before they normally would in autumn—yet by spring the tree puts out new leaves again. It's generally acknowledged in both folk wisdom and science that cottonwoods make good drought monitors. Depletion of their underground water source can cause the same problem. I watched this happen to cottonwoods during the summer of 2005, to a tree in the neighborhood as well as throughout the Colorado Front Range. Yellow clusters of dying leaves dotted the crowns by mid-July. I kept an eye on the tree a few doors down. The too-early yellow turned a sickly brown. Steady west winds brought only high dry air with storms full of thunder and lightning but no rain. The leathery leaves tore loose from their usually firm grip on the branches. They were holding on for dear life, even though that life diminished with every rainless day we endured another temperature reading around 100° F —hot enough to stop photosynthesis. The summer of 2005 brought the hottest, driest July on record in Colorado since 1878, surpassing even the parched and burning days of the Dust Bowl. The same thing is happening again this summer. In self-defense, cottonwoods let the leaves turn yellow and dry, sacrificing parts of the tree for the life of the whole. As members of the willow family they are consummate and expert seekers of water—but only when there's water to be found.

How Twigs Grow

As grows the twig, so grows the tree. That's the short version of how leaves grow. To understand how leaves grow, you have to understand how twigs grow. The next time you're out walking near cottonwoods, you can see this for yourself by picking up a twig and examining it. Even in winter, next spring's buds are already set, as they were last June, as part of the tree's master plan.

Find a twig about twelve inches long. That way, you can see how the whole twig factory—the tree—grows and gets its shape. Find a twig with a prominent bud at its tip—that's the terminal bud. When we look at a tree we usually view it from the trunk outward. In choosing a twig we've begun at the outer edge, the newest part. For the moment we'll work backwards. Such a twig remains neatly packaged, bundled tightly until the tree receives the hormonal message that the nights are getting shorter. Trees respond primarily to light as they begin to leaf out. In a few years, if all goes well, a bud attached to a twig will develop as a branch and then a limb.

Just below the terminal bud you'll find multiple buds on either side of the twig. These are the floral buds. If you were as well practiced as Tim Buchanan or researchers working to restore riparian habitat, you could cut the floral buds open with a razor and identify the sex of your tree by the size and shape of the catkin within. But for the moment look further until you find a "bump" on the twig. That's a leaf scar, the place where a leaf grew out of the twig last year. The horseshoe shape marks the remnants of the vascular bundle. The little dots that freckle the twig are lenticels, little "mouths" that help the tree breathe.

You should also notice rings around the twig that might remind you of the loose folds of skin around your own knuckles. The folds are technically known as bud scale scars or "girdle scars." How many girdle scars can you see? Each area above a girdle scar marks a season of growth.

In cottonwood trees, the bumpy leaf scars appear on alternating sides of the twig (that's why cottonwoods are described as having alternate leaves). Look up into the tree, as long as you're there. Backtrack. Notice how the twigs emerge from branches, branches from limbs, and limbs from the trunk. Then remember it all started with a lanky sapling—maybe not much bigger than the twig; probably not as big around as your little finger, sprouting its alternate leaves—the same pattern as the twig you hold in your hands. The twig is the basic unit of the tree. As the twigs stretch out, the circumference of the wood increases, as does the trunk. Now you see why I say, as grows the twig, so grows the tree.

If every twig's destiny was to become a limb, cottonwood trees would grow hopelessly top heavy and fall over. Luckily for the tree, not all buds succeed. Branches fall or are shed deliberately. Those that remain don't all grow the same length. Several factors influence the number of buds on a cottonwood tree in a given year. Wherever they grow together, trees display a habit called "crown shyness." Trees need their "space," and many try to keep from touching their neighbors. Studies have shown that trees whose crowns do touch tend to have fewer buds on that side. Another factor is light: not enough light, fewer buds. And who among tree lovers has not watched with trepidation as a sudden spring blizzard blasts new buds from the treetops?

From More Than a Seed

In the wild, cottonwoods grow from seed after pollen from the male trees sets off on the wind and gets captured by the sticky flowers on female trees. There are other ways to grow cottonwoods. In the final scene of the film *Enchanted April* the matronly character portrayed by Joan Plowright shoves her walking stick into the ground as the group of friends departs their rented Italian villa. The last shot fast-forwards through a year's worth of seasons, halting in springtime as green leaves sprout from the stick.

Similar stories exist about cottonwoods. The origin legend of the Balmville Tree in New York holds that it grew from a riding crop stuck in the ground. And in spite of rigorous laboratory efforts, the tree's most successful reproduction was accomplished by that same simple method shown in the film. That's one of the wonders of cottonwoods, as horticulturist Ray Daugherty puts it: "Just plant a branch in the ground and they grow!" No need to always wait for the wind.

Vegetative Propagation

Vegetative propagation is the name tree people (arborists, botanists, and horticulturists) give to growing trees in ways that don't require seeds or sexual reproduction, the way Ray Daugherty described. And though some trees reproduce this way on their own, in laboratory and field conditions the process is more formal. Alternatives to seed propagation include suckering, layering, reproducing from a stump, grafting, and micropropagation—better known as cloning.

Suckering

We've all seen examples of suckering. Tree roots do this when they send out new shoots through your lawn. Many bushes and shrubs in my yard have a habit of doing this (a bit troublesome, since at last count fifty-three of them share my faint half-acre), including two maple trees and two Colorado blue spruce in the front yard. Aspens and poplars are notorious for suckering, and can wreak havoc with yards and gardens by invading underground pipes and sprinkler systems. In the wild, one cottonwood relative prone to suckering—an aspen—holds a world record. According to the U.S. Forest Service, this massive clonal colony, consisting of a single male aspen (*Populus tremuloides*) occupies 106–170 acres in the Wasatch Mountains of Utah. This extraordinary growth is thought to weigh about 6,600 tons, or more than 13 million pounds. It even has a nickname: Pando, from the Latin word for "spread."

Suckering, which has been observed in Eastern Cottonwoods, happens frequently when branches or limbs around the trunk get cut. Lanceleaf Cottonwoods also tend to sucker, at an even earlier age. Young Plains Cottonwood trees have been known to "vigorously" sprout from roots and stumps. Narrowleafs get so "aggressive" that they are banned from planting in many cities. But what a wonderful quality this aggressiveness becomes in the wild, where streamside habitat has been eroded or degraded. In an open space in Boulder County, Colorado, Ray Daugherty challenged me to identify the youngest tree in a stand of Narrowleafs; and then, by working my way back through the trees, the oldest. We were standing under essentially one tree, which had been able to quickly and confidently reproduce itself in its natural habitat. Even the venerable Plains Cottonwood champion, also a Boulder County native—thought to be nearly two hundred years old—boasts an array of whip-like sprouts growing from one pruned limb.

Layering

Layering is a second way that trees reproduce without seed. This happens when a tree's branches touch the ground and rooting begins. Conifers seem to do this more easily than other trees, and it happens more often among trees in northern latitudes. Layering can also be accomplished in the laboratory. It's not described much in cottonwood literature, but let me tell you about a Plains Cottonwood I have observed since 1982 along the banks of Big Dry Creek in Westminster, Colorado. One fall day in 2005 I sat at the foot of this tree and summarized what I had witnessed.

"More than twenty years ago, not fifty feet from where I sit and write, I climbed into the bend of a cottonwood tree and lay down along the length of one sturdy limb, long enough and strong enough to hold me as it rose off the ground and stretched into a sturdy plank before it lifted once more and grew skyward. It stood firmly rooted on the banks of Big Dry Creek, a waterway that has etched its path across these plains since before the time we think of as the Ice Age. I can't climb the tree today. I can't cross over to sit beneath it unless I put on waders and slosh through the muck of a new marsh that's forming around what's left of the trunk. And though that Ice Age ended about 10,000 years ago, the land and the tree that stood before me once have changed completely in just two decades.

The tree I climbed with childlike glee in the early 1980s is gone—and yet it remains. A grandfather cottonwood I called it then—and I was right, though I didn't know it. The tree is an old Plains male: cottonless. All that's left of the original elder is part of a trunk, about breast high, as the arborists would describe the measure, 4.5 feet or so—and about half again as round as an elephant's foot. Over time, its triple spires of limbs aged and weakened. They collapsed in a heap about ten years ago. Traces remain, visible in a grass-covered limb carved by the woodworking skills of sun, wind, and water. Branches linger as skeletal outlines in the soil. Repeatedly struck by lightning, blackened limbs and withered branches could not endure the burn. Other limbs and branches lost their bark. The exposed inner wood faded to gray and then white, dying back in fantastic forms that would please a sculptor. The remains of insect galleries have etched the wood into tatters.

Yet still the tree found a way to send out life each spring. New leaves sprouted in the farthest reaches. Those territories had not gotten the message of the tree's decline. The tree once hosted great blue heron nests and provided both location and building materials for the rough-stick condominiums of magpies. Robins, sparrows, black-capped chickadees, wrens, finches, blue jays, flickers, crows, and starlings have all chirped, warbled, and urged the blood calls of territory and lust from these branches. Bald eagles wintered over, resting and then setting out to hunt mice, prairie dogs, and jackrabbits downfield. Naturalists with Boulder County Parks and Open Space told me that 80 percent of Colorado's bird species find shelter in the reaches of cottonwoods—as they do wherever cottonwoods grow. Mammals love cottonwoods, too. I once found a raccoon tucked inside grandfather's hollow trunk, keeping out of sight during the day. Plenty of other mammals have found shelter, even food, in the reaches of this old tree. Possums, surely, though I arrived too late to witness either them or the deer that may have browsed its bark or the beavers that once relished it as a food source along this meander—they had disappeared from these acres before I started hiking here.

Though that old tree I first knew is gone, a visit about five years ago revealed a marvel of cottonwood determination. From the place where the topmost limb collapsed, one steadfast branch took seriously some chemical signal to keep growing. In response, it kept pushing out new twigs, new buds, and new leaves each spring. The tree sent all its final energy to the branch, which, now upright, has become the new leader for the tree. Growing at the usual cottonwood rate of four to five feet a year, the leader stands more than twenty feet tall. It's pushed its way out of the shade of willow companions and pursued a straight and steady course as cottonwoods do in their early years—for the first fifteen feet or so. The straight line has relaxed as the tree eases into sunlight and air. The branches have begun to

spread, arching away from the trunk in a pattern arborists call "erratic." The trunk
has bent eastward, constantly pushed by the prevailing westerly winds that shoot
down the foothills of the Rockies and race along this open plain. Companion to this
cottonwood since its birth, the wind has served as midwife, chaperone, sculptor,
undertaker, and now sculptor again. Responding to the currents by balancing and
thickening, the trunk straightened up for a few feet and regained the east, a direction it has favored for the last three growing seasons. Near the top, the leader has
begun to straighten up once more, aiming for the North Star.

Is it fair to say that the grandfather cottonwood lives on in a new incarnation?
Is this really a new tree? Scientists ask the same question about that mass of aspen
suckers growing in Utah. The evolution of this grandfather tree is a natural
response to the circumstance. The death. . . well, but the tree lives on through the
branch that stood up once the old hulk fell down. With such a good start and its
trunk sturdy, it will keep reaching. The tree now sits in a slough of the new marsh.
The marsh is changing, too, and from the look of several trees on the south side of
the creek, beavers have found their way here again. The rounded carvings of some
cottonwood saplings and the dam stretching across the creek nearby give them
away. Will the beavers choose grandfather's offspring as part of their lodge
construction? Will the tree survive?

A Word About Cultivars

Left to themselves in the wild, cottonwoods reproduce in the same way they have
since the poplar genus first appeared on earth some 55 million years ago. Wind-
driven male pollen floats through the air in a seemingly random search for the small
tapioca-colored flowers dangling from female trees. Just about as sticky as tapi-
oca, the females capture the pollen and begin growing seeds in little green pods
that resemble beads on a necklace.

A tiny parachute of down allows the seeds to navigate by both wind and water.
They set loose from the mother tree, ultimately aiming toward clear, open ground
along a waterway. Cottonwoods have a great sense of timing. The seeds depart in
synch with spring winds and the melt and runoff of winter snow. And though this
method worked more efficiently in nature before nearly every river and stream in
the United States was dammed or diverted, cottonwoods have learned to work
around such obstacles. One practiced observer has noticed how older cottonwoods along a branch of the Virgin River in Zion National Park learned to delay the
release of their seeds, timed to the artificial rhythms of the river established by
humans. Some cottonwood species can replicate themselves in other ways. Like its

'Jeronimus' cultivars of Plains Cottonwood, Box Elder Creek Nursery.
Photo by Kathleen Cain

aspen cousins, *Populus angustifolia*, the Narrowleaf Cottonwood has a tendency to sucker. On the other hand, "pole planting" is a common way to grow cottonwoods by bypassing their normal reproductive methods. Poles—long, sturdy cottonwood branches—are cut from a parent tree and planted to a depth of groundwater. Research projects show that healthy roots establish themselves within six months. Cottonwoods can be benched, stooled, or coppiced (where you live determines what you call this process): cut the tree back slightly above the ground and it will reestablish itself.

The products of these artificial growing methods are called clones. Though these days we tend to think of cloning as something that takes place only in the laboratory, generating controversies about sheep and humans, pole planting is just one form of cloning used in arboriculture and horticulture to create an exact genetic replica of the parent tree. Other methods include grafting and air rooting.

Cloning is an old method used by foresters and arborists who are always looking for ways to strengthen and improve a species. The goal might be to make a tree more resistant to insects, disease, or drought. A particular aesthetic quality might catch the arborist's eye—fuller branches, or a straighter trunk. Continuing the work of Colorado arborist Harry Swift (who first succeeded in propagating native cottonwoods, as well as growing aspens from seed), the father and son team of Ken and Mike Jeronimus, in the nursery business in Colorado since 1953, concentrated on finding a paradox—a straight Plains Cottonwood tree. As Mike Jeronimus explains, though customers love the cottonwoods, the erratic nature of their growth can make the trees dangerous and hard to manage in both residential and commercial settings. In a suburban setting, straightness pleases the eye.

Why does Mike think cottonwoods grow in those crazy directions? Because they're such fast growers, he answers. They want to get up and out into the sunlight as fast as they can, and they will grow in any direction to catch the light. Like many people in the nursery business, Mike calls the Plains Cottonwood "Sargent's Cottonwood," one of the earliest names for the tree. Keeping focused on local native species, the Jeronimus' hunt proved successful one day along Turkey Creek near Morrison, Colorado. They took cuttings of a tree that grew straighter than any others, but soon found themselves following the old rule: "If at first you don't succeed...." It took several tries and ten years to develop what's known as a cultivar, an abbreviation for "cultivated varieties"—and in this case, one that's registered with the International Poplar Commission.

On nearly a thousand acres near Lochbuie, Colorado, the Jeronimus family business moved from its former headquarters in Golden, Colorado, to the Box

Elder Creek Nursery, a wholesale operation. Named for the historic Pony Express station—the whitewashed building still thick with sod walls serves as the office—the table of land runs three miles deep and half a mile wide. Box Elder Creek defines the landscape. The property is scattered with outbuildings, new greenhouses, nine miles of fence, and . . . trees. On the day I visit the temperature hits a record-breaking 70°F; not the usual March weather and worrisome to a tree man whose stock might act as if spring has arrived with too many more days like this. The next few weeks should bring more normal conditions—rain and chilly weather.

Mike Jeronimus provides a quick but thorough lesson in the arboriculture of the cottonwood cultivar that bears his name: *Populus sargentii* Jeronimus. We drive first to the "cutting block," a quadrangle of two rows of cottonwood trees nearly 50 yards long—150 feet, about half a city block. Like all the cottonwoods here, the trees in the cutting block are clones of the original parent, a cottonless male that Mike and his dad first gathered more than twenty years ago. Like nursery owners everywhere, whether bound by law or by customer preference, the Jeronimus enterprise does not sell the messy, screen-clogging female cottonwood trees. It's a little surreal to consider that nearly every cottonwood I'll see today is essentially one tree.

Does that bother him? I ask Mike. A little, he admits. Yet he's glad that cottonwoods still reproduce in the wild, male and female—there are more cottonwoods growing today than there were one hundred years ago, he tells me, waving a hand toward Box Elder Creek. And he sells his stock to groups involved in conservation and restoration. To reproduce his stock, Mike takes tip cuttings from the block. The cuttings measure 6 to 10 inches. He plants them until only a thumb's heighth of wood sticks out of the soil. Unrooted, they sell for a quarter each. Every two years Mike performs what he calls "stooling" (also called coppicing or benching). He cuts the trees on the block off a few inches above the ground and lets the stumps root out once more. One of the nurseryman's favorite things about cottonwoods is that quick-growth. In Mike's world, the rule is "head-high in a year" (5.5–6 ft.)

We drive to the "head-high" field. Row after row of thin, straight cottonwoods fill the line of sight. Mike walks into the field and yanks a tree up by its roots. Even in so little time, two roots have set off between rows; here's the "lateral growth" that all the textbooks describe. They're already on the hunt for water, although Mike likes the fact that the Sargent, having adapted to its native conditions west of the rain line, is set up to sit and wait until water's available when the dry times arrive. Each root is about as long as the tree is tall. "J roots," Mike calls them, for the shape they make in relation to the trunk. They will be cut off, he explains, forcing the tree to form a round root ball that makes the tree more stable. All the trees we're looking at, several acres' worth, will be pulled up, have their roots cut, and be moved to another field to grow.

Our next stop is the second-year field. We get out for a closer look. Mike points out the spot on the tree where the second year's growth has begun. The first year's bark looks tougher. The bark of the new growth glows, a light yellowish-gray. It's smoother, in spite of the characteristic ridges, so distinct that you can tell the species by closing your eyes and reading the Braille of the long tough lines. Mike hands me a bundle of another cottonwood cultivar grown here, *angustifolia* (Narrowleaf). The cool bark is silky smooth, the balsam aroma unmistakable. Natural incense—until you work around it all the time and the brown sap covers your clothes and hands. For trees in the second-year field, one of two things will happen. To meet customer demand, the trees will be pulled up and the roots cut off and sold; or the trees will be moved to a third field and grown for another year before they're sold intact.

Aside from growing cottonwoods commercially, Mike has found another use for them, as hedges throughout the fields, to protect the other nursery stock. A mowing machine keeps them trimmed at just the right height. Mike first saw this use of trees as hedges in New Zealand. It's a variation of the windbreak practice used since the early settlement of the western United States. At Box Elder Creek Nursery the hedges protect the young trees against microbursts, those Aeolian demons that appear suddenly out of nowhere on the eastern plains of Colorado, driving straight toward the ground and scattering through the fields at speeds fast enough to bring a jetliner down—or to level a field of hundreds of trees.

Microbursts present just one hazard to the tree business out here. Originally planted in corn, the land was subject to the unrelieved cycle of plow-and-plant, plow-and-plant—resulting in an accumulation of salts (which cottonwoods don't tolerate well) and the development of hardpan about five feet down. The site of the nursery had to be plowed that deep in order to break up the ground. Fortunately, cottonwoods do have a higher tolerance for and ability to absorb nitrates, a component of commercial fertilizer. The Jeronimus nursery uses wheat and barley for a cover crop between rows. The cover crop is plowed back into the soil, a way to restore the fields organically.

Getting the soil settled down and young trees established created an attraction for another species. The nursery suffered $30,000 in damage from browsing deer in one year. Cultivar or not, the sweet bark of young cottonwood trees is too tempting for deer to resist—and after all, in the wild, it's a natural food source. Nine miles of fence later, the deer problem seems to have been solved. Whether they grow in a nursery or in the wild, cottonwoods are susceptible to their own pests, particularly Cytospora. In Mike's experience, the Sargent's Cottonwood seems more resistant to these canker-causing bacteria—both in the wild and under cultivation—than other species. Diseases aside, other concerns affect the very heart of the business, and of the trees.

You can't talk about cottonwoods, even cultivars, without talking about water. A nurseryman all his life, Mike Jeronimus knows plenty about the interactions between the two. He owns both surface and well rights to water on his land. He represents his industry on local boards and committees that grapple with the water problems in Colorado and the western United States. He can tell you how many gallons of water mature cottonwoods drink: about eighty gallons per inch of diameter per day. He looks over toward Box Elder Creek when he says this, pointing out the cottonwoods that grow there naturally. He gets historical and philosophical for a moment, mentioning how there are far more cottonwoods now than there were a century or two ago. It's a problem that came with settlement. Before Columbus, Native Americans used range fires to clear and rejuvenate the land, right up to the edges of the creeks and rivers where cottonwoods grow. Cottonwoods can't tolerate fire, but they flourish on the open ground created by fire. Fire was a built-in control, acting like a natural predator. With European settlement came repression of the fires. Cottonwoods and other species began to flourish in a way they wouldn't have otherwise, with the result that more of them—at least in some places—take up more water, essentially competing with the rest of the natural world and with human demand. Water law, at least in Colorado, follows two paradigms: "first come, first served" and "use it or lose it." Efficiency of use is not a guiding principle of law; neither is sharing, even for a common good. Efforts to be more efficient are not encouraged, much less rewarded. It's tough; another paradox. Still, at our last stop, Mike points out the line of cottonwoods in the distance—not cultivars—that range along the banks of Box Elder Creek. It's a wetlands area that he's required to protect, though he would do it anyway, he says. He uses the word "stewardship" frequently. The Web site for the Jeronimus nursery states: "Our commitment is to maintain a healthy environment as we work toward ecologically sound growing and business practices." He's proud that his nursery has sold cottonwoods to Rocky Flats, to be used as part of a decontamination process at the former plutonium production plant. Regular customers include groups and organizations working on conservation and restoration efforts. But, back to the land along the creek: they were running cattle in there. The area was nearly ruined—the ground compacted, the creek foul. He's letting the land go back to itself, letting it heal.

Grafting

Grafting is such an accomplished part of tree science that even a comprehensive textbook like Peter Thomas's *Trees: Their Natural History* no longer provides its history. It's a way of connecting one kind of tree to another, with assistance from human hands.

The easiest way to explain grafting is that a "*scion*," or top, from one tree is attached to the "stock," or bottom, of another. Though the word scion defines a child or descendant, it bears more princely overtones—the scion of a family, for example, the young prince or heir upon whom all hope for the future rests. Stock has an ordinary ring to it: common stock comes readily to mind. In the science of grafting, the scion from one tree, noted for some specialty—it grows straighter, has more elegant flowers, or resists attack from a certain insect or fungus—is attached to the stock, the core, of another tree. Grafting has given us dwarf apple trees. According to the scientific literature, cottonwood grafting takes place more in the laboratory and the field, as part of ongoing research.

Cloning

With the appearance of Dolly the sheep in 1997, the word *cloning* entered our vocabulary in a way we haven't stopped talking about since. Nor have we stopped arguing about the moral consequences of cloning, especially as it applies to humans. Yet anyone involved with plants, from gardeners to forest researchers, knows that plant cloning is an ancient practice. It's been a way to create new plants at least since the time of the early Greeks, about 500 BCE. The Greek word *klon* means "twig." Cloning is a sexless way—no stamen, no pistil, no pollen, no muss, no fuss—to create genetically identical plants. A new plant grows from parts of an established parent rather than from seed. Buds, cuttings, stems, roots, or leaves can all be used. If you root a cutting from a house plant, you've created a clone. The Peace Rose, the Baldwin Apple, and the Concord Grape are all famous clones.

Cottonwoods are one of the easiest plants to clone. They even clone themselves, since the entire species tends to sucker to one degree or another. "Leaf peepers" who visit Colorado to see the aspen change in the fall are really oohing and aahing over clones, whether they know it or not. The hillside ranges of golden aspen trees, cottonwood relatives, developed from a single tree.

Cloning has become controversial. It's debated from all angles: social, medical, political, ethical . . . even economical. It's controversial in the tree world, too. Vegetative propagation, as professionals call it, can be accomplished in the lab as well as in the local nursery. Private and public research centers clone plant material, trees, and cottonwoods. At the federal level, one of the best-known centers is the Los Lunas (New Mexico) Plant Materials Research Center, a critical member of many research and restoration projects involving cottonwoods. The Champion Tree Project International, a private nonprofit organization, has cloned many national big tree champions of each species in the United States and endeavors, through partnerships with universities and botanical gardens, to study the genetic makeup of these unique trees. This latter effort is not without its critics, among them the venerable American Forests organization, a nonprofit conservation group active since 1875. Cottonwood clones are almost always used to restore riparian habitats, a practice that some have begun to question. Yet one of the first things environmental scientist Dr. Stewart Rood, who discovered 500-year-old cottonwoods in British Columbia, wanted to do was to clone these Canadian Methuselahs—though for study rather than commercial purposes. We'll learn more about cottonwood clone controversies in later chapters.

Cottonwoods grow easily from all the different means of vegetative propagation. For this reason, they are not always grown from seed under laboratory or field conditions. Yet seeding themselves in the wild is still the most important way for the trees to reproduce naturally so that they achieve greater diversity. Cloning poses the risk of creating monocultures of single-gender individuals in a tree community: all the same tree, all male or cottonless hybrids. Seeds repeat the basic pattern of a cottonwood's more diverse natural history and parentage. The end result of all that repetition: root, shoot, seedling, sapling, trunk, limb, branch, twig, bud, leaf, flower, fruit, seed . . . and back to root again, is survival. It's the urge of the life force that has made cottonwoods permanent inhabitants of Earth since the Eocene, otherwise known as the New Dawn of time. So before we depart for the future of cottonwood trees, let's drift back and take a look at the place where they began.

Sources

For the official USDA definition of a tree, follow this link:
http://plants.usda.gov/java/profile?symbol=PODEW#

Guinness Book of World Records 2006 describes the largest and smallest seeds on record, as well as the largest plant mass. Guinness World Records Limited. London. 2005.

Learn more about "Pando" from the U.S. Forest Service Web site at:
http://www.fs.fed.us/newcentury/organism.htm

Ron Smith's "Questions on: Cottonwood" Web site provides answers to all aspects of growing and living with cottonwoods, especially for residents of North Dakota. Read through the pages first; your question has probably already been answered. Hortiscope. "Questions on: Cottonwood." http://www.ext.nodak.edu/extnews/hortiscope/tree/cttnwood.htm

General information about all aspects of cottonwoods can be found in D. T. Cooper's extensive article, "*Populus deltoides* Bartr. ex. Marsh/Eastern Cottonwood"; Likewise, David F. Van Haverbeke's article, *P. deltoides* var. *occidentalis* Rydb. Both can be found online: http://forestry.about.com/library/silvics/blsilpopdel.htm

Information on the number of leaves on trees comes from Peter Thomas, *Trees: Their Natural History*. Cambridge University Press. Cambridge. 2000. p. 9

For seed size of the eastern cottonwood, D.T. Cooper's "*Populus deltoides* Bartr. ex. Marsh/Eastern Cottonwood" at http://forestry.about.com/library/silvics/blsilpopdel.htm cites E.J. Schreiner, 1974, "*Populus L.* in Seeds of Woody Plants in the United States." pp. 645–655. C. S. Schopmeyer, tech. coord. U.S. Department of Agriculture, *Agriculture Handbook 450*. Washington, D.C.

David F. Van Haverbeke describes seeds size of the Plains Cottonwood in "*P. deltoides* var. *occidentalis* Rydb" http://forestry.about.com/library/silvics/blsilpopdel.htm

See Thomas Ogren's *Allergy-Free Gardening/The Revolutionary Guide to Healthy Landscaping* for information on the allergenic properties of cottonwoods. Ten Speed Press. Berkeley and Toronto. 2000.

Gary Naughton discusses the range of Plains Cottonwood, as well as the information about the stomata, in his article, "The Cottonwood: Prairie Pioneer." *Wildlife and Parks*. 53 (3): 3–7. May–June 1996.

Peter Thomas provides a thorough explanation of seed growth in *Trees: Their Natural History*. Cambridge University Press. 2000. He also describes the large sucker mass in Utah.

The article, "branching out," about Colorado autumn foliage, appeared in the *Denver Post* on September 18, 2005: 27A, 31A.

During a "Cottonwood Walk 'n Talk" in April 2005, naturalists with Boulder
   County Parks and Open Space reported that cottonwoods provide habitat for
   80 percent of Colorado's bird species.

I visited and interviewed Mike Jeronimus at the Box Elder Creek Nursery near
   Lochbuie, Colorado, in March 2006.

An account of Dr. Stewart Rood's discovery of 500-year-old cottonwoods
   appeared in *The Lethbridge Legend.* "Rood Discovers North America's
   Oldest Known Grove of Cottonwoods." November 2003.
   http://www.uleth.ca/legend/Nov03/html/Nov03_RecordOnResearch.html

1.2- to 1.4-million-year-old fossil cottonwood leaf, *Populus fremontii* NMMNHP-
   12705. Courtesy of the New Mexico Museum of Natural History and Science.

3

DRIFTING BACK TO THE NEW DAWN

Eocene. It's a word that describes an epoch, in a scale so vast that it has its own zone of reality: geological time. As ordinary people living out our daily lives, we tend to think of time in terms of our own small allotment. We don't think of Earth's history unless we have to. We are most aware of generations, which genealogists used to define as about fifty years, and other sources describe as the time it takes plants, animals, and humans to reproduce and raise their own offspring, or about thirty to thirty-five years. In the United States, the average lifespan calculated by the CDC (Centers for Disease Control) in 2004 was 77.9; less than a century, though of course it's the centenarians who create the averages. In the Baby Boomer generation to which I belong, we had grandparents who were born at the end of the nineteenth century. My paternal grandfather was born in 1894—four years after the massacre at Wounded Knee and ten years after his parents had left Illinois to travel to Nebraska. In the year of my grandfather's birth, the drought and heat were so severe that spontaneous combustion flared up in the prairie grasses. Drought and heat defined his life. He lost his farm in the wake of double misfortunes: the Depression and the Dust Bowl.

Having heard my grandfather's stories and having examined land records, family documents, and histories of the time and place, I have some sense of my family saga. But our story or any family's, is a minor tale when compared with the history of the land—or, with an eye to my purpose here, to the history of the cottonwood trees my great-grandfather planted in 1884, ten years before my grandfather was born. He set cottonwood saplings to grow along a sometimes-watery embankment where they and their ancestors remain to this day. The Timber Culture Act originally required landowners in the western states to plant forty acres in trees, as a way to improve the land, prevent erosion, and protect new crops from wind and storms. The act was later amended so that the required acreage

1.2- to 1.4-million-year-old fossil cottonwood leaf, Populus fremontii *NMMNHP–12705. Courtesy of the New Mexico Museum of Natural History and Science*

dwindled to ten. Cottonwoods were a popular choice because they grow so fast. And whether my great-grandfather knew it or not, unlike he and his family (his father and mother had come from Ireland, exiles from *An Gorta Mor*, the Great Hunger), the trees were native to the place. He probably considered history to be the sum total of the generations he had come from and those he could imagine in the future: at least back to his Irish-immigrant father, born in 1827—and forward to the lifetimes his sons and daughters and their children were likely to lead. When he planted those cottonwoods along the "draw," I bet he wondered how long they would live. He was a farmer. Farmers plant hope. Most likely he thought of cottonwood time in terms of the future. Would they hold fast in the wind, or serve as firewood, if need be?

To think larger, we must turn to the work of scientists, geologists and paleobotanists, who can help us understand the Earth and what it contains. In studying Earth's history, told in the book of the rocks, as geologists say, we can learn about "cottonwood time." Geologists don't think in years or decades; nor do paleobotanists. Their work is just beginning with the contemplation—and then the multiplication—of millennia.

Even touching a cottonwood trunk is a way to time-travel, although there's been a change in thinking about when cottonwoods first appeared on Earth. And to highlight the sense of the time involved, I'm going to stray from the star path slightly to consider not just cottonwood species, but poplars, the larger group, or genus, to which cottonwoods belong. In my reading I have found brief statements, sometimes unsupported, that cottonwoods date to the Cretaceous Period—145 mya and possibly to the Jurassic—200+ mya. That sounded pretty exciting. I imagined (with full Steven Spielberg special effects, of course), dinosaurs munching on sugar-rich cottonwoods.

Age rings in cottonwood trunk. Photo by Kathleen Cain

But not so fast. To savor the journey, let me slow down and share with you how it began—and after so many visits to the place, I can. An exhibit at the Denver Museum of Nature and Science has held me spellbound since it first appeared— "Ancient Denvers." The exhibit, complete with a narrative and the best of botanical art, takes you on a journey back in ancient time. In a darkened room on the third floor, several intricately painted murals depict Denver from its earliest time to the present day. The purpose is to present the big geological picture and help us come to terms with big swaths of time. It helped me travel back through Earth history into cottonwood time.

One panel shows an ancient river scene, complete with beach-strolling dinosaurs and masses of ferns and broad-leafed trees. I thought I saw the tell-tale triangles of cottonwood leaves. Could they be? The exhibit, and a book by the same name, describes this scene as "Colorado's East Coast—Dakota Sandstone" and gives a date of 100 mya. I contacted Kirk Johnson, the museum's chief curator, also a paleobotanist (an expert in fossil plants) and a lead researcher in the project that resulted in "Ancient Denvers." His response was terse but packed with as much information as a block of shale containing a fossil leaf. Cottonwoods, he said, or rather *Populus* (the genus), date to the Eocene epoch (55 mya). The individual cottonwood species may be even younger, perhaps having appeared in the Miocene (24 mya).

Ah, the Eocene: the "New Dawn" as our Greek and Latin-loving forbears named it, an epoch that lasted about 15 million years and took place a mere 55 mya. I knew the Eocene from yet another museum exhibit, in still another time. Like anyone who grew up in Lincoln, Nebraska, I can tell you all about "Elephant Hall"; or, more precisely, Morrill Hall, home to the University of Nebraska State Museum. This hall of giants contains what all Nebraska schoolchildren remember first and most: the skeleton of an enormous mastodon. But a creature in many ways its opposite lives there, too. Known as the eohippus, the little "Dawn Horse," a relative of modern horses, stands only a few inches tall. The skeleton of this miniature prehistoric mammal, now extinct, survived to tell part of the story of North America—to which it and cottonwoods are both native—as well as that of the Eocene, to which it and the oldest known cottonwood relatives belong.

To drift back into the Eocene, we need to think like geologists and paleobotanists: in epochs, eras, and periods of time. But don't panic. Understanding the geological time scale is easier than you might think.

Epochs, which we also call ages, make up the smallest units of geological time. The Ice Age is a good example.

Combine epochs and you have periods. The Current (or Holocene) Epoch, and the one before it, the Pleistocene, make up the Quaternary Period.

Combine periods to make up eras. The Quaternary Period, which we are a part of now, and the one before it, the Tertiary, make up the Cenozoic Era. In a nutshell, that's it.

Let's look more closely, though, as any phenomenon in nature is always more complex (and more interesting, I think) when observed in greater detail. Besides, who wants to think in sound bites? Though geological time can be counted in millions, even billions, of years, the years are not equally divided as centuries are, for example. Geological time is determined by significant changes that occur within each one (the first appearance of seed-bearing plants, for example, or the later appearance of those that bore flowers). The Miocene Epoch—one of our destinations—began about 24 mya and lasted nearly 20 million years.

I don't know about you, but it's easier for me to understand something like a long time span by working from what I know back to what I don't know. Starting with the smallest and most recent unit of geologic time, we live in what is commonly called the Holocene (or Current) Epoch, which began about 10,000–25,000 years ago. For us that's a long time, but in geological terms it's not much more than what's required for the Earth to take a deep breath. Even that centenarian at the family reunion would have to live a hundred more lifetimes to approach the beginning of an epoch in which humans—never mind cottonwoods/*Populus*—have been in the development phase on Earth.

Imagine it, though: the Ice Age glaciers have melted, making life worth living again. The Great Lakes have taken shape. Land in the eastern United States has lifted up high enough to push the ocean back—and not for the first time. Humans have begun to explore all parts of the world, to hunt, to domesticate animals, and to start making use of the Earth's raw materials. But life was not always so easy

The geologic time preceding the Current Epoch is called the Pleistocene Epoch, a.k.a. the Ice Age. Although there have been several ice ages, this is the closest one to our own existence on Earth, which extends from 10,000 years ago to about 2 mya. Though nearly 2 million years is a long time, we humans are not yet a regular feature of all landscapes, having traveled only as far as current-day Europe from Africa. Sheets of glacial ice have ebbed and flowed like tides and still cover many places we will eventually live when the ice begins to melt and the Earth warms up enough for us to keep moving north. But if we are not yet everywhere, wooly mammoths and rhinos occupy many parts of the world. Together, these two epochs, the Holocene (Current) and the Pleistocene, make up the Quaternary Period. The Quaternary is one of several periods within the Cenozoic Era.

Stay with me now as we move back into yet another epoch, the Pliocene, which began 5 mya and lasted for 3 million years. The world is a busy place. The number and size of mammals is on the rise. Elephants, horses, and camels move across many different parts of the Earth. Erogeny, or mountain–building, is continuously taking place in North and South America. Volcanic eruptions cause the Earth to cool as it prepares for that shift into the Pleistocene Epoch—the Ice Age.

The Miocene Epoch is next, taking place about 24 mya and lasting about 20 million years. The Miocene was warmer than the Oligocene which preceded it or the Pliocene which followed. By now grazing mammals have appeared, along with grasslands and kelp forests. Though no humans are yet alive to see them, the Sierra Nevadas and the Rocky Mountains have emerged. The Cascades are beginning to form from the great eruptions taking place, along with the lava plains of the west. Primitive elephants wander through North America. Asia and Africa are home to the apes. Redwoods appear in Colorado (yes!) and other places where they haven't been seen since.

Patterns change all over the Earth, including the circulation of ocean waters around the North and South poles. The Antarctic polar cap has come into being. Seaways have changed, bringing animals from different continents into contact.

Flowering plants look more like they will long into the future. It's here in the Miocene, at least one fossil plant expert says, that the species known today as *Populus deltoides*, the cottonwood, has appeared. If the smaller group species has appeared then the larger group genus from which it emerged, also exists even farther back in geological time.

Back into the Oligocene Epoch, then, which lasted 10 million years and took place about 34 mya. In spite of low lands and mild climates, active volcanoes rumble and roar, creating the Rocky Mountains. On the other side of the world, the Alps and Himalayas have begun their long ascent. Creatures whose descendants will become elephants have arrived in Africa. Many animals that live in what will become the western United States thrive and then disappear, leaving only their bones behind. And look out, over there! It's a saber–toothed cat!

As we cross over the Oligocene border, we enter yet another Period, the Paleogene, which contains two more Epochs: the Eocene and the Paleocene. We'll pause inside the Eocene Epoch, the New Dawn and our final destination, to consider the appearance of the genus to which cottonwoods belong, *Populus*.

Here in the Eocene, which lasted more than 20 million years and occurred about 55 mya, we can find mammals that will develop into the modern forms we know—though they are much smaller, like the tiny eohippus, the Dawn Horse, that at two feet long and eight to nine inches tall at the shoulder, looks more like a dog than a horse. Time does rise again. Mountains built up earlier have already eroded and left deposits of sediment and clay behind in huge basins. The seas have receded once more, as they have done so often over time, leaving more land exposed. A warm climate gives a boost to life; animals begin to grow larger. Look closely, for along the shorelines of departing seas and rivers, we should be able to spot a cottonwood ancestor, too. Ancient tides have left ripple marks. At the edge of streams, leaves that tumbled into the once-mucky earth, now shale, have left their imprint. It's been a long journey. Let's sit down by the stream and consider a few things about this ancestor. What did *Populus*, the poplar genus from which the cottonwood species would eventually derive, look like?

This streamside is the perfect place to find answers to this question, here in the still-open spaces of western Colorado, eastern Utah, and southern Wyoming. Here the Earth reveals, among all its rough-layered skins, the middle Eocene. And within the deposits of prehistoric shale, set adrift by summer winds along the shores of an Eocene waterway, appear the earliest fossil evidence of *Populus* (if not quite yet *deltoides*). Three scientists who study fossil plants have found a new (though now extinct) species and member of the *Populus* genus: *Populus tidwellii* sp. nov. (species nova = new species). The remnants of this female tree carry a prophecy of plant life to come.

Loren Eiseley, an anthropologist as well as a gifted writer, once imagined what it must have been like when flowers first bloomed on Earth. Wouldn't he have loved the Internet and the chance to visit NASA's Earth Observatory Web site at: http://earth-observatory.nasa.gov, where a view of the Earth in all seasons can be seen just beneath one's fingertips?

To touch even the trunk of a cottonwood tree is to reach through a veil of time and touch the Earth as it was growing rich and specific with grasslands and animals that could fly, crawl over land, and swim through water. The litany is exorbitant, filled with fur, fang, claw, and wing. Still in their primitive forms were bats we would not recognize, along with camels, cats, tiny horses, rhinoceroses, and out in the deep, leviathan—whales. By now the cone-bearing gymnosperms, their seeds as nakedly exposed as their name implies, are well established. Ferns, too, have long been part of the fantastic landscape. Flowering plants had, as Eiseley imagined (long before NASA gave us the view) added the shifting green to our otherwise blue planet—the colors of truth and hope, as we would come to symbolize them, respectively.

What's the ratio of 4.6 billion years to 55 million? The first number is the current scientific estimate of the Earth's age; the second is the time when, according to this most recent evidence, anyway, *Populus* appeared. As paleobotanist Kirk Johnson has indicated, the species *deltoides* arrived later, in the Miocene, a mere 24 mya. Not a long time given the history of the Earth; yet far longer than human memory can recall. It's humbling to recognize that, genetically speaking, *Populus* has a much longer memory than our own.

How do paleobotanists know this is a new species, one that provides the earliest record to date? They describe *P. tidwellii* as their Rosetta Stone. The original Rosetta Stone, discovered in Egypt in 1799, contained a passage written in three identifiable scripts: Egyptian hieroglyphics, Egyptian demotic, and Greek. It provided the breakthrough in translating hieroglyphics. Steven Manchester and his colleagues have not only found abundant samples of *P. tidwellii*, they've discovered the rare fossil that provides the translation: a twig with leaves and fruits intact. Before this discovery in 2003, leaves and fruits were found separately, widely scattered in different locations. The twig provides complete and reliable points of comparison previously unavailable. *P. tidwellii* can be compared with other "texts" in nature—even to extant *Populus* species—and the similarities and differences determined. In this way, she is a prophet, telling what had already happened in the natural world, and predicting what would happen some 54 million years later, along yet another waterway farther to the south.

Another group of scientists has also published the results of their discovery near what is today the airport in Albuquerque. The landscape has changed since the Early Pleistocene, about 1.2–1.4 mya. Though the area is dotted with pumice from an ancient volcanic explosion to the northwest, the fossil plant remains were discovered near a pond. The research team found both the Fremont Cottonwood (*P. fremontii*) and the Narrowleaf (*P. angustifolia*). Though far younger in geological time than the extinct poplar relative, *P. tidwellii*, the New Mexico findings proved that the "bosque"—the cottonwood groves along the Rio Grande—are much older than scientists suspected.

Descriptions of the Fremont leaves sound like those in a contemporary field guide to trees: deltoid-shaped, about as wide as they are long; highly defined, pointed leaf tips; from six to fifteen teeth (those teeth again); flat leaf stalks (petioles) about as long as the leaves; the distinct pattern of veins in each leaf, from the conspicuous mid-vein to smaller ones that alternate on either side. The comparisons resulted in assigning these leaves, the most numerous found at the site, to the Fremont Cottonwood species.

The Narrowleaf Cottonwood fossils were scattered and fragmented, less abundant at the site than those of the Fremonts. Yet both species live today, as they did when they were locked into the stone after the volcanic explosion, at elevations of 6,000–7,000 feet, following the water paths that run through the canyons between high and low ground.

From nearly 1.5 million years to 55 million years ago is a stretch of time that's hard to imagine. Yet with the help of scientists, whose technical work can be translated and told to us like a story, we learn the saga of the long existence of cottonwoods on Earth. They are not alone, these trees. They are like many living organisms that have come so far in time. They were here, waiting for us, for millions of years. They continue to grow and develop, some into amazing creatures that we might not expect.

Sources

Information on the average life span in the U.S. comes from the Centers for Disease Control. Center for National Health Statistics. http://www.cdc.gov/nchs/products/pubs/pubd/hestats/prelimdeaths04/preliminarydeaths04.htm

Basic information on the eohippus can be found at the Illinois State Geological Survey at www.isgs.uiuc.edu/ faq/fossils/pdq261.html.

For more information on "Ancient Denvers," visit the museum exhibit in person or online at: http://www.dmns.org/main/minisites/ancientDenvers/index.html. The book *Ancient Denvers* by Kirk Johnson and Robert G. Raynolds, published by the Denver Museum of Nature & Science in 2003, is also available for sale in the museum gift shop.

A geological time scale is available from the UC–Berkeley Museum of Paleontology Geological Web Time Machine at http://www.ucmp.berkeley.edu/help/time-form.html. I also turned to that old reliable, *The World Book Encyclopedia*, for help in understanding geological time.

See Loren Eiseley's essay, "How Flowers Changed the World," in T*he Immense Journey.* Vintage Books (Random). New York. 1957. pp. 61–77. For a view of the Earth from space, see: http://earthobservatory.nasa.gov.

Information about the age of *Populus* and *Populus deltoides* (cottonwood species) comes from e-mail correspondence with Kirk Johnson, Vice President of Research and Collections, Chief Curator and Curator of Paleontology Chair, Department of Earth Sciences, Denver Museum of Nature & Science.

The manuscript "Foliage and Fruits of Early Poplars (Salicaceae: *Populus*) from the Eocene of Utah, Colorado, and Wyoming" by Steven R. Manchester et al. details the discovery of the oldest known *Populus* fossil currently on record. Florida Museum of Natural History. University of Florida. Gainesville, Florida.

Information on the discovery of fossil cottonwoods in New Mexico comes from "Early Pleistocene (Irvingtonian) Plants from the Albuquerque Area, New Mexico." Paul J. Knight, Spencer G. Lucas, and Anne Cully. *The Southwestern Naturalist.* 41(3): 207–217. September 1996.

4

HOW TO MEASURE A COTTONWOOD TREE

It's the middle of May. My father and I are off to search for a cottonwood tree growing along the Blue River near Dewitt, Nebraska. We head west out of Lincoln to Highway 77, travel south for a few miles, then turn west again for a few dozen miles and work our way through Saline County to the Big Blue. Saline County is home territory for my father. His family lived in Wilber for many years. He has visited the county regularly since he left home in 1941—the same year he last saw the cottonwood tree we're hunting for today. His father, then county extension agent for Saline, took him to see the tree, already old and oversized more than sixty years ago.

Dad doesn't remember the exact location, but the sight of a gravel road that doglegs off the highway between Wilber and Dewitt stirs a memory. We follow it across the Blue and wave to a guy who's parked his SUV on the bridge while he fishes from the bank. On we go to a T junction nearly half a mile away. Some signal's gone off on Dad's radar. The road's not right. So back around we go, toward the man on the bridge who's packing up his gear, getting ready to leave. Dad steps on the gas so fast I'm afraid he'll scare the guy. We definitely get the fellow's attention. He stops what he's doing and steps back off the road. As we skid to a stop we wave and smile to let him know we're friendly. You're just around the corner from the tree, he says. Go back across the river and turn at that dirt road you missed.

Set in the midst of a cottonwood gallery that stretches half a mile along the gravel road, our tree doesn't look like much. Not until we see the trunk and a limb that arches farther across the road than the road is wide. It's a beauty. Multi-trunked. The trunks appear conjoined before they divide and ascend, defying both gravity and verticality. We are astonished to find a giant among so many ordinary

91

J. A. Cain, in front of Eastern Cottonwood near Dewitt, Nebraska.
Photo by Kathleen Cain

trees of the same kind. The others in the gallery are likely a tribe of children and grandchildren, for evidence on the ground and among the branches proves this is a female tree. Her dangling green beads have already opened to reveal tiny nests filled with cottony seeds.

What makes her endure for so long here? Two massive limbs extend from the trunk in opposite directions. A third has collapsed in cellulose chaos. Shattered branches stretch along the fall line—downed by wind during one of the fierce storms, summer or winter, that roar through this flat farmland. Judging by the size of the skeleton in the grass—long, thick, old, a third of the tree—she has enjoyed more life than many of her kind. Perched above a creek that wanders out from the Blue, she doesn't lack for water. Her roots still perform their streamside duty, to keep the bank from caving in. She shades and shelters other trees and vegetation in the understory. Ash, elm, sycamore, currant bushes, and grasses all thrive in her shadow. Several cavities, a result of the heart rot to which her tribe is so suscepti-ble, provide time-share housing for mammals and birds. Raccoon, opossum, and skunk are the most likely residents on the lower floors, though they're not visible today. And though we can't see any nests overhead, cardinals, crows, western kingbirds, flickers, and finches discuss our arrival in their woods. Spiders and black ants go about their silent work in the deep ravines of her heavy brown bark.

Dad estimates that the tree is 105–110 feet tall. I'm not great at estimating height. I am, however, most of the time meticulous and thorough when it comes to research. Today I've brought pens and pencils, notebooks, specimen bags for leaves and catkins, field guides, a magnifying glass, a camera (Dad has two), sunscreen, and water. But between the two of us we've forgotten the most important tool: the measuring tape. Aargh! Curses!

For a moment, we feel like Lewis and Clark when they lost their compass. Yet we share the ability to enjoy the moment. Like kids on a field trip, we spend a couple of hours admiring the tree, the quiet setting, and the day. We take pictures: black-and-white and color, panoramic shots of the tree from top to bottom, in our best James Balog style (the tree is too large to capture in one frame); silhouettes of the "snag" side of the tree against the eerie gray light, flecked with gold and pink, of a summer thunderstorm moving north, so fierce it will set off the sirens back in Lincoln. We snap each other in front of the trunk, arms spread to show perspective of the oversized bole. With the length of his garden hose in mind, my dad estimates the circumference at fifty feet. Too big, I tell him. Nebraska's (and the nation's) Big Tree Champion Eastern Cottonwood measures about thirty-nine feet in circumference. I've seen pictures of that tree, which lives just one county over to the west. Grand as it is, the one before us is definitely smaller.

Once they're developed, my dad takes the pictures to the dining room table and searches for the one of him with his arms extended. He has an idea. Equipped with a compass (the kind with a pencil fitted into one hinge and a sharp, pointed metal piece in the other) and formulas for finding diameter and circumference, he sets to work. Here are his directions for how to measure the circumference of a cottonwood tree when you have forgotten your tape measure but brought your camera along!

Problem: Calculate the circumference of a tree, with some known factors.

Known factors:
Circumference = Pi (3.14) x diameter
Height of figure standing by the tree: 5 ft. 7 in., or 67 in.

Using a compass, measure the height of the figure standing by the tree; since the full height of the figure cannot be measured (ankles and feet concealed in weeds and grasses), measure the armspread, which is equal to the height.

Also using a compass, measure the diameter of the tree in the picture. Compare the compass measurements to those on a ruler.

Using this comparison, create a ratio:
the measured height of the figure—2 in.
is to
the measured diameter of the tree—2.6 in.
or
2 : 2.6

as the known height of the figure—67 in.
is to
the unknown diameter of the tree (X)

2(X) x 67 in. x 2.6 in. = 174 in.
174 in. : 2 in. = 87 in.
C = 3.14 (Pi) x 87 in. = 274 in., the circumference of the tree
the circumference in feet = 274 in. : 12 in., or 22 ft., 8 in.

Wanting to be fair to both science and the cottonwood, we return to "the Dewitt Tree" two months later—after checking twice to make sure we've packed the measuring tape. "Take two!" my brother Sean warns. A project director in the residential housing industry, he remembers more than once when the tape broke. We make it a family affair. My mother and sister have also grown curious about the tree.

The tape measure is a fancy new Black & Decker battery-operated model that extends and retracts at the push of a button. It's perfect for urging around the circumference of a gnarly old cottonwood. We're trying to follow guidelines established by American Forests, a national nonprofit conservation group that has maintained the National Register of Big Trees since 1940. Champions on the register are determined by calculating points assigned for a tree's circumference, height, and one-fourth of the average crown spread. We don't have the special equipment needed to measure height and crown spread, but we can manage circumference and diameter. And it's not a matter of just wrapping a measuring tape around a tree. American Forests has established a protocol.

Circumference should be measured at 4.5 feet above ground level, in inches. This is an old forester's measurement, "d.b.h.—diameter at breast height." If a tree forks before reaching 4.5 feet, measure the circumference of the largest branch at 4.5 feet. Such a measurement is not impossible for the Dewitt Tree, but achieving a consistent d.b.h. is tricky. The bole is more exposed on the woods-side than it is on the side near the road. Between the three of us—my father, my sister, and me—we manage to smooth the metal tape into a constant height around the tree's middle.

How close will we come to the paper-and-pencil reckoning, formulated without a calculator or—horrors!—a computer? Our first measurement comes in at 24 ft. 11 in., or 299 inches. But wait, there's a wrinkle; a hinge of bark has twisted the tape. We rearrange. We hold tight. We double-check. The second reading measures 24 ft. 6 in., or 294 inches. We triple-check. Though the girth turns out to be less than we hoped for, we submit to the numbers. The final measurement seems to be 22 ft., or 264 inches—8 inches short of the estimate. Of course, we're new at this, so we'd love to be proved wrong!

Measure by Official Measure

Some months after we measured the Dewitt Tree, I met Keith Wood through e-mail correspondence with the Colorado Tree Coalition. As an assistant staff forester with the Urban and Community Forestry office of Colorado State University, he works with the coalition to officially measure and document the largest native species of Colorado trees. He offers to teach me how to take an official measurement of a long-lived cottonwood that grows near where I live in Arvada, Colorado. With the help of Craig Hillegass, the Arvada city forester, and the kind permission of the tree's former owner (the land is now passive open space for the city) we meet one crisp winter morning along a canal that has nourished a nearby stand of cottonwoods for at least six decades.

Keith has brought along three essential forester's tools. The first is called a diameter tape. It provides diameter measurements on one side and circumference measurements on the other. Foresters, as well as American Forests, always measure a tree's circumference in inches. The second tool is a handheld, hundred-foot measuring tape that unrolls from a spool. This second tape is used to determine the height of the tree from a distance, as well as the crown spread. The third tool in Keith's kit, and the most unusual, is called a clinometer. About the size and shape of a small tape measure, the kind you'd take along shopping, the clinometer has a built-in trigonometric formula that measures tree height. Inside the tiny lens, two scales appear side by side: one that's 60 feet, the other 100 feet. Keith explains that some foresters prefer (and some situations require) a 60-foot measure. He likes to calculate from 100 feet.

The men wrap the diameter tape around the cottonwood's trunk. The tape has a pointed end, perfect for hooking into one of the deep furrows. Well practiced at this task, they stretch the tape around the tree at a consistent height of 4.5 feet with little effort. The result is 109.2 inches.

Keith hands me the 100-foot spool and instructs me to walk it out to its length, making sure I stay on level ground. At that stopping point, he uses the clinometer to measure the height of the tree and then hands the instrument to me to do the same. An accurate measurement requires a steady hand and a good eye. It's like looking through binoculars. You have to keep both eyes open, using the left to sight the highest branch on the tree (determined by agreement beforehand and not necessarily the one closest to you) and the right to see where the needle falls on the scale. The sun's bright stare is unrelenting this morning and I am unpracticed. My hand's a little shaky. It takes me longer than it took Keith. We agree on 98 feet for the top. The formula requires a second measurement taken at stump line, where the trunk meets the ground. This is a negative measurement, -2 feet. When subtracted from the top reading, we get a final measure of 100 feet.

The third measurement reveals the average crown spread, determined by measuring the longest and the shortest branches, then figuring an average. Here's where the art of forestry comes in. It's a subjective judgment. It's not always easy to tell which branches—and they must be living branches—are the longest or the shortest on either side of the tree. Keith and Craig have the trained eyes of professionals, though. It's easy to agree that they've made the right choices. Once again we unroll the 100-foot spool from the tree trunk to the drip line—the place where water drips off the tree—to the ends of the shortest and longest branches.

The longest branch exceeds the length of the tape measure: 109 feet.

The shortest fits the tape perfectly: 100 feet.

The combined length, 209 feet, divided by 2, equals 104.5 feet. We need one more calculation. American Forests uses one-fourth of the average crown spread as the official measurement: or, 26.13 feet.

American Forests uses a point system to evaluate all the big trees. Keith does some quick number crunching. He converts the trunk measurement to circumference by multiplying the diameter by Pi (3.14). The result is 342.90 inches. Here are his results. Each measurement equals points that are then added together for a final score.

    342.90   (circumference in inches)
    100   (height in feet)
    26.13   (1/4 average crown spread in feet)

TOTAL POINTS = 468.93, rounded to 469

According to the 2006 state list for Plains Cottonwoods that Keith compiled, this tree could take fifth place, slightly behind a tree in Cortez, Colorado, with 474.22 points.

The National Big Tree Register

Why measure trees? Those who work with trees for a living need to know the results of their efforts in the lab, the nursery, the field, and the forest. It's just good science. It's also the American way! We love to find and celebrate what's bigger, faster, better—that was even the theme of the 2006 Winter Olympics. We only have to remember the super-sized lumberman Paul Bunyan and Babe, his big blue ox, to understand why big trees still stand tall in the American imagination.

Since 1940, American Forests has celebrated this uniqueness by accepting nominations, from ordinary citizens and professionals alike, for "big trees," the largest of their species. The list includes nearly eight hundred species that are native and naturalized to the United States, categories that exclude natural hybrids such as the Lanceleaf Cottonwood (although many states do recognize their Lanceleafs—and Nebraska needs a champion in this category!). Through forest services and various state organizations such as Tree New Mexico or the Colorado Tree Coalition, for example, Big Tree Coordinators in each state oversee the nomination, measurement, and reporting of big trees.

Though the Big Tree Register may be its best known feature, American Forests does more than keep track of big trees. Its mission is "to protect, restore and enhance the natural capital of trees and forests." But it's hard to resist the fascination with big ones, hard not to wonder how and why these big trees got that way. Keith Wood answers that their survival proves a combination of superior genetics, the right environmental conditions—and, as Craig Hillegass adds—luck.

Activity on the Big Tree Register is ongoing. By working with the Big Tree Coordinators in each state, residents can nominate trees each year. Christine Meyer, Big Tree Coordinator for Nebraska, knows that the ranking state champion in any category can change from day to day. Champions come and go. A larger specimen is discovered to unseat old champions. Older trees succumb to disease. They topple over in storms and get carved up by lightning. They get cut down to make way for houses, roads, and shopping malls. Some have even been vandalized and poisoned. Cottonwoods in particular are susceptible to disease, windthrow, and the ravages of insects. Before it fell in 1991, the national Big Tree Champion Eastern Cottonwood was an Illinois favorite that grew along the Michigan and Illinois Canal. Hollow at the base, it was big enough so that schoolchildren on a field trip could crowd inside the trunk.

To view the current list of the eight Big Tree Champion cottonwoods (twelve total for the genus *Populus*), visit American Forests at http://www.american forests.org and click on the link for the Big Tree Register. Search the register page for *cottonwood* or *populus*.

Meeting the Champions

Eastern Cottonwood

When she greets us at the door, Susan Hackbart offers to walk us down to the Eastern Cottonwood tree that is the Big Tree Champion—the largest of its species—in Nebraska, the U.S., and perhaps the world. We follow a trail ("it's soft today," she warns) that drops down beside a stream and leads through a slight woods straight to the champ. Susan and her husband Daryl do not farm, but they have purchased land from a man, now deceased, who grew up under the cottonwood we are about to see. His original plan—altered when the young couple bought extra acreage to save the tree—was to cut down the champ and create more tillable acres. If the tree had a nickname, it died with this man—though "Lucky" would fit. If there were stories about it, they too are gone. Susan conjectures that no one is left who might know more about it than what the statistics say—that according to the National Register of Big Trees, this is *the* big Eastern Cottonwood. Like royalty, the national champion keeps it secrets.

How do you describe a tree that when last measured in 2003, rounded out at 444 inches in circumference, stood 93 feet tall, spread 103 feet across and received a total point score of 563? Mammoth, huge, massive, immense, gigantic,

---

In Search of a Champion

Christine Meyer reports that Nebraska has no Lanceleaf Cottonwood champion. Though the Lanceleaf is a natural hybrid and as such does not qualify for inclusion on the National Register of Big Trees, Nebraska does recognize champion status for the Lanceleaf at the state level. Meyer especially encourages big tree hunters in western Nebraska to be on the lookout for such a specimen and reminds searchers that the tree "does not have to be an enormous giant, only the largest of its species in the state." For more information, contact the office of the Nebraska Big Tree Coordinator through the Nebraska Champion Tree Program at: http://www.nfs.unl.edu/CTProgram.htm.

Kathleen Cain and Big Tree Champion Eastern Cottonwood, Seward County,
Nebraska. Photo by John Vaske. Reprinted with permission.

gargantuan, enormous, colossal, oversized, Homeric . . . no adjective fits. As we
walk in under the drip line I realize I cannot view it in a single glance—the way the
camera cannot take in its height, breadth, or depth in a single shot. You need a
panoramic camera, everyone tells me. You'd need a winch and tackle, I don't tell
them. It's winter, so the look of this old sylvan survivor is like that of an ancient ship
with its sails down and the rigging exposed. Even now, sea and ocean similes linger
in the Great Plains. Along nearly every creek sails a cottonwood, though none like
this one that could lead the entire fleet.

From a distance the multiple trunks form a W, the split-letter signature of
cottonwoods (they also love Ys and Vs). The boles divide before they lift, each one
stretching up and out, the dynamic that, even leafless, gives the crown such a lofty
appearance. Since the division has taken place before the tree reached 4.5 feet tall,
the trunk counts as one, not two. The cottonwood has lost enormous limbs the way
smaller trees lose branches. Twigs by the dozens have been cast off in reaction to
drought. Staring up into the top of the tree makes me dizzy. Wind has been hard at
work here, even though the creek flows down through a sheltered area, into a slight
valley between the subtle rise and fall of surrounding hills. Lightning found a
tender spot, making a direct hit where the trunks conjoin. Bark and cambium have

erupted from the inside out, like a volcano. The electrical jolt tore the tree open, boiling the sap and splintering the woody shield. The owners fear the tree will not survive. Susan points out more strikes higher up in the tree. One limb has been amputated, and another is twisted and torn. The tree, thought to be nearly two hundred years old, bears the scars like a battle rig.

A friend who has driven me out here observes that there are few other cottonwoods in the vicinity. He recognizes the bare trees by their bark—ash, red maple, elm, hackberry. Maybe that's why this one has grown so massive, he speculates, in answer to my constant: Why? Why does one succeed so well where others do not? How does it defy the odds of its own weaknesses—soft, brittle, tending to live not more than one hundred years, susceptible to heart rot, borers, chewers, diggers, as well as canker-causing bacteria, fungus, slime mold, you name it—as well as the marauding weather forces that sweep across these still-open plains? It stands in the face of natural powers strong enough to wear down mountains and change entire landscapes. And then I remember what Ray Daugherty has taught me: "Science cannot answer why . . . it can only answer how." And although I have worked as a volunteer naturalist, I am not a scientist. So, why?!

Is it just because a tiny, tufted bit of life-containing germ inside a seed dropped down here one day late in spring or early summer and found everything it needed: water, sunlight, the right mix of nutrients—and laid claim to this streamside territory by putting down a root and sending up a shoot? This is lowland terrain. In addition to the stream, water drains off from all the higher fields around, into this shallow declivity. It's "soft" today because it's wet. And though we can't see them, the roots of the cottonwood are working beneath us. Double or even triple that crown spread of 103 feet for the province the roots have colonized in search of water. Beneath the ground, they stretch in the same directions as the limbs and branches. We're standing on them. We walked above them as we approached the tree from about three hundred feet.

But why does one succeed to such massive proportions when all around the rest are about the size you might expect? Are trees like people? Perpetuated by some genetic message that makes one taller, stronger, and more able to stand and live longer in one place? Is it as my friend says, that there are few other cottonwoods here? Is there such synergy between this tree and its companions that it has benefited the community and receives benefits in return, some co-op of nature? Or is it a fluke—an exception in a natural world so full of exceptions? Is this an example of the variation among species that Charles Darwin described? Or is it an anomaly—not superior at all—but a sign of abnormal genetics? As gigantism is in humans . . . caused by some wildness in growth hormones not seen in other trees?

"Something" has tried to nest in the upper branches, Susan points out. She worries about her kids when they scramble through the tree, showing the route they take from the right wing of the big W. Once the kids are up there they can climb to just about any limb. When we walk around the left side of the W, she spots another child. The carcass of a fawn, the bright bone of its tiny skull exposed, lies folded in a small cove between two extended walls of the trunk. Though the eastern side of the tree provides shelter from the blustery west wind and the relentless, prevailing south wind, sometimes the shelter is not enough.

Americans don't go in for royalty much. But if ever a tree deserved a royal title, surely this one qualifies; Lucky, the Earl of Seward (for no one has reported any cotton), perhaps, in honor of both fate and county. I should have curtsied as I came down the path. I should have asked his permission to step across the land where his roots grow beneath me. He is the royal *genius loci*, the spirit of the place, both guardian and atmosphere. He dominates the streamside community of trees and grasses. He is their reason for survival, as they are surely part of the reason for his endurance; water, light, the company of others that can be counted as friends, even allies. Who or what could ask for more when life means standing so long in one place without being able to move except to wave? The cottonwood is the ranking noble of the streamside. He holds a longer genealogy than most, and a biological memory stretching back at least 24 million years. At the very least he deserves a nod of respect.

When I return later in the year, in August, to see Lucky in full bloom, Susan Hackbart's fears have come true. The lightning strike at the place where the old tree's trunks are conjoined has become an ever-widening split that is literally pulling him apart. Eventually, my respect will turn to memorial observance. It's the way of life in these riparian woods.

Plains Cottonwood

Five hundred miles away, within view of the foothills of the Rocky Mountains in northern Boulder County, Colorado, the riparian woods keep a late winter silence. The ninety acres of open space surrounding the woods will soon fill with live choruses of birdsong. Someone has even reported a heron rookery nearby. Shorebirds, water fowl, and raptors will arrive, making up a list that includes more than thirty species, ranging from the Common Snipe to the Bald Eagle, though none are visible on this January day. Likewise, the list of local mammals seems exorbitant when compared with other places where development has edged the critters out of their home territory. The plant communities, too, are lush by comparison with others, and growing more so with help from the Boulder County Parks and Open Space department. Conscientious management of these acres is part of an overall

*Foot of the Big Tree Champion Plains Cottonwood, Boulder County, Colorado.
Photo by Kathleen Cain*

plan to increase the natural biological diversity of the land. Oak, cherry, and willow trees have been planted to complement native plants like prairie cordgrass, big bluestem, yellow Indian grass, switchgrass, and peachleaf willow. Efforts to reduce invasive species are underway. A native, *the* native, gets its own paragraph in the description of the area, but there's not much fanfare. It's "award-winning," which refers to its rank as the Big Tree National Champion Plains Cottonwood.

The newest measurements for this tree, taken in fall 2005 by Neil Bamesberger of the Colorado Tree Coalition, reveal a circumference of 393.6 inches, a height of 95 feet, and an average crown spread of 99 feet. These measurements give the tree a total point score of 513.35. It has been listed on the National Register of Big Trees since 1967. T-shirts available for sale at the grocery in the small town nearby publicly proclaim this as "the world's largest cottonwood tree."

Plans are underway to create a walkway and viewing platform that will allow the public to visit sometime in 2007. I have arranged for the staff-guided tour of the site that's currently required. My guide is Pascale Fried, Education and Outreach Coordinator for Boulder County Parks and Open Space. She has the unmistakable enthusiasm so obvious among those whose workplace is nature. Like others I have met, she is generous with her time and knowledge, even willing to meet me at the end of her shift and introduce me to the tree.

This "Gentle Giant" as it's nicknamed, is yet another venerable elder. I feel like bowing, and this time I do. The tree has secluded itself in the place its seed first landed near an irrigation ditch at the bottom of a steep embankment—how many years ago? No one knows for sure. The county forester suspects the Giant has been here at least as long as the ditch. First water rights date to 1864 or 1866. It hasn't been possible to "core" the tree (to drill a core sample to test the age), Pascale explains. Boulder County doesn't have the necessary (and expensive) equipment— the same equipment needed to core a redwood. History of the area helps establish a timeline. The open space was formerly known as "Laramie Crossing" for the passage over nearby St. Vrain Creek. The name dates from the 1860s, when the Overland Trail from Denver to Laramie, Wyoming, tracked through here. By then the cottonwood was probably already peeking over the top of its embankment, though travelers then might have been as unaware of it as they are today. Unless you know what you're looking for, the champion's crown is just another bunch of branches sticking up through tangled treetops.

Some people look at a cottonwood and think "cottonwood," or maybe even more vaguely, "tree." I'm not one of them. Every tree has a unique personality. Champion trees exhibit this trait more than others, and the Gentle Giant proves the point. Pascale says it first, how the gnarled foot of the trunk, overgrown with generations of rough bark, reminds her of an old man's knobby hands—those of her grandfather, or a hard-working farmer. The calluses look as if they might harm the tree. I saw similar growths on several geriatric Eastern cottonwoods in Nebraska. Tree experts explain that this "knobbing" is a way for the trees to contain a fungus. When I knock on different parts of the Giant's trunk, several hollow echoes reply. Pascale points out how the ground beneath the tree has been trampled—evidence, like the worn trail leading down the embankment—that people have been visiting for a long time. Such packed down soil harms the roots. Pascale and others worry about the tree's safety—and that of any unauthorized visitors. Cottonwoods are notorious for dropping limbs without warning. Only a month earlier, during a sudden, wet, heavy snowstorm in Denver, the limb of an ancient cottonwood fell and fatally injured its owner as she shoveled snow. Beneath the Giant, a single limb that crashed down measures the same size as an average tree. He's been pruned on one side but the county wants to keep the site in as natu- ral, yet safe, a condition as possible. No guy wires, no supports that would spoil the setting are visible. The educational focus will help preserve the location by teach- ing visitors the importance of stewardship.

It's silent, this tree. Not only a Gentle Giant, but a reticent one. Perhaps it's because the woods are so still today, except for last year's grasses talking back to the wind that sweeps down from the foothills. The top branches of the tree exposed above the embankment click and sway in stiff winter rhythms. Down below the irrigation ditch, the cottonwood has dug in. Its roots long ago moved out beyond the reach of the road, far beyond the width of its crown spread. By the time the stage to Laramie had a regular schedule the roots had already begun traveling north into what is now open space wetlands. East and west, the Giant has anchored along the lower embankment, extending into landscape that in other places would be called a dell or a dale but here is still called a draw or a gully. There's plenty of water—from the irrigation ditch, from old gravel pits, from groundwater, from nearby St. Vrain Creek. It was the perfect place for that little seed to land and sprout before any other green or growing thing caught up with it. And though now more like an old man who needs the sun on his skin, he still stretches toward light, without which he could not survive, then or now. And if passengers from the Laramie stagecoach couldn't see him from the road above as he grew, so much the better. That's one of this old man's secrets of survival. He, too, is clearly the *genius loci* of his surroundings, the guardian spirit to which all others—animal, vegetable, and mineral—accede. One day they will inherit the Giant's realm. But not yet. Big enough to house a tribe of Hobbits, and still growing, though weak, he keeps a steady, brooding watch, as he has for at least decades, possibly centuries. If the Giant could talk, what would come out might be the language of time itself.

Our Lady of the Ditch

There are champions, and then there are the underdogs . . . or, undertrees. "Our Lady of the Ditch," as Albuquerque residents Matt Schmader and his wife have nicknamed a local holy woman among trees, is such a one. This gorgeous Rio Grande Cottonwood grows along the Griegos Drain (or ditch), not far from the river, which is its namesake. I have driven down from Taos to see her. Though the visit is brief, I am smitten, easily surrendering my awe to the tree the Schmaders also call (with playful reverence) "the Virgin of Wood-alupe." She planted herself along the drain, part of a network of irrigation canals—called acequias in this part of the country—perhaps eighty to a hundred years ago, and settled down to a long, full life. Matt and his wife came upon Our Lady while out hiking. As Superintendent of the Open Space Division of the Parks & Recreation Department for the City of Albuquerque, Matt has seen plenty of cottonwoods. He knew Our Lady was special.

On the warm May afternoon when Matt takes me to visit Our Lady, a clutter of trucks and men in orange work bibs obscure her from view as we walk along the

Rio Grande Cottonwood, "Our Lady of the Ditch," Albuquerque, New Mexico.
Photo by Kathleen Cain

ditch path. As we get closer the frame of her massive crown begins to dwarf both men and machines. I experience the same element of surprise that Matt and his wife did when they first saw her. She is a mansion, a cathedral, a sacred dwelling. She measures 32.4 feet/384 inches in circumference and stands 64 feet tall. Her crown spread is 88 feet. It's hard to imagine how anyone could not respect her.

But the irreverent are everywhere. And though few, they are powerful. The small group of men is a trimming crew from the conservancy that owns the ditch. They surround Our Lady, looking like armed guards sent to watch the palace after the government has been overthrown. A pile of Our Lady's limbs, already cut into rounds, nearly fills one truck.

Matt keeps calm and greets the men with respect. He asks whether they know this is one of the largest living cottonwoods in the country. They do, although one counters that there's a bigger tree in Fort Davis, Texas.

Another, lounging at the foot of a sister tree nearby, says he knows where there's one even bigger than the Texas champ.

Where?! Matt's response is a cry, not a question, one that springs instantly to the lips of big tree hunters.

It's in the hills somewhere, the man answers, describing two-thirds of New Mexico. Suddenly he can't remember.

Matt and the men discuss trimming the tree. The men point to a huge adobe house, built next to Our Lady years after she took up residence on the drain. The owner is nervous, they say, and wants the tree cut down. Matt has talked to the man before, he tells them, and explained the story of this tree. The man has seemed to understand.

Like all who treasure trees, Matt worries that these men, sent out with their saws and trimming poles, expected to fill their trucks with limbs and branches, have little knowledge about trees or habitat. He doesn't blame them; it's just the way things are in trying to balance nature and human action.

The men are not arborists or foresters. Through no fault of their own, they lack a judicious sense of balance. Our Lady of the Ditch is getting regular amputations on one side. Since cottonwood roots spread more widely than deeply, such trimming without benefit of professional advice could destabilize her. And given Our Lady's heft, it's not an imbalance you would want to create if you could help it.

Our Lady has been measured many times, as part of the fierce competition among big tree hunters. The story that drew me to Albuquerque is an account posted on the American Forests Web site. In June 2003 Matt and Suzanne Probart, executive director of Tree New Mexico, among others, hopeful that they had a national champion, measured Our Lady and submitted the results to American Forests. New

art on her leaves. Her teeth are rounder, less coarse, and fewer than those of
her cottonwood cousins. As I have seen along the canyon road from Taos to Santa
e, these native trees smooth out the harsh desert angles and fill the water courses
ith green. And though the men with the saws have cut into her at the time of year
hen all her energy is devoted to producing seeds, large green beads dangle from
er branches. Compared with the fruits of her Plains cousins, she could be grow-
ıg grapes as against their dried peas. Her story is not finished yet. Matt and
uzanne are likely to have the last word on her behalf.

Preserving the Champions

Since some champions like the Eastern Cottonwood in Nebraska are on private
›roperty, and others like the Plains Cottonwood in Colorado are on public land,
:fforts to preserve the trees take different approaches. Visits to private land always
·equire permission. And even on public land, restrictions are often in place to
›rotect these valuable natural resources. If you want to find out about cottonwood
champions in your state, visit the American Forests Web site at http://www.ameri
canforests.org and follow the links for State Registers. While the register is a
popular feature, American Forests does more than keep track of big trees. The group
participates in public policy efforts related to forests. It stocks a nursery of trees
cloned from historic originals—without a focus on the big tree champs. A clone of
the Dwight D. Eisenhower Cottonwood (*P. deltoides*), from a tree that shaded the
future president's Texas home, sells for less than $40. The Web page provides infor-
mation from growing zones to no-ship zones in the United States. A citizens group
at heart, American Forests teaches how essential trees are to life on Earth. Every tree
works hard, taking in carbon dioxide and giving back planet-sustaining oxygen.
Trees are the lungs of the Earth—cottonwoods even more so, since they grow so fast.
Trees clean the water and absorb toxic materials in the soil. They provide cool shade
and shelter for every category of wildlife. They even help keep the energy bills low
(when you visit the Web site, take a look at the energy savings from even a single big
tree champ). Honoring the giants through the register is just one of American
Forests' many efforts, from helping with "Katrina ReLeaf" to providing assistance
worldwide, or supporting long-range conservation efforts.

David Milarch, head of yet another organization devoted to the big trees and
an arborist from Copemish, Michigan, has taken a different and somewhat
controversial approach to preserving the champions. In 1996, Milarch and his son
Jared formed Champion Tree Project International (CTP). One goal is to create
clones from as many existing champions as possible—of all species—and to make

How to Measure a Cottonwood Tree

Big Tree National Champion Rio Grande Cottonwood, Fort Davis, T?
Photo by Oscar Mestas, courtesy of the Texas Forest Service.

Mexico enthusiasts thought Our Lady might challenge a Rio Grande Cott
Fort Davis, Texas, that had been on the champ list since 1971.

Texas big tree hunters immediately called for an official remeasu
Mestas, an official with the Texas Forest Service—with New Mexico witne
ent—measured and re-measured Our Lady—some say six times. With onl
separating Our Lady from a new title, all agreed that the Texas tree still rei
does today. "Don't hold that visit against me," Oscar wrote back good-
when I queried him about the incident. How could I? After all, a champic
champion tree! Plus, he sent along a picture of the Fort Davis tree, a state
the Big Bend Country, and yet another national cottonwood treasure.

Champion or not, Our Lady still stands her ground in her own enchar
even if all do not adore her. In spite of the indignities she has suffered, s
tains her composure. Her furrowed bark stretches skyward in impressiv
Her glistening leaves—still sticky with resin but not aromatic like the Narr
jostle calmly in the wind. She's softer, showier, and, as Suzanne Probart s;
species in general, more "gracious." Unlike the Plains Cottonwood, wl
bottom is often straight enough to use for measuring, the Rio Grande w

the clones commercially available. They have special concerns about urban areas that have suffered the loss of forests. Chesapeake Bay and the Rouge River in Detroit are two examples. As they point out, with only 3 percent of old growth forest left in the United States, the Milarchs have their work cut out for them. Several "Living Libraries," as they call the plantings, are already in place: at the Henry Ford Museum, the site of the 2002 Winter Olympic Games in Salt Lake City, Arlington National Cemetery, the Pentagon, and on several university campuses. A reforestation effort at Mount Vernon, the historic home of George Washington, included planting a clone of a white ash tree that Washington apparently planted by hand. The stated mission of the project is to "be the leader of urban and community environmental sustainability by protecting, propagating, and planting a living legacy of our champion trees." Articles about the Milarch family (wife Kerry and son Jacob continue to run the Michigan tree farm) have appeared in newspaper articles nationwide, including the *New York Times, Washington Post,* and *USA Today.* Working with the U.S. Forest Service, they attempted to clone "Methuselah," the 4,600+ year-old California bristlecone pine—and acclaimed oldest tree in the world. As of October 2005 the project has cloned and planted more than 125 species.

Milarch believes—though he admits his controversial theory remains to be proven—that the champions have survived because they contain superior genes. American Forests shies away from any notion of a race of "super trees" and views Milarch's theory and efforts with skepticism. Many arborists and foresters suggest that environmental conditions and pure luck are as likely as genetic makeup to determine a tree's success in a given place, though little research has been done to test such a theory.

When Milarch first contacted tree professionals with his idea, posed as a question, he says they laughed at him. Conventional wisdom holds that the older a tree gets, the less vigorous it becomes, and that cloning is best done when trees are young. Yet the champions have survived and surpassed expectations even in unlikely places; in urban environments, for example, where trees might often live less than ten years. Milarch likes to point out a champion white poplar in downtown Leland, Michigan—happy and healthy and growing near a busy intersection. He counters many arguments with the essential benefits that trees bring to human life—and the inherent dangers that their continued loss will create. He's not alone with his questions or his concerns. And though they once laughed at him, nurseries, arborists, and the U.S. Forest Service have all cooperated with different efforts to clone the big tree champions. Cloning is, after all, a longstanding practice in the world of trees.

While the Milarchs work with many different species, one of their colleagues has a special affinity for cottonwoods. Martin Flanagan, champion tree hunter and western director for CTP, has worked as a nurseryman for many years, and resides in Big Timber, Montana, a town north of Yellowstone National Park, named for the cottonwoods. He writes:

I definitely see the greatest need for the restoration of cottonwoods is in people's minds and hearts. They are a pioneer species that have been abused, neglected and mostly over-looked and unappreciated. . . except by a few. . . . Any of the major water ways that have been dammed have a definite need for cottonwood restoration if it's possible.

The genetics of these trees need restoring in our shade tree industry. This movement is beginning to take shape. . . . This is good news. Some genetically engineered or hybridized trees could have catastrophic effects on our native species, if they haven't already.

The issue of genetic studies also arises among cottonwood champions of another kind. Though focused on age as well as size, a Canadian researcher is interested in probing big-tree genetics. A grove of 500-year-old cottonwoods—previously thought to be a mere 400—was discovered a few years ago in British Columbia. The oldest grove found so far in North America, these trees displace the Balmville Tree in New York state, a youngster of only 300+ years. In his quest for understanding these extraordinary trees, Dr. Stewart Rood, leader of the Canadian research and discovery team, intends to examine the genetic code. He wonders whether trees able to live long have any unique genetic traits—in addition to what he knows about the generous environment provided by the Elk River, along which these ample Black Cottonwoods grow. International interest has prompted the sequencing of the poplar gene—a Genome Project for trees—using the Black Cottonwood as a model. Understanding poplar genetics has many implications—one of which would be to improve the commercial qualities of hybrids, and thus pulp and paper products. Public interest, as well as media interest in the Canadian trees, along with early planning, helped gain protection for the grove as part of Morrissey Provincial Park.

The practice of identifying and registering big trees has been an American pastime for more than sixty years. It reflects the human fascination with the unpredictable, the unusual, and the unexpected. Officiated by American Forests, the search brings out the tree treasure-hunters—and the competitive American spirit. Just read the news section of the American Forests Web site to see the lively banter among big tree hunters. I have met and corresponded with Big Tree Coordinators who work with American Forests as well as with Martin Flanagan of CTP. Through their efforts I have visited a few champions, as well as a few trees defeated by circumstances. I have also learned much about cottonwood problems—and some possible solutions. I have seen firsthand the pride and care with which these people interact with trees. We are luckier than we know to have such dedicated and knowledgeable arborists, foresters, horticulturists, nursery owners, researchers, tree farmers, and volunteers working on our behalf and on behalf of trees, no matter what the size.

Great enthusiasm, as well as great wariness and skepticism, exists about the discoveries and possibilities of continuing to clone trees. Since they are not always easily grown from seed in lab or nursery conditions, cloning has been a primary way of propagating cottonwoods—and not just the champions. And as Dr. Rood reports, the allure of learning the genetic secrets of 500-year-old cottonwoods is irresistible. Cloning is a method at least as old as the people who gave us the word from Greek. It is unlikely to diminish. Modern science offers too many great possibilities that will take tree cloning to new levels. Such possibilities are never without risk or free of challenges. Learning more about Big Tree Champions may help us learn more about native cottonwoods. Learning more about cottonwood genetics will help us learn more about the landscapes the trees inhabit. In future chapters, "Trouble in Cottonwood Country" and "Good News," we'll see how that's true. For the moment, let's consider how cottonwood trees have long been champions of the spirit.

Sources

Cain, Jerome A. Calculations of circumference of cottonwood tree at Dewitt, Nebraska.

"Measuring Guide." American Forests.
    http://www.americanforests.org/resources/bigtrees/measure.php

For information on the Colorado Tree Coalition, see:
    http://www.coloradotrees.org/.

Information on American Forests comes from the organization's Web page at:
    http://www.americanforests.org/

Information on the former Illinois champion Eastern Cottonwood comes from
    Native Trees for North American Landscapes from the Atlantic to the Rockies. Guy
    Sternberg with Jim Wilson. Timber Press. Portland and Cambridge. 2004.
    p. 333.

Measurements for the Great Plains Cottonwood tree in Colorado were taken in fall
2005 and verified by Keith Wood, as per e-mail correspondence in January
2006. Discrepancies between these measurements and those listed on the
National Big Tree Register are the result of measuring the trees and updating
the register.

Personal visit to the champion Eastern Cottonwood tree in Seward County,
Nebraska, on December 28, 2005.

Basic facts about the Plains Cottonwood champion in Boulder County, Colorado,
can be found in the "Pella Crossing Fact Sheet" printed by the Boulder Parks
and Open Space Department. July 2004. Additional information about this
tree was provided by Pascale Fried, Education and Outreach Coordinator for
Boulder County Parks and Open Space during a site visit on January 11, 2006.

The tragic death of former Denver Post reporter Ginny McKibben was reported in
"Cottonwood removed after fatal accident" by Manny Gonzales. *Denver Post.*
October 2005. p. 4B

Conversation with Suzanne Probart, executive director of Tree New Mexico and
Matthew Schmader, superintendent of Open Space Division of the Parks &
Recreation Department for the City of Albuquerque, in Albuquerque, New
Mexico. May 8, 2006. Subsequent field trip with Matthew Schmader to visit
"Our Lady of the Ditch."

"Texas vs. New Mexico." Rio Grande Cottonwoods. American Forests.
http://www.americanforests.org/resources/bigtrees/facts.php

For activities of Tree New Mexico, visit: http://treenm.com.

The mission statement for Champion Tree Project International is taken from the
project's Web site at: http://www.championtreeproject.org.

Information about the 500-year-old cottonwoods comes from the University of
Lethbridge Legend. "Rood Discovers North America's Oldest Known Grove of
Cottonwoods." http://www.uleth.ca/legend/Nov03_RecordOnResearch.html
and from an interview with Dr. Stewart Rood, "Discovery of 500 Year Old
Cottonwood Trees." www.innovationalberta.com/article.php?articleid+424.

Comments from Martin Flannagan from e-mail correspondence.

5

THE COTTONWOOD STAR:
HIDDEN CENTER TO SACRED CENTER

"Have you ever seen the cottonwood star?" my father asked, as we were out walking one day.

The question caught me by surprise. No, I told him. I hadn't.

"Here." He stopped and picked up a twig from the ground. He turned it over. He was looking for something. "You have to find one with a sturdy knuckle on it."

That's exactly what the joints that mark each growth spurt on a cotton-wood twig look like: miniature knuckles surrounded by pouches of bark that resemble the skin on our fingers.

He pulled a tiny silver knife out of his pocket. "You have to cut cleanly," he instructed. "No hacking. Not jagged. One cut is best."

With deft expertise, he sliced through the center of the most promising protuberance, his physician's hand steady from long years of practice and patience.

"There, now. Look." He turned the twig so I could gaze directly into its center. Running crosswise through the middle of the small piece of wood, the cut revealed a reddish-brown and nearly perfect five-pointed star.

Though I didn't know the technical name for that part of the twig, I knew sap flowed there. A star-shaped stream of life moved up from the roots through the trunk and the branches, eventually reaching the twigs of the cottonwood tree each spring. I'd cut an apple sideways before and found that beautiful pentacle of seeds and casings—the core of the fruit. But what a surprise inside the cottonwood!

I asked my father where he had learned this secret of nature. He didn't remember. Maybe he'd always known it, or discovered it on his own. Maybe his

"Cottonwood Star" by Dan Cain. Reprinted with permission.

father had told him. Having grown up on a farm in south–central Nebraska during the 1930s, he is full of country wisdom. His grandfather had planted a stand of cottonwoods in an effort to improve land purchased in 1885. Those cottonwoods still stand along an unpaved county road that borders the north side of what was once part of his "proved–up" quarter section. My father grew up beneath those trees. He remembers chopping dry limbs for firewood, how easily they split. From the unpaved county road, the remnants and descendants of that long–ago planting still wander back along a draw that fills, as regularly as Nebraska summers allow, with water.

Most likely my father learned the secret of the cottonwood star from someone else—if not his father, then his mother, perhaps. It's the kind of thing she would have known. In spite of her deeply held Catholic faith, her Irish folk wisdom remained intact. Though she probably also said her beads (rosary) over such a blemish, she still buried potato eyes in the garden to rid her children of warts, as my uncle recalls. She also warned her children not to explore the far side of the Republican River, which flowed a mile south of the family's farm near Republican City, Nebraska. Known as "Indian Hills," the off–limits side of the river was known to be a place where Pawnee Indians, once the most powerful tribe between the Missouri and the Rocky Mountains, had lived until they were forced into Indian Territory in 1874—just eleven years before those cottonwood trees were planted along the draw. Local wisdom had it that a burial ground lay concealed among the bluffs overlooking the river. As such, my grandmother warned her children, it was sacred ground, to be respected in the same way as the cemetery a few miles up the road where the children's own relatives lay buried.

That star would have been no secret to the Pawnees who lived along the Republican River, or to other tribes that inhabited the Great Plains for so many

"Daniel's Cottonwoods" near Republican City, Nebraska. Photo by Kathleen Cain

thousands of years, long before the European settlers arrived. The tree was a part of daily living, as evidenced by one practical Pawnee use reported by nineteenth-century chronicler George Bird Grinnell: a garland of branches wound around the head made a perfect sun visor. One of Edward S. Curtis's famed photographs shows a Cheyenne man named "Porcupine" wearing such a visor. Cradleboards made of cottonwood kept Pawnee infants safe and snug. Robert Adams, a photographer who devoted an entire book to the stark and beautiful illustration of cottonwood trees in black and white, says the Arapaho believed that the stars in the sky originated in the cottonwood, because of how the sap catches the sunlight and sparkles in late winter, as the skeleton tree comes back to life. If you've never seen this, try to get out next year just as that golden halo begins to form around the trees—in just the right angle of sun, the glint and sparkle of stars is pure, natural magic. Adams recounts that a healing force for the Hidatsa was the shade of the cottonwood; on a hot, summer day, such shelter still wields the power of healing. Writing earlier, Sir James George Frazier, the collector of lore that came to be known as *The Golden Bough*, gave a different meaning to the "shade" described by the Hidatsa Indians. In his under-standing, "shade" meant spirit as well as intelligence. Cottonwoods along the upper Missouri—great trees of a mighty river—if asked in the right way, could provide a source of helpful power, not merely protective shadow. Adams also describes how Native Americans taught the new white strangers that horses could survive harsh winters by feeding on cottonwood bark and leaves—"power food" rich in sugar and starch. Native people would also have known that cottonwood was part of the standard food supply for beavers and wild turkeys. To the Lakota, the sound of cottonwood leaves in the wind was not just pleasant chatter but the voice of the Creator. The Plains tribes, living among all things and not apart from them, knew all the secrets of the cottonwood, practical as well as spiritual. They knew that here, revealed by a simple cut in the wood, hid a tiny star, so much like a mirror that could be held up to reflect the continuity in all creation.

Black Elk's Cottonwood

A sense of how sacred the cottonwood tree was (as it still is) to Native Americans comes by way of the renowned Oglala holy man, Black Elk (Nicholas Black Elk, Hehaka Sapa, 1863–1950). Two years before he died, Black Elk asked Joseph Epes Brown—who lived on the Pine Ridge Reservation in South Dakota for eight months during 1947–48, and who later founded the first Native American religious studies program in an American university—to transcribe seven rites of the Oglala Sioux. According to Brown, Black Elk revealed these usually secret ceremonies because he was afraid that his people were falling away from the old ways and truths. He hoped that sharing the rituals would restore wholeness to a people bent—but not broken—by a changing world. The rites had come down through oral tradition to Black Elk from his teacher, Elk Head. Among them was one entitled "*Wiwanyag Wachipi*: The Sun Dance."

I first learned about the Sun Dance through the film *A Man Called Horse* (1970). What stuck with me was the focus on the Sun Dance as a ceremony of torture and mutilation. Even today, the popular Internet Movie Database Web site summarizes the film this way: "A man called 'Horse' becomes an Indian warrior in the most electrifying ritual ever seen!" During the intervening years, as the celebration of the Sun Dance has continued to be practiced by many tribes, and as Black Elk's narrative reveals, the Sun Dance is an important religious ceremony. As Kablaya (Spread), the man whose original vision was passed down to Elk Head and then taught to Black Elk, the Sun Dance was a "new way to pray." At the center of the prayer stood a cottonwood tree.

The Sun Dance took place in June or July, months described by Black Elk as the "Moon of Fattening" or the "Moon of Cherries Blackening." One of the most important Oglala rituals, it was to be observed during a full moon. Elaborate detail governed the ceremony. Ritual preparation required four days. Specific tools and equipment were essential, right down to blue paint, a flint axe, and eagle bone whistles. Every element involved, material or spiritual, was critical to the power and success of the ceremony. In Kablaya's original vision the cottonwood (*wagachun*), known as one of the "standing peoples," stood at the center of the ceremony not just because it was a beautiful tree but because it symbolized the "way of the people" and the people themselves. It was rooted in the earth but pointed toward the sky. Here stood the sacred "World Tree" that appears in the spiritual beliefs of so many cultures worldwide.

Kablaya's vision gave direction about which tree to select, information he shared with a helper who then marked the tree with sage. A scouting party was organized and sent out to "capture" the tree. Black Elk explained to Brown why the cottonwood was held in such high regard by the tribe, since it had taught them so much. As the great conservation pioneer Aldo Leopold would later comment about another cottonwood, the tree provided a great "library." Black Elk told how a group of elders, watching children at play, observed the youngsters using cottonwood leaves to make tiny make-believe houses. A later observer, Melvin Randolph Gilmore, writing in the *Thirty-Third Annual Report of the American Bureau of Ethnology* (1911–12), did:

> They split a leaf a short distance down from the tip along the midrib: at equal distances from the tip they tore across from the margin slightly: then, bending back the margin above the rents for the smoke flaps, and drawing together the leaf-margins below the rents and fastening them with a splinter or a thorn, they had a toy tipi. These they made in numbers and placed them in circles like the camp circle of their tribe.

According to the tradition passed on to Black Elk, from this simple observation came the inspiration for the shape of the tipi, and thus shelter and protection for the tribe. This knowledge has been passed on in a way you might not suspect, to yet another generation in another time. Teachers in Kansas have developed an entire lesson plan that teaches children how to make these cottonwood leaf tipis, in the context of learning more about Native American life and the life of the cottonwood tree. Black Elk's people knew more than what the leaves of this tree could teach. They knew that cutting a twig revealed the five-pointed star, for them a clear sign of the Creator's presence. And in the rustling of the tree's leaves, in its special voice, a necessary part of living could be heard—the reminder to pray all the time.

Following the directions in Kablaya's vision, four warriors were chosen to surround the tree and begin cutting it down. Each man had to declare his own courageous deeds, thus proving his worthiness for such a sacred task. By contrast, a

Sun Dance participants carry a cottonwood tree across a soybean field near Hallam,
Nebraska, July 2004. Reprinted with permission of the Lincoln Journal-Star.

quiet person, often a woman, was selected to deliver the final blow to the tree.
Because it was sacred, the tree was not allowed to fall to the ground. Nor was anyone
allowed to step over it before it was carried reverently to the site of the Sun Dance
lodge. Black Elk describes an elaborate liturgy, of how the cottonwood tree, chosen
as the sacred representative of the way of the people, was to be dressed and blessed.
His description resounds with a sense of wonder and awe. Red paint, representing
Mother Earth, and buffalo fat, from the animal whose life sustained that of the tribe,
were applied to the tree. A cherry tree—representing fruitfulness and food for the
people—and the skin of a buffalo calf, covered with symbols representing a man and
a buffalo, were tied to the cottonwood. Hoisted with honor to stand at the center of
the Sun Dance lodge, surrounded and connected by twenty-eight posts, each of
which represented some element of creation (the sun or the moon, for example), the
holy tree transformed the space into a living re-creation of the universe. What
better creature to duplicate the cosmology of the universe than this member of the
"standing peoples" with a secret star embedded in the hidden realm of its branches?

　　With its focus on only one aspect of the Sun Dance ceremony, the piercing, *A
Man Called Horse* created a popular misunderstanding of the Sun Dance, one that

has been corrected with time as the dance continues once again. According to Black Elk, the part of the ceremony where young men bound themselves at the shoulder, chest, and back with thongs that eventually tore loose as they danced their prayers to the Great Spirit represents the suffering that all people must endure. Such a sacrifice might be compared to the Christian belief in Christ's suffering for humanity or the Buddhist idea that all life is suffering. Participants in the Sun Dance suffered on behalf of their people. Their sacrifice represented the tribe's sacrifice. For people who were advised by Kablaya that the closest relatives were Grandfather and Father Wakan Tanka (Great Spirit) and Grandmother and Mother Earth, it should be no surprise that the cottonwood, a most sacred and prominent creature connecting earth and sky, should be held in such esteem.

More than fifty years later, Black Elk's message may have been taken to heart more seriously than he ever dreamed it would. The Sun Dance practice not only survives but has grown among Native Americans and non-natives alike. According to one estimate in 2004, more than sixty Sun Dance ceremonies now take place during the summer months. Native elders of several tribes are concerned. Some feel that the Sun Dance should be reserved only to Native people, and that to maintain the sacred aspect of the tradition, fewer dances should be held. At the other end of this practice stands Leonard Crow Dog, a Lakota medicine man. During July 2004, Crow Dog led a Sun Dance ceremony outside Hallam, Nebraska, a town leveled by a tornado two months before. Crow Dog made it clear to a reporter that "This is not a Lakota Sun Dance" in the spiritual sense, since he opened the ritual to participants of all races. An invitation was required, but Crow Dog believes that Lakota ceremonies should be shared, at least in spirit. In a post-9/11 world, perhaps the time has come, once again, to restore the old ways and truths. The newspaper article that describes a ceremony still recognizable from Black Elk's description features two photographs: one shows more than two dozen participants carrying the ceremonial cottonwood through a soybean field, careful to keep it from touching the ground. The

Words for Cottonwood

Álamo, Alamos, Alamillo, Alamillas
(Spanish)
Maa zho^n (Omaha–Ponca)
Natakaaru (Pawnee)
Paako (Hopi)
Wága cha^n (Dakota)
Wagachun (Lakota)
Tiis (Navajo)

(Sources: *Uses of Plants by the Indians of the Missouri River Region*. Melvin R. Gilmore. University of Nebraska Press. Lincoln and London. 1977. From *33rd Annual Report of the Bureau of American Ethnology*, for Maa zhon; Natakaaru; Wága chan)

other, in full color, highlights the decorated tree being hoisted to its position of sacred honor as *the* center of the ceremony. Kablaya's vision endures, and the lessons of Black Elk are still being taught. And for yet another tribe, a vision lives on with a cottonwood tree at its center.

The Real Omaha

In 1888, a terrible thing happened to the Omaha people. Times had been hard enough. They suffered through smallpox epidemics in the early 1800s. They separated from tribal allies, including the Quapaw and Ponca. Their lands had been invaded by European immigrants. With the buffalo destroyed, traditional ways of living had been broken. And then they suffered the loss of their holiest object, the Sacred Pole. The pole, along with its companion, the White Buffalo Hide, had lived among them since even the elders could remember.

Though population decline and loss of tribal ways contributed to the separation, the actual physical loss of the Sacred Pole was brought about by Alice Fletcher and Francis La Flesche. Fletcher was an anthropologist affiliated with Harvard University. La Flesche, an Omaha himself, was also the first Native American anthropologist and ethnologist who meticulously documented the ceremonies and traditional ways of his people. Tribal members today feel their most sacred objects were stolen, but Fletcher and La Flesche said they acted to preserve the objects because they feared the Omaha would not survive. The Sacred Pole was sent to the Peabody Museum at Harvard University in 1888, where it remained for a century. There it stood on public display. What the Omaha had relied on for spiritual and psychological sustenance became a genderless artifact that could be viewed by anyone, without honor, without reverence, without understanding.

As part of his 1919 report on the uses of plants by Native Americans living along the upper Missouri River, Melvin Gilmore noted that the Sacred Pole of the Omaha was made from cottonwood. Gilmore compared its importance and power as a sacred object to the Ark of the Covenant for Jewish people. His comparison can be extended to include the consecrated host of Roman Catholics or the sacred stone at Mecca that Islamic pilgrims are obliged to visit at least once in their lives. Yet another comparison might be the omphalos, the round and phallic stone at Delphi, site of the oracle that marked the center of the ancient Greek world. Like the omphalos, the Sacred Pole of the Omaha is male, a symbol of the virility of life. Yet such symbolism is only one of the pole's many powers.

The Sacred Pole is not an "it," but "he," named *Umon'hon'ti*—"the real Omaha" and "Venerable Man." The names reflect his status as the most important elder. He is the center of the tribe and, like the cottonwood of the Sun Dance, the center of the cosmos, the power of unity which keeps the people together (ironically, during the time the Sacred Pole was absent, an American flag took his place in any ceremony). We have been privileged in our time to learn firsthand from many Native Americans the nature of certain spiritual beliefs. One deeply held principle is contained in the phrase "all my relations," sacred wording used for sacred ceremony. But it's more than a saying. The words express a reverence for all creatures that goes beyond merely acknowledging their shared presence in the world. All of creation, from the grass to the water and the sky—and all that inhabit each realm— are regarded as relatives. Trees are part of this sacred kinship. And the Omaha have no greater relative than the Sacred Pole. He had stood at the center of the annual buffalo hunt, undertaken by the whole tribe. There he leaned on his own staff, part of a careful, quiet ritual that would not frighten away the herd on which the tribe's well-being depended. The last hunt took place around 1877, eleven years before the Sacred Pole was surrendered by his last keeper and taken off to the Peabody.

The way the Sacred Pole first came to the Omaha is a story that anyone who remembers the tale of Moses and the burning bush will understand. Drawn by a sacred urging, Moses was called to Mount Sinai to obtain the Ten Commandments during a time of great trouble for the tribes of Israel. Along the way, he experienced the divine presence in the form of a burning bush. Also during a time of tribal disunity, the son of an Omaha chief traveled through a forest late at night and became lost. He was drawn to a "burning tree" as he described to his father and the other chiefs. Animal paths led to the tree. The Pole Star (North Star) hovered above it. The chiefs interpreted the event and determined that the tree offered a symbol for their own unity, a living representation of their need.

In a narrative that invites comparison to the Sun Dance, the Sacred Pole was "captured" in a ritual manner and brought to live among the Omaha. He remained with them until he was taken away in 1888. A sacred keeper was trained and authorized to care for him. He was fed and clothed, given buffalo meat (red with life) for sustenance, consecrated with buffalo fat (a sign of abundance), and carefully wrapped with a special shield braided from wicker and filled with down feathers. A scalp lock hung from his top, as it did from that of any brave warrior. He was the sacred person around whom the tribe gathered and kept itself together. He represented the individual standing alone as well as each member making up one part of the whole tribe. He brought about the unity of opposites: men and women, light and dark, day and night. But as the buffalo disappeared and the hunts ceased, a way of life also vanished. The U.S. government applied unrelenting pressure on

Native Americans to assimilate, to change even the ways they held their land and conducted their religious life. The memory of old ceremonies began to fade. And then the Real Omaha was taken from home. Whether stolen, kidnapped, or "rescued" (as those who took him claimed), he was gone.

In 1988, a wonderful thing happened to the Omaha people. Some of their members were reunited with the Sacred Pole. Even after all those years standing up in the Peabody Museum, the power of the Real Omaha had not diminished. It touched yet another person, an anthropologist named Robin Ridington. Drawn to learn about the Sacred Pole, Ridington eventually contacted the Omaha people and became acquainted with the tribal historian, Dennis Hastings (In'aska). Each man shared what he knew. One thing led to another, and in 1989 Umon'hon'ti returned to his people, where he lives near them yet today. No longer viewed as merely an object, the Real Omaha has once again begun a relationship with his people. Like any relationship, there are ups and downs. Upon his return, some tribal members feared that Umon'hon'ti was too powerful, dangerously so. Many of the old rituals and ceremonies regarding his care and presence have been lost—and Omaha ritual must be performed to perfection. Yet tribal leaders persisted in trying to re-establish a relationship with this most revered elder. Where Umon'hon'ti once presided over the annual buffalo hunt, he took his place at the annual renewal ceremony in August, where he could be viewed publicly—though briefly, and with honor. His long absence and return is a spiritual miracle, for he has come home to a tribe that has not only survived but now numbers nearly six thousand, a Native American nation still living on its own ancestral lands. The Omaha have not vanished. And they have not merely survived. They thrive. And however they decide to continue the relationship with Umon'hon'ti, he is home among them once again.

Kachinas

South and west of the Great Plains, among the nineteen Pueblo villages of New Mexico and the three Hopi mesas of Arizona, the root of the cottonwood tree has since ancient times held a unique and original place of honor in a special religious tradition and ceremony. That tradition and ceremony revolve around what we have come to call the Kachina. Say the word and different carved figures come to mind: an eagle maybe, or a dancer, or a black-and-white-striped clown eating a water-melon. Created from metal, clay, and even yarn these days, the Kachinas traditionally appeared as figures carved from cottonwood root, painted in earth tones with natural materials such as ochre. Older figures, the kind you find in museums, more sacred than commercial, appear somber, even a little dull when compared with the more artistic, sometimes glitzy contemporary style. The older figures stand straight inside their block of cottonwood root, unmoving. Their colors show the real earth tones of paint made from brown or yellow mud, or red clay. Modern figures, painted with bright acrylics, appear for sale in art galleries, museums, and gift shops all over the world. Since James Stevenson first collected and catalogued two dozen Kachinas for the Bureau of American Ethnology in 1879, other collections have been gathered for public and private museums from northern Arizona to Berlin. Notable collections in the American Museum of Natural History and the Heye Foundation in New York have been transferred to the new National Museum of the American Indian. Senator Barry Goldwater was known for his collection.

Kachinas of all sizes and shapes dance their way through paintings and other art forms, including jewelry, ceramics, and crafts too numerous to describe. Contemporary Kachinas of the commercial sort dance and turn: "action figures," in the vernacular of pop culture. They lift a foot, a leg, or a hand. One whole side of the body stretches up, ready for the next dance move. They look behind. They stare straight ahead. They lower a head in praise or song, in time to the drumbeat. They have, much to the chagrin of traditional Hopi and other Pueblo people, been used for entertainment and advertising, even showing up in Marvel Comics and on packages of tortilla chips. Although it wasn't always so, they've been carved and sculpted to represent everything from a field mouse to Mickey Mouse.

Dolls. That's the word usually associated with Kachinas. With a little more investigation, it's easy to learn that the Kachinas—or *Katsinas*, as the Hopi people explain on their Web page, are not dolls at all. They are "supernatural beings who are believed to visit the Hopi villagers during half of the year" when they come down from the San Francisco Peaks in Arizona and other sacred mountains where they live. As Hopi artist and author Alph Secakuku and others try to teach, the tradition of the *Katsinas* is unique to the religious practice of the Pueblo peoples. Powerful spiritual messengers, the *Katsinas* hold sway over the realms of nature, crops, and rainfall in a desert region that receives only five to seven inches of precious moisture a year. The *Katsinas* also influence the everyday lives of the Hopi—working to bring those who stray from social and moral standards back in line and serving as intermediaries between the realms of earth and spirit. Secakuku also instructs that the *ch* sound does not exist in the Hopi language. Thus the pronunciation and spelling *Katsina* is more correct.

These spirit figures visit the villages in disguise. Men of the tribe dress in masks and costumes that allow them to assume the personas of the *Katsinas*. These masked spirit representatives give carvings that the Hopi call *tithu*, or more formally, *katsintithu*, primarily to young girls and sometimes to infant boys, new brides, and expectant mothers. These carvings of the *Katsinas* who visit the villages, made by the same men who bring them, are given as gifts to help children learn about the different spirits, and thus about Hopi spiritual belief. Not intended as toys, the gifts are hung with honor on the walls of the homes of those who receive them. A simpler (and safer) form of the *katsintithu*, described as a "flat doll," is given to babies still in the cradle. Three-dimensional *katsintithu* offered during the Bean Ceremony are given to boys, though only in infancy. As two early observers mentioned, the *katsintithu* figure is really a three-dimensional prayer or blessing. The figures made available for sale commercially, whether carved by Pueblo people or non-natives, lack any spiritual element, and are not, properly speaking, *Katsinas*.

Sources generally agree that there is no way to absolutely date the appearance of the carved figures in Hopi culture, although archeological evidence indicates a presence between 1300 and 1400 CE. Historical documentation from non-Hopi sources dates to the 1850s. By 1900 the figures were bought and sold by non-natives. Called Early Traditional, these figures were made from flat pieces of wood with minimal carving from the traditional cottonwood root (*paaku*, in the Hopi language) and painted with natural, earth-colored pigments.

Since the 1930s, when the first commercial market opened for Hopi carvers in Arizona, the commercial Kachina figures available for sale have become some of the finest artwork in the U.S. Prices have followed suit. Once sold for $1.00 an inch, Kachina figures currently fetch hundreds, even thousands of dollars. Among Native carvers, traditions and styles are proudly maintained—and modified— among families and friends. Demand for more elaborate figures changed the carving style.

By the 1940s and 1950s the fashion had shifted to what Jonathan S. Day, the self-described son of an Indian trader who also became a trader and Kachina collector, calls Early Action figures. Dimensions changed from two to three. Limbs began to emerge from the carvings, arms and legs lifted in dance steps, often fixed to a round piece of cottonwood. The action style increased and the figures became more elaborate up through the 1960s. The next evolution in style, still popular, was to use a single cottonwood root to carve a single figure. In these easily identifiable sculptures, the carvers adhere to the importance of the mask at the top of the sculpture but let the curves of the root create bodies that possess an otherworldly appearance.

In the 1990s the change in style shifted to what is called Modern Contemporary. One piece of cottonwood root is still used by the carver. Additional

During a trip to New Mexico in 2003, rather than trying to choose a Kachina from among the overwhelming array, I decided to see whether one might choose me. In one shop, I passed a case where a small, blue-faced figure caught my eye and tugged at my heart. A female figure shaped like an ear of corn, she kept her arms and feet modestly concealed. I left the store and returned later. As I walked by the case, the spirit cry issued again. I was brought up a Roman Catholic. My ethnic heritage is Irish. Even when uttered in a different tongue, though, the cry of the spirit is not foreign to me. I could recognize its nature from another realm, and I have learned the hard way that it is

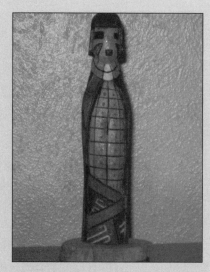

The Blue Corn Woman. Photo by Bill Mekelburg. Reprinted with permission.

unwise to let such biddings go unheeded. On a more practical level, I checked my pocketbook. Though the original *katsintithu*, the sacred representations of the *Katsina* spirits that visit Pueblo villages at certain times of the ritual year, are spiritual figures, what I was seeing throughout New Mexico were the commercial versions, the "Kachina dolls" that have acquired significance as an art form, many fetching multiple thousands of dollars—nothing my poor pockets could afford.

I asked the young woman behind the counter for help. Could she tell me the story of this figure? She was just learning about the Kachinas herself and welcomed any opportunity to share what she knew. Non-native, she was just beginning to meet the carvers, who taught her a little more each time they spoke with her. She opened the case and let me hold the six-and-a-half-inch corn woman, standing on a medallion of cottonwood less than three inches across—the same wood from which she was carved. The corn woman's open red robe, edged in black, revealed squares outlined with a wood-burning tool, made to resemble rows of kernels on a full ear of corn. Inside each square, three delicate dots of paint—one red, one yellow, one turquoise blue—highlighted the kernel-of-corn design.

The figure rose from a crisscross design near the bottom of her tiny plinth, one that at first glance seemed to be the robe crossed in front of her. Or could they be red ➤

roads, lifting up to the Hopi mesas? Below them, outlined in white, on green inside black triangles, were those lengths of planted fields? Was she the corn spirit rising up out of village life? Hovering over it? Sustaining it? Or was the mix of color and design a matter of artistic inspiration translated into carving? The cottonwood round was marked on the bottom: Blue Corn it read. Hopi. 2002. A signature of sorts . . . V . . . Luz perhaps, was visible, but impossible to read for certain. The last name flowed in a script that favored anonymity rather than identity.

Something about the elongated shape of the corn woman soothed and inspired, as it does still. Her tendency toward roundness reminded me of psychologist Carl Jung's saying that all things in nature, even stones, tend toward roundness. Black Elk had remarked:

> Everything
> The Power of the World does
> is done in a circle.

And yet, whatever muse or spirit guided the carver of this tiny sculpture from cotton-wood root, nothing about her is left to chance. From the top down, she is identifiable as a female in several ways, the young saleswoman pointed out. There's her hairstyle. Viewed from the front, it's squarely cut, blunt and straight at the bangs and sides. Turn her around, though, and you see the cascade of jet black hair flowing over her robe. The robe features black and red trim at both top and bottom. The rich golden brown of varnished cottonwood root shows through in the middle. A red sash, trimmed in green and decorated with black symbols, hangs from her right side. On her right side, in the back, about where a hand would be if it hung down, a tiny circular blemish remains: the site where a branch once grew from the living wood. From the root emerges an image of yet another kind of life: of stalk and stem, of the precious blue corn.

Multiple symbols abound, all well and beautifully incorporated to form a holistic design. First, the cottonwood root is carved into its disguise as the Kachina "doll." In this secular form the root bears some, though not all, of the elements by which a Hopi girl would recognize the spiritually infused gift given to her by the *Katsinam*— Hopi men, her father perhaps, or her uncles, assuming the form of the *Katsina* spirits who visit the Hopi villages at certain times of the year. Such a distinction between the secular and the spiritual is not hard for me to understand. In the practice of Roman Catholicism, statuettes of Jesus, Mary, and the saints abound. But unless they are blessed by a priest, they are just painted plaster, carved wood, or sculpted stone. You can buy them in any religious goods store. Catholics do not worship statues any ➤

more than the Hopi worship the *Katsinas* or the *katsintithu*. It is the essence of the blessed spirit these figures represent that is revered. Only a ritual or a blessing from a priest or makes such a figure sacred. The "disguise" cloaks a more powerful divine presence and provides a way for humans to recognize and catch a glimmer of the supernatural. And what better wood to use for the carvings than the cottonwood, familiar companion of these dry desert lands even yet? All through its life, the root searches for the spirit of water, without which life in these dry places would not exist.

While Catholic statues are recognizable for their human (if romantically stylized) features, the sacred *katsintithu* and the commercial Kachinas are more abstract. The emphasis is on depicting the essence of spirit, not realism. The Blue Corn Woman's face is blue-green—more turquoise, really. Not the deep tones and shades of blue corn; but then she represents the spirit of the corn. Her eyes are two long black slits. Not human. Not meant to be. Anonymous, the gaze of spirit. Carved into both cheeks, one red, one yellow, tattoo-like marks called hachures resemble miniature stalks of corn. Her mouth is an open, dark square, as if she is about to speak or sing. Around her neck—and I wouldn't know this except for the sales clerk—another sign of her gender: a necklace of turquoise and white shell.

Through her open robe, the carver's tools and paints have created four rows of corn. And without fully understanding the deeper significance a Hopi viewer would have for such a figure (especially if it represented one of the *katsintithu*), I realize that mine is a secular carving, blessed by the artist's talent. Yet still a little window has opened onto another world, and I have been granted a glimpse of the eternal and the everlasting in disguise. The figure represents the life-sustaining corn, whose kernels can sprout after lying dormant for several years. She also manifests the spirit of growth and the cycle of life, carved from the cottonwood root, one of the oldest trees on the North American continent. The cottonwood was already an old being by the time humans arrived on earth—when the Hopi people themselves emerged into this world. What perfect sense it makes that this tree companion, still familiar to the canyons and riverbanks of the Southwest, would be the one chosen for carving. It still grows in the wild, though less and less so in many places along creeks, streams, and canyon beds that have not been disturbed by too much demand for water. What better choice than the cottonwood with its soft heart and determination, and, like the Pueblo peoples, native to the continent? And though my little Blue Corn Woman, with her face of mystery, anonymous in the spirit of life, is the result of a commercial carver's work, it would not surprise me at all if the spot on her back right side suddenly began to sprout.

tools are employed. Some carvers even use a wood-burning tool—although traditional carvers equate burning the cottonwood root to burning their own children; sacred kinship remains strong. Now, in the early twenty-first century, a style known as New Traditional has begun, as carvers return to the older ways known and practiced since the beginning. One near constant in this stylistic evolution is the use of the traditional cottonwood root to carve the figures. Sometimes pine is used and sometimes aspen, but it's primarily cottonwood that lies beneath the paint, feathers, stones, shells, and fur, unchanged by style or time.

However different the *Katsinas* they represent—and the count is currently between 300 and 500 (compared with more than 200 mentioned by well-known collector Barton Wright in the 1950s), the figures have one thing in common. They are all carved from the root of the cottonwood tree. Other woods have been used without much success, such as aspen or balsa. And though the Zuni carvers have been known to use pine, the Hopi continue the tradition of using cottonwood root.

Though all sources are clear about the use of cottonwood root for carving the sacred katsinthithu given to children, I have found only one who has indicated why the root is required. Helga Teiwes, a former staff photographer for the Arizona State Museum, explains that in addition to following religious tradition, use of the root has practical application. It's soft, which makes it easy to carve. Compared with the often-brittle branches, once dry the density of the root prevents the wood from splitting, making carving much easier. One occupational hazard is a root that takes in sand with water. Sand embedded in a root, often in pockets, challenges any carver's skill. Because cottonwood is so porous, each carving has to be "primed" with a layer of white paint called kaolin before other colors specific to a costume or a figure can be applied. Materials, methods, and styles continue to evolve. Even the sacred figures, the *katsinthithu*, come and go as different *Katsina* spirits are "danced." Children only receive carvings of figures that have appeared during a spirit visit.

The availability of cottonwood provides another answer to the question "why." In the past, roots were easy to find along creeks and streams. They were gathered in a special ceremony undertaken by the carvers, who traveled to the canyons and along streamsides to find them. Grand Falls was once a favorite collection site along the Little Colorado River in Arizona, where Hopi men could find them already scoured and dried. Teiwes mentions that some carvers preferred to search the old way, by checking the washes and canyons below the Hopi mesas as they tended livestock. Others explored farther west of the mesas, as demand and drought made the trees scarce. A fast-developing commercial market tapped many local supplies and forced carvers to purchase wood from other states. As the distances have increased, so have prices. During the years following World War II commercial figures sold for as little as $1.00 an inch—an increase from earlier times when the unsigned carvings were often given away, in a gesture that separated the sacred from the secular. Within three decades, commercial Kachinas had begun to fetch prices of $1,000 or more for action figures—a price that has not declined as the carvings have grown ever more valuable as works of art.

Barton Wright compared the per-foot price increase for cottonwood root that measured less than 12 inches in diameter. In 1965 it was $1.50. By 1977 it had jumped to $50.00. Before 1990, when the Bureau of Indian Affairs began imposing annual fees and permit requirements specifically on non-native suppliers, both Navajo and non-native dealers brought cottonwood root to the carvers. While the Navajo dealers remain today, many others have ceased their trade due to the high prices.

Choosing cottonwood root also fits within Hopi and Pueblo spiritual belief. Reading like a minor lesson in quantum physics, harmony and the wholeness of nature lie at the center of the belief that everything in the physical world has a counterpart in the realm of spirit. What more perfect medium to teach children about the *Katsinas* and the world of spirit than the once-plentiful tree that graces creeks and streams, the tree that whispers and prays all the time, the tree with its soft heart but long survival on earth? It's a worthy companion and mediator, as are the *Katsinas*, between the natural world and the spirit world. And although it's presumptuous to assume that because the Oglala Sioux accorded the cottonwood tree sacred significance that the Pueblo people did too, there are enough beliefs about nature shared by many tribes to realize that reverence for the cottonwood tree is held in common. The cottonwood remains full of the spirit of life, sharing

Prayer Sticks

Another sacred use of cottonwood by Pueblo people is to make prayer sticks. Like many native people, the Pueblos believe there are many ways to pray. Prayer is an essential part of daily life, not just an activity reserved for certain days of the week or special occasions. Use of a prayer stick allows constant prayer. After being ritually prepared and painted, the prayer stick is often dressed in a way that reflects its intention; feathers to help summon clouds and rain, for example. Used in both public and private devotion, the prayer stick is taken to a location appropriate to the prayer, from the walls of a new house or a field about to be planted.

equally in the blessings of the weather and the precious rain, suffering, too, when the rain does not fall. The star inside the cottonwood mirrors the hidden tree inside the *katsinthithu*. Yet Native Americans were not the only ones to call forth the sacred with carvings of cottonwood.

The Santos

I had a hard time finding a good working definition of *santos*. The most distinguished scholars and authors of this traditional folk art, still prevalent in New Mexico and Colorado, are so well versed in their subject that they often begin in the middle of things, without providing a basic meaning. Even the famed *Dictionary of Art* in its newest incarnation does not offer an individual entry or index reference. *The Encyclopedia of Folk Art* came to the rescue, though, providing articles on the *bultos* and *retablos*, which together make up the religious art form known as the *santos*.

Is a definition too obvious? *Santo* translates from Spanish as "holy." Maybe everybody knows that *santos* means "saints" and refers to carved figures of popular patron saints as well as Christ and *Nuestra Señora*—Our Lady, his mother—even in her various identities such as the Virgin of Guadalupe. As *retablos* these figures appear painted on pieces of wood about the size of a small notebook or as large as an altar piece for a church. According to some experts, cottonwood was an early and preferred choice, with pine becoming a later favorite—although other sources say just the opposite. And, as any colonial history reveals, necessity often strikes hard and more than once. In New Mexico, two events contributed to the creation of the *santos* by local people (mostly men) from local materials: independence from Mexico in 1848 and the destruction of the churches after the Pueblo Revolt of 1680. Settlers from Spain and Mexico began to paint and carve on their own. They imitated a religious art they knew from the home country, but they began to create a distinct iconography, recognizable to this day. And though the work of the *santeros*, carvers and painters of holy images, declined in the late 1800s, a century later their sacred art began to flourish once again and, like the commercial Kachina figures, grew into a commercial art form. The names of modern practitioners take up a page in a current text, a counterpoint to so many anonymous forbears.

The *retablos* can refer to painted wooden panels as well as to specific pieces of furniture used to display religious objects. Such objects include *bultos*—three-dimensional carvings or sculptures. The *bultos* were often carved from a single piece of cottonwood root, chosen by the *santeros* for the same reasons that the Pueblo, Navajo, and Hopi carvers selected the roots to create the sacred *katsinthithu* and later created a commercial art tradition. The root is dense and easy to carve. It doesn't splinter like other woods. It's less likely to shrink. Plus, it was locally available. Some *bultos*, like the ceremonial *katsintithu* and now the commercial Kachinas, have been carved and pieced together from different woods. Another thing these religious figures share is that they are often painted and clothed.

The *santos* take their place in daily life in different ways, as the scholars reveal. Like the *katsintithu* given to young girls of the Pueblo, Navajo, and Hopi tribes, the *santos* were first used to teach religion. They represent Christ, his mother, and the saints, all known to help with special needs: St. Francis of Assisi, for example, protects and watches over the animals. St. Anthony helps find lost items. St. Michael protects against evil. The holy figures represent the link between the human and the divine. In the churches, they are still honored, even implored for what their lives and spirits represent. At home or in the fields, while such honor is no less respectful, it can be less formal. A display at the Millicent Rogers Museum near Taos tells the story of farmers who took a *bulto* of the Baby Jesus around their newly planted field in a procession, asking for his help with a successful crop. That night, as the story goes, the rain poured down without mercy and washed away the seeds. Next day, the farmers took a *bulto* of the Blessed Mother out to the field, showing her all the damage her boy had done and asking her to fix things as they replanted the seed.

The work of the *santeros* continues to this day, depicting the holy people not just in wood but also in tin, on embroidered cloth, canvas, and stone—all the materials at an artist's disposal. But those first early figures so many of the *santeros* created, like those in the renowned collection on display in Denver, Colorado, known as the "Regis [University] *Santos*" turned to that old reliable of the Southwest, the cottonwood tree, in the same way Native American carvers had already done for hundreds of years.

The sense of the sacredness of trees, represented in these accounts of the use of cottonwoods, is an enduring part of the Native American and Hispanic cultures that have survived and been shared with the culture at large. In 1997, Dr. Belden Lane, a professor of theological studies at St. Louis University, made a plea for including trees in no less a body than the Christian communion of saints. His entreaty, titled "Open the kingdom for a cottonwood tree," cited chapter and verse from scholars, saints, philosophers, and environmentalists. While Native Americans might wonder what all the fuss is about—why the need to prove so logically and historically that trees have spiritual value—they would certainly understand the experience that helped Professor Lane develop his corollaries for the sacred personhood of trees: personal acquaintance with a cottonwood. Likewise, all the tales shared in a collection called *Tree Stories* tell how individuals came to have an intimate relationship with a particular tree. Each tree served as teacher, nurturer, childhood landmark, companion, and memorial (many of them cottonwoods). Cottonwood trees have been helping human beings step across the spiritual threshold for a long time.

Cottonwoods and Imagination

Cottonwoods hold the spirit in thrall in many ways. In his essay "The Brown Wasps," the poet-scientist Loren Eiseley recalls a special tree from his youth:

> I have said my life has been passed in the shade of a nonexistent tree, so that such sights do not offend me.... It was planted sixty years ago by a boy with a bucket and a toy spade in a little Nebraska town. That boy was myself. It was a cottonwood sapling and the boy remembered it because of some words spoken by his father and because everyone died or moved away who was supposed to wait and grow old under its shade. The boy was passed from hand to hand, but the tree for some intangible reason had taken root in his mind. It was under its branches that he sheltered; it was from this tree that his memories, which are my memories, led away into the world.

Later in life, Eiseley could not resist the memory of that tree growing during all the years he lived away from that town. He bought a ticket and returned. He found the street, the house, even the white picket fence. But no cottonwood stretched its branches and limbs up into the sky as it had in his mind all those years. What a fine Jesuitical argument his discovery would have made: If a tree once planted as an act of faith survives only in the mind of its planter, does the faith endure? If the question had been put to Eiseley, he would doubtless have answered a resounding Yes! That the tree he would plant as a boy was a cottonwood is not insignificant. Years on and far away from the place of his boyhood, he would always identify himself with that tree and the true Middle West that had given birth to his spirit.

Cottonwood trees have captured and held other creative spirits. Two of our best-loved cultural icons were born beneath a cottonwood. Without one of them, my generation of Baby Boomers probably wouldn't know how to spell E-N-C-Y-C-L-O-P-E-D-I-A. ➤

Jiminy Cricket and Mickey Mouse first appeared in the imagination of Walter Elias Disney while, as a boy growing up in rural north-central Missouri, he conducted "belly botany," studying the wildlife beneath his "Dreaming Tree." Walt's tree is still there. To help keep some of that dreaming alive, American Forests offers a clone of the Disney tree for sale at its Historic Tree Nursery.

Back in Nebraska, cottonwoods were planting seeds in yet other dreamers. They held sway over the writer Bess Streeter Aldrich:

> I grew up under the cottonwoods and I love them. They're the happiest, merriest trees in the world. When everything else is still and doleful and pessimistic, they dance and laugh and twinkle. I think sometimes we don't appreciate the things we're used to . . . don't see our commonest things the way they are.

Author Wright Morris rooted his novel *Ceremony at Lone Tree* on an event that took place near a cottonwood tree, in a place named for it that no longer existed. For a fiction writer, is there any better setting than one that remains only in memory? Willa Cather, the best-known Nebraska writer (before Ted Kooser received two appointments as the nation's poet laureate, anyway), had a minor love affair with cottonwood trees, which she often calls "poplars" in her novels (she knew her genus and species). And why wouldn't she love them? After she moved from tree-luscious Virginia to the open Nebraska prairie, she quickly learned how cottonwoods growing along the Republican River and streams near Red Cloud brought not only shade and relief, but the sound that had grown so rare in her life—rushing water. In the rustling of cottonwood leaves she heard rain and the cheerful celebration of water. Beneath such trees her heroes and heroines lived through both great and tragic lives. Writers are not the only ones to have cottonwoods work such magic on their imaginations. Visual artists have been spellbound, too. Maynard Dixon, one of the most prominent western artists of the early twentieth century, proclaimed that "Nature is your starting point." He was a man who believed that even the "the wind of the wastelands has color," a man who explored the western United States by every method possible, from shank's mare to the Model T. As dedicated to solitude as he was to his art, Dixon inevitably celebrated the cottonwood trees that kept him company. As a symbol, cottonwoods can be found in his work more often after 1930. One of his favorite times to go into the desert was in the fall, when the ➤

cottonwoods take on that golden luster that shines out of his work. As biographer Donald Hagerty wrote for a 1998 exhibit catalog of Dixon's work:

> Dixon understood the tree's promise; its leaves, rotating and rattling, might foreshadow rain; its figure on the horizon was a signpost for water, firewood, shade and shelter. The cottonwood stands alone or in small groves along watercourses. It prefers solitude, as did Dixon himself. He made the cottonwood a personal symbol in his art in the last fifteen years of his life, painting many canvases of a tree which tolerates little between it and the world.

Another artist whose name and work are synonymous with the Southwest is Georgia O'Keeffe. And, as one biographer has recorded, during her first visit to Mabel Dodge Luhan's house in Taos, O'Keeffe found shade and shelter in an open-air studio beneath cottonwoods, trees that still shelter Luhan's "Los Gallos" today. According to O'Keeffe scholar Sarah Whitaker Peters, O'Keeffe once told artist Marsden Hartley, "I wish all people were trees and I think I could enjoy them." Considered in that light, her cottonwood portraits are mystical, as she was reputed to be herself. At the Georgia O'Keeffe Museum in Santa Fe, I purchased postcards of her work. Even in that small form, in "Cottonwood Trees in Spring," painted in 1943, an ethereal veil of yellow-green hovers over the tree as it leafs out. Already the new leaves move, each branch flowing like a river in the wind. Salmon-colored bark peeks through spaces between the limbs; a shred of blue sky appears above, a rag of cloud floats by. Painted the same year, "Dead Cottonwood; Abiquiu" offers a contrast. Closest to the viewer, the partially hollow stump of a snag, an old cottonwood, rises right out of the picture. A hole in the wood provides a binocular view to the far side of the painting, to a thriving cottonwood grove. A scorched piece of hooked wood extends from the front of the bole. And yet this dead trunk, denuded of bark and bleached almost white, remains strong and supple. The curves move toward roundness. The long steady arm of a branch reaches toward something only the artist can see. In 1954, O'Keeffe painted another view of cottonwoods in "Winter Cottonwoods East, V." Roxana Robinson, another O'Keeffe scholar, finds the cottonwood series less successful than some of the other subjects painted more than once. The reason? A haziness, less clarity than O'Keeffe's other natural objects. Yet, that's how Rio Grande cottonwoods look in the spring, or in the wind of any season. A soft, dreamy quality always surrounds them, even in the fall sunlight that sharpens their gold against the azure New Mexican sky. ➤

Though their work was a study in contrasts, Maynard Dixon and Georgia O'Keeffe shared some common traits with their cottonwood subjects. Peripatetic by nature, both trees and artists wandered the streams, rivers, and canyons of the Southwest, looking for sustenance. They had that ability to "pioneer," to go first and alone into uncertain ground and thrive there; to provide a beacon, one in nature and the other in the world of art; to be solitary, disliking too many neighbors nearby who could crowd out the light or the view; and though softer inside than might be suspected, also able to defy gravity and the expected pattern of growth in a predictable way— able to fence with the wind, absorb the rain, withstand storms and stand up to whatever the world might bring.

Cottonwood trees still tempt the modern artistic imagination. A new novel by Eugene Guerin titled *Cottonwood Saints* opens with an invocation of "los santos"—those sacred images of Christ and the saints carved from cottonwood. A little collection called *Tree Stories* recounts personal encounters with trees, many of them cotton- woods, as teachers, healers, and guides. Ted Kooser, former U.S. poet laureate, collaborated with fellow poet Bill Kloefkorn to co-publish a collection titled *Cottonwood County* in 1979. Even the worldly Joan Didion had her cottonwood dream. In an essay entitled "John Wayne: A Love Song," she remembers: "We went [to the movies] three and four afternoons a week, sat on folding chairs in the dark- ened Quonset hut which served as a theater, and it was there, that summer of 1943 while the hot wind blew outside, that I first saw John Wayne. Saw the walk, heard the voice. Heard him tell the girl in a picture called War of the Wildcats that he would build her a house 'at the bend in the river where the cottonwoods grow.' As it happened I did not grow up to be the kind of woman who is the heroine in a Western, and although the men I have known have taken me to live in many places I have come to love, they have never been John Wayne, and they have never taken me to that bend in the river where the cottonwoods grow. Deep in that part of my heart where the artificial rain forever falls, that is still the line I wait to hear." As long as cottonwood trees grow, they will continue to dwell in the artistic spirit.

Sources

The Night Country. Loren Eiseley. Charles Scribner's Sons. New York. 1971.
Bess Streeter Aldrich. *The Rim of the Prairie*. University of Nebraska Press. Lincoln.
    1960. p. 82 ➤

Sheldon, Addison. *History and Stories of Nebraska.* Lincoln. The University Publishing Company. 1926. pp. 92–93

Information on Maynard Dixon can be viewed at:
http://www.MaynardDixon.org/articles/mdixon3.html.

Jeffery Hogrefe remarks on O'Keeffe's first visit to Taos in *O'Keeffe/The Life of an American Legend.* Bantam Books. New York. 1992.

See Sarah Whitaker Peters, *Becoming O'Keeffe.* Abbeville Press. New York. 2001. 2nd ed. p. 88

Robinson, Roxana. *Georgia O'Keeffe/A Life.* Harper & Row. New York. 1989. p. 478.

Jacobs, Warren David and Karen I. Shragg. *Tree Stories/A Collection of Extraordinary Encounters.* SunShine Press Publications. Hygiene, Colo. 2002.

Kloefkorn, William and Ted Kooser. *Cottonwood County.* Windflower Press. Lincoln, Nebraska. 1979.

Sources

The digital image of Porcupine is from the Northwestern University Digital Library Collections. "Porcupine–Cheyenne." The North American Indian (1907–1930) v. 06, The Piegan. The Cheyenne. The Arapaho. ([Seattle]: E. S. Curtis; [Cambridge, Mass.: The University Press], 1911), plate no. 216. To view the image, go to the American Memory Web site at: http://memory.loc.gov and click on Native American History/Edward S. Curtis collection/then keyword search: Porcupine.

Adams, Robert. *Cottonwoods.* Smithsonian Institution Press. Washington, D.C. 1994.

Grinnell, George Bird. *Pawnee Hero Stories and Folk-Tales.* University of Nebraska Press. Lincoln. 1961.

Sir James George Frazier's account of the Hidatsa view of cottonwood intelligence is from *The Golden Bough: A Study in Magic and Religion.* Collier Books. New York. 1922. Available online at: http://www.bartleby.com/196/pages/page111.html.

Black Elk, Nicholas. *The Sacred Pipe/Black Elk's Account of the Seven Rites of the Oglala Sioux.* Recorded by Joseph Epes Brown. University of Oklahoma Press. Norman. 1953.

Gilmore, Melvin Randolph. "Uses of Plants by the Indians of the Missouri River Region," *Twenty-Third Annual Report, Bureau of American Ethnology*. Smithsonian Institution (1911–12).

For the lesson plan developed by the Kansas teachers, see "Cottonwood Tree." http://www.kshs.org/teachers/trunks/pdfs/symb_jtree.pdf

Abourezk, Kevin. "Native Sun Dance, rare in the area, is being held." *Lincoln Journal-Star*. July 2004.

I have necessarily summarized a complex account of an elaborate liturgy surrounding the Sacred Pole and the restoration of other sacred objects to the Omaha people. For the complete stories of the real Omaha and the true evocation of this sacred being, see *Blessing for a Long Time/The Sacred Pole of the Omaha Tribe* by Robin Ridington and Dennis Hastings (In'aska). University of Nebraska. Lincoln and London. 1997. For history as well as current information about the Omaha tribe, see the Omaha Tribe of Nebraska Web site at: http://www.omahatribeofnebraska.com/index.html. For a better understanding of "all my relations," see chapter 7 of the Ridington book, as well as Linda Hogan's essay, "All My Relations," in *Dwellings*. W. W. Norton & Company. New York and London. 1995. pp. 36–41.

Hopi Tribe Web page. http://www.nau.edu/~hcpo-p/arts/kachina.htm

A Man Called Horse (review). Internet Movie Database. http://www.imdb.com/title/tt0066049/

Mankato State University E-Museum. http://www.mnsu.edu/emuseum/cultural/northamerica/pawnee.html

Naughton, Gary. "The Cottonwood: Prairie Pioneer." *Wildlife and Parks*. 53(3):3–7. May–June 1996.

Pearlstone, Zena, ed. *Katsina/Commodified and Appropriated Images of Hopi Supernaturals*. UCLA Museum of Cultural History. Los Angeles. 2001.

Teiwes, Helga. *Kachina Dolls/The Art of the Hopi Carvers*. University of Arizona Press. Tucson. 1991.

Wright, Barton. *Hopi Kachinas/The Complete Guide to Collecting Kachina Dolls*. Northland Press. Flagstaff. 1977.

Paul Horgan describes the Pueblo use of prayer sticks in *Great River/The Rio Grande in North American History*. Wesleyan University Press/University Press of New England. Hanover. 1984. p. 27.

Dickey, Roland F. *New Mexico Village Arts*. University of New Mexico Press. Albuquerque. 1990 (first printed in 1949).

Steele, Thomas J. S. J. *Santos and Saints*. Ancient City Press. Santa Fe, New Mexico. 1994 (first printed in 1974)

Visit to the Millicent Rogers Museum in Taos, New Mexico, in 2003.

Jacobs, Warren David and Karen I. Shragg. *Tree Stories/A Collection of Extraordinary Encounters*. SunShine Press Publications. Hygiene, Colo. 2002.

6

THE COTTONWOOD MAGICAL
HISTORY TOUR

During a bus ride through southern Illinois, the great conservationist and nature writer Aldo Leopold glanced out the window in time to see two men cutting through the trunk of a huge old cottonwood tree. Leopold envisioned the tree as a "buoy in the prairie sea" and imagined that William Clark, co-captain of the Lewis and Clark Expedition, had sheltered beneath it. Leopold could picture buffalo cooling off in the great tree's shade and birds filling its branches. He went on to describe the cottonwood as "the best historical library short of the state college." Leopold is gone, but his idea of the cottonwood tree as a historical library remains. All aboard for the Cottonwood Magical History Tour!

Lewis and Clark

It's hard to find a group of people or an event that benefited more from cotton-wood trees than members of Meriwether Lewis and William Clark's Corps of Discovery, during the first expedition directed to explore land west of the Missouri River from 1804 to 1806. A search of the online version of *The Lewis and Clark Journals/The Definitive Nebraska Edition* retrieves 141 hits for "cottonwood" or "cotton wood" and 30 for "cotton trees," just two examples that variant spellings provide. After reading different editions and interpretations of the Lewis and Clark journals, and watching documentaries—including the riverside seat afforded by the IMAX screen and the steady journey of the Corps of Discovery's progress presented by filmmaker Ken Burns—I have often wondered how the course of American history might have changed if Lewis and Clark had not found a cottonwood to camp beneath—or to rely on in so many other useful and life-saving ways. And what might we not know about cottonwood trees if they had been less attentive to detail?

Lone Tree Monument near Central City, Nebraska. Photo by Kathleen Cain.

As for the natural history of their mission, though Meriwether Lewis obtained his first lessons in botany from his mother, a practiced herbalist, Thomas Jefferson sent him to Philadelphia to learn the scientific ways of collecting and preserving specimens in the wild. His tutelage under Benjamin Smith Barton, author of the first textbook on North American botany (a book Lewis lugged across the continent) paid off. The specimens that remain include hundreds of pressed plants and examples of cottonwoods, kept today in the Academy of Natural Sciences in Philadelphia. Lewis and Clark described nearly two hundred plants unknown to them. Among these was a species of cottonwood.

Meriwether Lewis provides many descriptions of plant life along the river route, but on June 21, 1804, Clark describes, in a manner befitting any modern naturalist, the cottonwoods (probably Eastern, given the location), which he calls "cotton," one of the tree's common names at the time. He depicts their favored riparian habitat and lists their riverside companions, in a place thought to be near modern Wellington, Missouri. He describes the bottomland preferred by two poplar species—"cotton" and willow. He even mentions the second shelf of growth where cottonwood companions tend to grow—walnut, ash, hackberry, mulberry, and sycamore.

Less than a month later, on July 18, 1804, after getting an early start and measuring the current of the Missouri near present-day Nebraska City, Nebraska, Clark again sees cottonwoods. There isn't much timber around except in the usual low points he's described previously, and on islands in the river and along the creeks. He wouldn't recognize the spot today, located several miles from the rerouted flow of "the Big Muddy," as locals call the modern Missouri. He might not even recognize the river. It has been reshaped to suit the economic needs of shipping. It's been dredged, its curves and oxbows straightened to create "the Big Ditch," eight hundred miles of fast-moving water. If you want to see the Missouri as Lewis and Clark saw it, you have to travel farther north, up near Ponca, Nebraska. One thing Lewis would recognize—and he could stand on the deck of the "Captain Meriwether Lewis" (a dredger named for him and put into permanent dry-docks as a museum near Brownville, Nebraska) to do it—is the unbroken gallery of cottonwood trees across the river. His descriptions of two hundred years ago still fit—the tallest tree in the gathering of river trees, keeping to higher ground, sheltering their arboreal familiars, growing into a mature riparian forest.

By September 1804 the Corps of Discovery reached what is now Brule County, South Dakota. Here, on a "Dark drizzly Day," Clark records that Lewis killed a porcupine as it fed on the leaves and "bowers" of a cottonwood. The leaves of this tree and those of other cottonwoods had been consumed—by the porcupine, he presumes. Scientists have since confirmed that the porcupine is one of several mammals that love starchy, sugar-rich cottonwood leaves. As they pass island after island, Lewis and Clark note the constant presence of cottonwoods. By October 14, 1804, in what is now North Dakota, they notice that only the cottonwoods still have leaves. Lewis repeatedly describes what naturalists and foresters today call the understory of a riparian habitat, complete with elm, ash, and box elder, as well as small-leafed willow, serviceberry, and "redwood" (red osier dogwood). In May, Lewis repeats a similar description near Elkhorn Point in Montana. His reiteration keeps him true to the task of providing Jefferson—and future generations—with a consistent description of the country so new to them all—comparable to the Apollo missions to the Moon, the late historian Stephen Ambrose mused, adding that Lewis and Clark had less information about their destination than the Apollo astronauts did. Although the Ambrose view is legitimate, in reading the journals it's good to consider the advice given by modern Native Americans: to remember that what was so new for the Corps of Discovery was and had been daily life for the tribes of indigenous people for thousands of years. Such knowledge came to serve the Corps well. Caught up in the beauty and splendor of the terrain while exploring Rainbow Falls and Colter Falls in what would become Montana, Lewis trudges on until he sees an island in the area of Great Falls. He's been told about this place by the Hidatsas: look for an island on which a tall cottonwood grows—a cottonwood in which an eagle has built her nest. Lewis finds the island, the cottonwood, and the nest, exactly as it's been described. Now *that's* knowing your country, to be able to direct strangers over a great distance to an individual tree holding a particular nest.

Other members of the Corps add their observations of cottonwood habitat, or lack of it, to the journals. On May 17, 1805, in Montana, Patrick Gass records a by-now familiar scene. Though he notices that the land is growing poorer and the grass shorter, the presence of cottonwoods and their characteristic companions remains the same from the riverside view—the expedition's main vantage point. Lewis has previously noted how the cottonwood presence has diminished on the plains. He distinguishes the broad-leafed from the Narrowleaf Cottonwood as the altitude changes. The Narrowleaf prefers elevations of 5,000 to 10,000 feet. We take such knowledge for granted today, but in the journals Lewis describes the preference and the distinction for the first time. Though he knows the tree is a cottonwood, he distinguishes its slender, tapered leaf from the broad, triangular form of the species he's more familiar with at lower elevations.

The job of natural historians goes on for the Corps as, by November 1805, they find their way to the western side of the Rockies. In what historians and botanists have decided is near present-day Clark County, Washington, Clark continues to document—along with the number of canoes a certain tribe owns and the results of test-tasting a new root that makes a good substitute for bread—the presence of cottonwoods. Here the trees appear in a woodland setting; fewer than in the usual riparian habitat. In April 1806, in what is now Multnomah County, Oregon, Lewis and Clark notice that male cottonwoods are losing their flowers. In each place they camp and observe they remain faithful to the mission of describing the country. On July 26, 1806, as the time at "Camp Disappointment" (where two rivers have failed to come together as expected) comes to an end and Lewis prepares to move on, he remarks upon the differences between several species of cottonwood. He describes the Black Cottonwood more common to the Columbia and one he never observed along the Missouri. It's unlike the narrow-leafed species of the more mountainous regions, he notes, and bears other marks of distinction from the familiar broad-leafed variety of the east.

Even though the primary purpose of the Corps was to further Thomas Jefferson's version of economic development, it's hard to put a price on the natural history that the expedition brought back to the "United States." Cottonwood trees made for a significant part of the commentary. You could say that cottonwoods served as organic members of the expedition. Just as today's Olympic teams choose team symbols, the cottonwood could certainly have served as Lewis and Clark's "Corps tree." You don't have to wonder much, or for long, how Lewis and Clark and their companions would have fared without cottonwoods during the unexpected winter they spent at Fort Mandan during 1804–1805. Most likely the Mandan or Hidatsa tribes would have given them shelter if the need had become too great. Tribal members often appeared with timely gifts of buffalo robes, meat, and other food. But if hospitality had not been forthcoming, the Corps' adventure might have been a footnote in American history rather than the foothold on the continent it became. The "Cotton Timber" as they described the planks they were able to hew and saw into walls, was all they had. Though not known for quality or reliability as a building material (even now the wood has a bad reputation), it had to do. The Corps was able to make cottonwood timber into tables, benches, shelves, and other furniture. They used its hot, quick-burning logs to keep warm. And those few inches of soft, friable, lumber so easily given to warping, breaking, or bending were all that stood between them and a North Dakota winter—during which they recorded temperatures between -10°F and -42°F. Members of the Corps listened to the pop and crack of fragile cottonwood timbers that froze and thawed through the short days and long nights.

Another kindness that the Mandans and Hidatsas extended to Lewis and Clark regarding cottonwood trees was knowledge of the natural world. As Clark recorded on November 9, 1804, the Indians showed the Corps how the horses could feed on the sugar-rich leaves and bark. It wasn't only porcupines that could survive on such a diet. This was an important lesson in a strange country with a harsh climate, where the life of a human being depended on the well-being of a horse. When given a choice between moistened feed or cottonwood, Lewis watched the horses choose the tree bark. He also described the common practice among the tribes of having plenty of cottonwood available as feed; leaves, bark, and boughs were all edible. Humans could benefit from the nutritive value of the cottonwood bark, as well as from its medicinal qualities. An active ingredient of the inner bark is salicin, which helps control fever and pain (modern aspirin contains salycillic acid). Is it too dramatic to suggest that Lewis and Clark would not have survived that winter of 1804–1805 without the benefit of cottonwood trees? After all, they were trained, experienced military men used to innovating on the spot. They would probably have found other ways to survive, as they did time and again during mishaps in the course of their journey. They might have retraced their steps to save themselves and their men, seeking shelter with trappers and traders who lived along the Missouri. Perhaps the Mandans and Hidatsas, who were generous to them in so many ways, would have helped them stay the winter. But it is not overly dramatic to say that the cottonwood helped them; and if the tree didn't save some lives along the way, it certainly made them easier.

Early in the journey, before Fort Mandan, Lewis had wondered aloud in his journal what this tree, with its "parrishoot" of cotton and its "spungey" texture, was valuable for, other than building pirogues (boats)—as if finding enough of the only wood available to build the boats was not enough. Before leaving Fort Mandan, the Corps was able to obtain enough cottonwood to build six pirogues in which they labored upstream toward the Yellowstone. Later, during the difficult portage along dangerous waterfalls in Montana, Lewis describes the luck of finding a single cottonwood, nearly two feet in diameter, sizeable enough to make wheels for the carriage hauling the party's cottonwood canoes. Though by now well aware of the wood's soft, brittle nature, Lewis doubts that another tree within twenty miles. could match its size If you've ever had to stop in mid-journey and change a tire, you know it's no fun. Imagine having to stop, chop down a tree, make your own wheels from the wood, and still be ready to travel the next day. (The cottonwood wheels lasted five days.)

After the portage, cottonwoods came to the rescue again when Lewis's portable, iron-framed boat failed to "answer"—it sank miserably in its first test when a storm tore its covering apart. Clark led a group up the Missouri from the Upper Portage camp below Great Falls, until they found two cottonwood trees suitable for building dugouts—yet another survival skill learned from Native Americans. Though a little smaller than they'd hoped, the new boats increased the size of their fleet—they had cached the iron boat along with two other pirogues that survived the journey. There were other practical uses for cottonwood, also learned from Native Americans. The wood could be carved and shaped into implements and tools, ranging from spoons and bowls to even an oar when the original went overboard.

Cottonwood trees are tied to the fate of another member of the Corps of Discovery. Only a few Narrowleaf cottonwoods grew at Three Forks, the place on the Missouri River where Sacagawea, the Corps' interpreter and the woman Clark called "my guide," was taken captive by the Hidatsas as a young girl. In one account, Sacagawea was said to have fled with her family to a shelter of cottonwoods that ultimately failed to protect them from the war party's advance or discovery. Had Sacagawea not been captured, how different the history of so many might have been.

As for my earlier-stated "cottonwood thesis," even if Lewis and Clark had not been able to find cottonwood logs to construct Fort Mandan, it's clear from the determined tone of the journals that they would have gone on. And if they had not found enough cottonwood timber to build dugouts and continue along the upper Missouri before winter arrived, as Lewis concluded, if the Native Americans who lived in these regions could survive, so could the Corps of Discovery. In spite of capsized pirogues, sinking iron boats, lost journals, wet clothing, unpredictable weather, miles full of prickly pear cactus, cranky grizzlies, alternating bouts of "biliousness" and diarrhea, twisted ankles, sore feet, lack of food, and constant wrong turns in an alien geography, the two captains would not have given up. Lack of the proper timber, when all was told, was just one more item on a long list of troubles. Yet cottonwood trees should get high marks and special notice for all they helped the Corps achieve. And I am not the only one to think this way. Naturalists and historians who have spent years studying the Corps' accomplishments all agree that the cottonwood was the tree that most contributed to their success. For the bicentennial celebration of the Lewis and Clark journey, the North Dakota Forest Service recognized the value that this tree—more than any other—provided to the expedition by publishing a booklet entitled "Lewis & Clark Cottonwoods." Had Aldo Leopold traveled farther north and west, he would have been able to see a cottonwood tree near where Lewis and Clark really did camp at Smith Grove near Washburn, a site now owned and managed by the North Dakota Fish and Game Department. As we will see later, in the chapter titled "Good News," the booklet examines the life and times of the cottonwood in North Dakota in the context of its own natural history, one eventually tied to Lewis and Clark's river, the Missouri.

The Balmville Tree

In 1699, long before Lewis and Clark set off on their westward trek, a cottonwood tree growing much farther to the east was on its way to becoming a branch library of American history. Still known as "the Balmville Tree," this venerable elder gave its name to the surrounding area, a hamlet of Newburgh, New York. In its earliest days people called it "the Balm Tree" or "the Balm of Gilead," common names for the balsam poplar that refer to the fragrance of the leaves. And though cottonwoods do belong to the genus of poplars, experts have long since agreed that the Balmville Tree is an Eastern Cottonwood. They also concluded that a celebration of its three hundredth birthday in 1999 was accurate. Written sources have proved the tree's status as a living witness to American history since before the Revolution. By then it had already passed the expected midlife of such a tree, normally fifty to a hundred years. Scientific sources agree, having confirmed the tree's age through a core sample tested in 1953.

If Leopold's bus had passed through Newburgh and Balmville, he might have let us stop, get out, and walk around beneath this tree, which is one of the four best ways to view a cottonwood—two others are from a distance in an open space and from within the tree itself. I'll tell you about the fourth view later.

Life has changed in Balmville since 1699. The cottonwood stands at a crossroads, overlooking the place where Native American trails became settlers' tracks, tracks became dirt roads, and dirt roads eventually got paved. There's not much room beneath the tree, which resides on a tiny, official island, nearly 350 square feet of space. Standing inside the stone wall built around the tree, we can still look up into the limbs and branches, and imagine, as Leopold would have, what might have taken place beneath it. When first described, the Balmville cottonwood was estimated to be 105–110 feet tall, with a circumference of 20 feet, 6 inches, its crown spreading 113 feet across. About a hundred years later, the official measurements were 83 feet high, with the circumference nearly 25 feet. Another measurement in 1998 showed that the tree had grown one foot and one inch in circumference, and maintained its steady height of 83 feet. By comparison, the Washington Monument stands over 555 feet tall. It would take seven Balmville Trees to equal the height of the monument.

Why mention the Washington Monument? Well, just by standing so long in one place, the Balmville Tree has stored in its library some history involving America's first president. While plenty of venues might be able to claim that "George Washington slept here," the residents of Balmville can say that Washington passed beneath the Balmville cottonwood—not once, but many times, on his way to and from a headquarters he established in nearby Newburgh in 1779. Another Washington—whose last name was Irving—defined by some as the "first American man of letters" and author of "The Legend of Sleepy Hollow" and "Rip van Winkle"—looked up into the branches of this tree. A second U.S. president and New York native, Franklin Roosevelt, was fond of it. So was the folksinger Pete Seeger. And supposedly Matthew Vassar, the namesake of Vassar College, had a flash of inspiration beneath the tree, one that contributed to his rags-to-riches transformation.

A lesser known—though in some ways more important—admirer of the Balmville Tree is a man named Richard Severo, who lived near enough to the tree to be able to look right into it (the fourth best view). By the mid-1990s the Balmville Tree faced what so many historic trees often do: a sentence of death by chainsaw, issued by proclamation of a municipal council. Being truly good neighbors, Severo and other citizens asked for a second opinion on the tree's health. Yes, with special care, representatives of the New York State Department of Environmental Conservation concluded, the Balmville Tree could be preserved. A root feeding system was installed in the pavement surrounding the tree. Guy wires hold precarious branches and limbs in place, to protect them from wind damage. Behind a small stone fence barricade, the Balmville cottonwood has made a little history of its own: it constitutes the smallest state forest in New York, having been declared a "public historic park" in 1976.

The tree is holding its own. It continues to grow new wood and foliage each year, in its urge to surpass its success at living more than three times the average maximum of its species. Not bad for a tree that legend says got its start from a riding crop stuck in the ground. As for successors, even though multiple sophisticated and scientifically controlled attempts were made to reproduce the Balmville Tree, the one that succeeded was the result of an effort by that good neighbor, Richard Severo, who planted the old way: by sticking a branch in the ground. And who knows? Maybe in another three hundred years someone will be writing about the Balmville Tree's successor—and the continuation of American history. If you can't visit in person, you can see the Balmville Tree online at http://www.newburghrevealed.org. Until recently the Balmville Tree was considered the oldest Eastern Cottonwood in North America. But it has been displaced by the discovery of five hundred-year-old cottonwoods in

British Columbia. As you might expect, the Canadian trees are the subject of intense research. We'll learn more about them in chapter 8, "Good News."

Scythe Trees

The scythe was once a symbol of American agriculture. Before the days of air-conditioned tractors equipped with computers and GIS locators, fields were often cut by hand, using the big curved blades with the wooden handles. In the eighteenth and nineteenth centuries, few respectable farms would have been without one. They're still used occasionally. I've seen one or two swung in Connecticut meadows too small for a tractor. As we leave Newburgh and the Balmville Tree behind, and travel to north-central New York, a little below Lake Ontario and just east of historic Seneca Falls (famous gathering place for women's rights activists in the nineteenth century), we'll find American history remembered by scythes and cottonwood trees.

The plaque on a particular tree (this time it is a Balm of Gilead poplar, though a "cottonwood" to many) in Waterloo, New York, tells such a story. In 1861, the year the Civil War began, "James Wyman Johnson came from the fields one morning, hung his scythe in the crotch of a small cottonwood tree and told his parents to 'leave the scythe in the tree until I return.'" He enlisted in the Union Army and went off to fight. The young soldier died three years later, a patient in a Confederate hospital. He had been wounded in battle at Plymouth, North Carolina. His grieving parents left the scythe in the tree, where it remains today.

Following Johnson's tradition, toward the end of yet another war, in 1918, the brothers Schaffe—Raymond and Lynn—also hooked their scythes in the bark of the Waterloo Tree. Luck stayed with them, however. World War I ended the same year they departed. They returned home, but they never came back to reclaim their scythes.

The tree has absorbed all three blades into its sturdy hide, lifting them nearly 10 feet off the ground as it grew. The handles, rusted with the years and the seasons, still show through the bark. The tree serves as a local point of interest, celebrated enough to become the subject of a postcard and, in today's delivery methods, a Web page.

Apparently the habit of leaving a scythe in a tree was not uncommon. Richard Shelley of Merengo, New York, left his in a tree at about the same time, and for the same reason as James Johnson. But the Shelley Tree did not survive and was blown down in a storm in 1998. At least one more scythe tree has been recorded for posterity, but we'll have to travel west to find it.

Lyman Wetmore of Lincoln County, Kansas, didn't go off to war and leave his scythe hanging in a tree. Instead, he was taken ill while cutting weeds. Planning to return and finish the work, he hung his blade up in a young cottonwood (only a couple of inches in diameter at the time) and went home. He died not long after. The scythe was left in the tree until 1896—thirteen years later—when it was reported in the local paper. By that time the cottonwood had grown to nearly two feet in diameter, making the blade irretrievable and the story a Kansas original.

The Ties That Didn't Bind

Throughout American history, cottonwoods were put to every use possible, first by Native people and later by European immigrants. As so often happened, one of the most unusual uses came out of desperation. During the building of the transcontinental railroad (completed in 1869), engineers discovered they were running out of hardwood to build the railroad ties set beneath the track. Someone came up with a solution: at a ratio of 5:1, mix cottonwood ties in with those milled from harder woods. The short-lived result was disastrous. A tree that lived its life so full of water wasn't strong, couldn't hold a spike any better than it could hold a nail, and, as the locals joked, began to rot the minute it hit the ground.

On the Bosque

In continuing our tour, let's turn south and travel to New Mexico, to old Fort Sumner (not to be confused with Fort Sumter of "rockets' red glare" fame). The fort was one in the chain of military installations used to control the western United States and subdue Native American tribes in the 1800s. What's left of the fort stands in a hip-high maze of adobe walls, built long ago within sight of the muddy Pecos River. The river flows west of the fort and spends part of its five hundred mile length twisting through a landscape still known as the Bosque Redondo. A Spanish word, *bosque* (bos-kee) means a wooded place—a grove. *Redondo* describes the shape—a round grove. The phrase refers to all the trees and shrubs that grow along the river. Like the river water they take in through their roots, the native cottonwoods have witnessed and been part of what happened here along the Bosque Redondo. Members of the Navajo Nation have another name for this place, however. They call it *Hweeldi* (hweel-deh). Though one scholarly source says the Navajo word comes from a variation of *fuerte*, the Spanish word for fort, today we will learn that the word means simply "the sorrow."

Cottonwood relict from the Bosque Redondo near Fort Sumner, New Mexico.
Photo by Kathleen Cain

The lush look of cottonwoods growing along this part of the Pecos caught the eye of Major James Carleton, a U.S. Army officer who had as his dream the plan to create an Indian reservation here as early as 1850. Cottonwood trees have a mirage-like quality about them when they move and shimmer in the distances of open desert country like eastern New Mexico. They look more alive than other trees. They even seem to beckon. Like the Navajos and the Mescalero Apaches, the trees could not resist the overpowering force of the U.S. Army. But Carleton's dream became a nightmare. By 1864 that nightmare, that *Hweeldi*, translated into the Long Walk of the Navajo and the imprisonment of the Apaches in their own land. With help from Kit Carson (who in turn had help from some members of the Utes, Hopis, and Pueblos—traditional enemies of the Navajos)—the U.S. Army forced the Navajos to walk four hundred miles from Fort Defiance, Arizona, to Fort Sumner. Accounts of the number of people who made the journey vary: A current New Mexico county newspaper reports 7,000; the state booklet commemorating the Bosque Redondo Memorial says 8,500 people made it to Fort Sumner; a tourist guidebook says 8,600. Yet another source says that 9,000 people started out on the journey. Sickness, being forced to cross three rivers, including the Rio

Grande, and the generally harsh conditions without adequate preparation or shelter caused many deaths. Once at the fort, life was not any better. The army was unprepared to feed, shelter, or care for so many people. The flour was tainted. Native people were unused to cooking with or eating the kind of food provided. Shelter meant digging a hole in the ground. The Pecos, notoriously alkaline, was undrinkable. In Carleton's agrarian utopia, the crops failed year after year.

If the cottonwoods on the Bosque provided any respite or relief for the prisoners, who held tightly to their traditions and beliefs just to survive, such relief did not last for long. Though other wood for construction was brought in from the Capitan Mountains, most of the cottonwood grove that gave the Bosque its name was cut down and used to build the fort, established by 1862. After they arrived in 1863 and 1864, Navajo and Apache men were ordered to cut down what was left of the cottonwoods, essentially deforesting the place—an act that must have been as painful to them as if they were ordered to kill members of their own clans and families. In Navajo and Apache belief, the inhabitants of the natural world, human as well as arboreal, are all relatives. The U.S. Army didn't share such a worldview; consequently, a fuel shortage occurred at the fort early on, adding to the misery. Next came Carleton's order to plant trees for fuel, as well as along the *acequias* (canals and irrigation ditches), where cottonwoods do another of the many jobs they perform in their watery natural habitat: keep the ditch banks from caving in. More than twelve thousand trees were replanted. Photographs from the time show cottonwood saplings set along the edge of the canals. The fort served as a prison camp until 1868, when a treaty was negotiated with the Navajos, who began their long walk back home in January 1869. The Mescalero Apaches, feeling no obligation to comply with broken promises, had departed one full-moon night in November 1865.

Like the round grove itself and like the replenishment of the cottonwood trees, the story of the Bosque Redondo continues, this time with a new ending. On the morning of June 4, 2005, as we drive from Santa Rosa, New Mexico, to the site of old Fort Sumner, a distance of a little more than forty miles, a friend and I pass a man who is walking. He carries the flag of the Navajo Nation. He is several miles from the old fort. We follow the line of cars, park beneath cottonwoods, and walk toward the new Bosque Redondo Memorial building.

The walk from the parking lot to the memorial is not far; maybe two blocks. But with each step, anyone who has come here today, especially the hundreds of Navajo people whose ancestors were forced to walk the four hundred miles that these grandchildren and great-grandchildren have just driven across from Arizona, cannot help but dwell on all the hard steps of that long-ago journey.

Bits of conversation float through the air like the cottonwood fluff that drifts everywhere; the female trees have opened their strings of green beads in time for today's ceremony, to release new life on the wind. "To think they walked ..." one woman begins. "Here, where we have to have our air conditioning in our cars...." Many of the people were barefoot. They walked through carpets of prickly pear cactus and over stones that cut their feet. A woman whose great-grandfather hid in the Grand Canyon to avoid capture says that many of the people could not swim. Yet they were forced to cross three rivers.

We step in and out of the shade of cottonwood trees. The New Mexico landscape and cottonwood trees are partners in nature. Step out of the blistering heat, so much more intense at this high-desert elevation, and the relief is immediate, almost magical. Shade, shelter, and the soft music of the tree called *Ti'is* (tees) in Navajo, are all offered at once. Did the trees protect those people from so long ago?

We keep walking on a paved road that winds around to the memorial. On our left an ancient remnant of a cottonwood tree, a relict trunk, has been turned on one side. One of the rangers says it is an "original," a log from a tree that was here in those awful days. The log stretches about thirty-five feet long and about fifteen feet around. The red earth beneath, in contrast with the white-gray hue of the tree's skeleton, has been plowed. The tough old trunk is full of the patterns and furrows of age. It must have heard the weeping of all that *Hweeldi.* Cottonwood saplings of various sizes surround it, a tribute to the strength and resiliency of the people who survived their time of slavery and imprisonment. Some of the saplings are set in black plastic buckets. They are for sale, part of the fundraising effort of the Friends of the Bosque Redondo Memorial. The cottonwood, after all, is the fastest-growing hardwood, even around here.

They hold much in common, the people of the *Hweeldi* and the cottonwood trees. Both are native to this place. And though loving and flourishing in sunlight, air, and the freedom to grow, both are able to endure harsh conditions—bad water, poor soil, not enough to eat or drink. "Plant a stick in the ground," one of the rangers says, pointing to the buckets, "and the roots will grow." When I mention the replanting of twelve thousand cottonwood trees here on the Bosque as part of the restoration of land and spirit, she corrects me: "I want to say fifteen thousand." Later, as speaker after speaker—including Joe Shirley, Jr., president of the Navajo Nation; Ellen Big Rope, representative of the Mescalero Apaches; Bill Richardson, governor of New Mexico; and Senator Pete Domenici—talk to us, we learn how the stick of tradition, replanted by courage and resilience and belief, and watered by the desire for home, helped the Navajo and Apaches survive.

Forgiveness is asked for and granted. Pledges are made never to let such a tragedy happen again. If the Navajo returned home as 7,000 people, their nation has now grown to 325,000. Once confined to the 40-square-mile Bosque, the Navajo Nation today encompasses 25,000 square miles. As they grow up and replenish the Bosque, the cottonwood trees sift and sigh with what they know of this place; with what has been replanted in the earth. They will hold, too, the cries of sorrow brought to us by a woman, wrapped in a blanket, who followed behind that man we first saw out on the road, the one carrying the flag of the Navajo Nation. In the midst of Senator Domenici's talk, the woman in the blanket interrupts, her wailing heard in the distance as faint as the cry of a child. As she got closer, her cries carried more than the voice of a single woman. She carried the grief of all of those who took the Long Walk. She put her song into the air so we could all hear it, people and trees alike, the *Hweeldi* of those days.

The new memorial, designed by David N. Sloan, a Navajo architect, is simple and elegant. At its center rises a tipi-shaped cone made of metal and glass. The glass apex lets natural light shine down onto the circular floor below. The tipi cone is flanked by a rectangular building, giving it the appearance of being set into an adobe dwelling, planted in the earth. Wooden posts, like the beams of a grape arbor or drying racks, frame the entrance, which faces the position of the sun at winter solstice. The memorial sits at a respectable distance from what's left of the old fort. A portico at the rear of the new building looks out onto the Pecos. Like a red rope, the river flashes and whips along. Paths and walkways wind along it, providing everyone the chance to walk and remember what happened here. Many walk in silence. Across the river, cottonwoods wave in the hot summer wind.

As George Thorson recounted, Lewis and Clark were not the only ones who learned to make the best of what they had, and thus incorporated cottonwood into their buildings. Plenty of cottonwood timbers were found during the excavation phase of the historic preservation effort at Bent's Old Fort near La Junta, Colorado. Researchers noted that the cottonwood was found mostly in the older part of the fort, and surmised that it didn't take long for the builders to discover cottonwood's propensity to bend, warp, and split. Newer portions of the fort were found to contain pine, which had to be hauled from greater distances than the cottonwood growing along the nearby Arkansas River. Although cottonwood was used mostly as support beams, known as vigas, a stairway that led to the rooms of one of the principals of the fort, Ceran St. Vrain, was reconstructed of solid cottonwood.

Custer's Observations

In spite of the lessons he ultimately failed to learn from his life on the plains, George Armstrong Custer was an astute observer and avid recorder. Like other scribe-conquerors such as Alexander the Great and Julius Caesar, he faithfully recorded life in the Seventh Cavalry as he systematically tracked down tribes of Native Americans. Custer the botanist is a little hard to imagine, but nevertheless, as clear-eyed as Meriwether Lewis, he made several observations about cottonwood trees. He noticed that in the western terrain certain species (the Plains) appear "dwarfed." He accurately described the dominant trees, cottonwood and poplar, and even referred to them by Latin designations: *Populus monilifera* and *Populus angulosa*. *Monilifera* is part of the current name used by the USDA to identify the Plains Cottonwood. Custer gave special credit to the cottonwood, which "performed a service for which no other tree has been found its equal." The service was an aid to survival. The cavalry's horses and mules were able to feed upon the inner bark and leaves during the winter, when grass and other forage was unavailable—a lesson he had learned from the Native Americans. Custer offered a longer description of an Indian pony feeding on cottonwood:

> *The limb being usually cut into pieces about four feet in length and thrown upon the ground, the pony, accustomed to this "long forage" would place one forefoot on the limb in the same manner as a dog secures a bone, and gnaw the bark from it. Although not affording anything like the amount of nutriment which either hay or grain does, yet our horses invariably preferred the bark to either, probably on account of its freshness.*

Fremont's Cottonwood

In both its ordinary and its scientific names, the Fremont Cottonwood (*Populus fremontii*) still bears the name of the man who first described it, John Charles Fremont (1813–90). Though Fremont's reputation was challenged by a court martial, he was an independent man of many paths. He was an explorer, a military officer, and a politician. He knew cartography, geology, linguistics, mathematics, and botany. In his many travels across the country (he was nicknamed "the Pathfinder of the West") he was as attentive to his note-taking as Meriwether Lewis had been eighty years earlier. In January 1884, while camped near Pyramid Lake in what is now Nevada, Fremont wrote the first description of the tree that would share his name. The scout Kit Carson was along. He and Fremont had explored the valleys around Pyramid Lake and found a suitable camping place that had both grass and water. Fremont wrote:

> *Overshadowing the springs were some trees of the sweet cottonwood, which, after a long interval of absence, we saw again with pleasure, regarding them as harbingers of a better country. To us they were eloquent of green prairies and buffalo.*

The sweetness referred to the bark of the tree, which, like that of the Plains Cottonwood, was favored over grass by horses. Three months later, in April, having reached the San Joaquin Valley in California, Fremont again described a good camping spot with a fine stream flowing through it, and large cottonwoods standing beside it.

Lone Trees

You can't understand the value of a lone tree until you travel west of the Missouri River for a couple of longitudes and get out into an open space all by yourself. Merrill Mattes, master chronicler of the *Great Platte River Road*, as both the trail and his book are titled, documented three lone trees along the emigrant trails that paralleled the Platte during the mid-1800s. A few miles from the current town of Central City, Nebraska, one of these three trees still stands—in memory. A historical marker two miles from the site describes the Lone Tree "Standing on the north side of the river." You can see the river from the monument. Though it used to be only about "80 rods" (100 ft.) from the tree, the river now flows about a quarter of a mile away.

The ten-foot-tall monument, carved from yellow Vermont granite and made to resemble the trunk of a cottonwood (by someone who had apparently never seen one) declares that

ON THIS SPOT
STOOD THE
ORIGINAL
"LONE TREE"
ON THE OLD
CALIFORNIA ROAD

Wayfarers said they could see the tree from twenty miles out, east or west. And though it served as a guide and a refuge, the emigrants carved the record of their passing into the tree's skin. Someone recorded a circumference of 10–12 feet and a height of 50–65 feet. The closest branches were said to be 20 feet off the ground. Wayfarers hacked off pieces for timber, firewood, and souvenirs. Part of the leftover trunk was taken to the nearby train station, where tourists carried it off, too, bit by bit. If any pieces remain, they are hidden.

In 1863 the tree refused to leaf. In 1865, the year the Civil War ended, it came down in a storm. Though Lone Tree gave its name to a post office and a stage station, the town was platted as Central City in 1875. Its early incarnation provided a setting for the fiction of the town's best-known native, novelist Wright Morris, author of *Ceremony at Lone Tree.* The tree's memory survived for nearly fifty years after its death, when townspeople erected the monument in 1911. People just couldn't seem to forget. Thirty years later, on Arbor Day, 1941, P.S. Heaton planted a new cottonwood tree in the old tree's place. The "new" tree still presides over the site, having now stood there longer than its predecessor did from 1833 to 1865.

Trail Trees

During the settlement of the West "trail trees" like the Lone Tree were well-known markers along the California Road, the Oregon Trail, the Mormon Trail, the Great Platte River Road, the Chisholm Trail, and the Santa Fe Trail. New Mexico travelers found their way from grove to grove of cottonwoods, and sometimes from tree to tree. In Marion County, Kansas, yet another citizen could not forget a place that had marked the road to Santa Fe. A place on the trail once known as Cottonwood Crossing was first dedicated with a marker in 1906. By 1965 the carved stone grew faded and unreadable. John Borton, whose older brother had attended the original dedication ceremony, thought the crossing should be remembered. At his own expense, the marker was sand-blasted, cleaned, and fitted with long-lasting bronze plaques. Though it's fiction, the life of a single cottonwood tree, told in Holling Clancy Holling's *Tree in the Trail,* is one of the best sources I know for also telling the story of all who passed along the Santa Fe Trail. Whether you're six or sixty, you'll enjoy this evocative tale that begins when a young Native American boy finds a cottonwood sapling near a buffalo wallow. Suzanne Probart, executive director of Tree New Mexico, uses this book in her organization's educational programs. There's no better way to learn about either the Santa Fe Trail or the cottonwoods that marked its route than in this charming and timeless tale.

"Remember the Cottonwood!"

Translated into English, that's what the famous slogan, "Remember the Alamo!" means. The saying refers to an epic battle in the Texas Revolution against Mexico that ended on March 6, 1836, although the Alamo had residents long before then. The site was established as a Spanish mission as early as 1724. By 1793 government officials returned the land to Native American residents. In the early 1800s Spanish cavalry occupied the fort and renamed it in honor of their home town, Alamo de Parras Coahuila. Cottonwoods still grow near the site today, with a note in a booklet about the flora of the site that the Alamo cottonwoods are cottonless— and thus all males.

Buffalo Bill's Cottonwoods

Memorial cottonwoods throughout the west do not always mark a loss or battles. Outside North Platte, Nebraska, at the Scouts Rest Ranch, survivors and descendants of the "Buffalo Bill Cody Cottonwoods" still provide beauty on the landscape and the cool relief of shade. The trees are part of a special group designated by the Nebraska Forest Service as "Nebraska Heritage Trees."

Buffalo Bill Cody Cottonwoods, Scouts Rest Ranch, North Platte, Nebraska.
Photo by Kathleen Cain

Buffalo Bill built his two-story Second-Empire-style house as a retreat in 1886. He needed a place to rest between his famous Wild West shows. Early photographs on display in the barn (the Nebraska Game and Parks Commission operates a museum on the grounds) illustrate an anomaly—a beautiful house, complete with all the architectural flourishes money could buy, sitting alone on the proverbial flat and treeless plains. To soften the landscape, Cody planted quick-growing cottonwood trees, probably gathered as saplings from the North Platte River, which still flows within view of the ranch. By 1890, when they would have grown to about twenty feet tall, the trees offered enough shade for picnics. They still shelter the grounds. Some lean at acrobatic angles before their trunks straighten into sky towers. Among the younger trees, a preference for angularity makes itself obvious in the way limbs and branches form Vs and Ys, like Martha Graham dancers throwing up their hands in some prairie ritual.

It's fitting that one of the best-known Nebraskans would choose to plant a native Nebraska tree. He is gone but the cottonwoods remain, the planting paths obvious—set in rows, so many feet apart. The trees chatter in the constant wind. It doesn't take much to imagine the stories they could tell, of Sitting Bull and Annie Oakley, of Cody himself. Slayer of the great buffalo herds, he outlived his own time. When the frontier was gone, he was still there. Now that he is gone, the trees remain.

Council Trees

Nebraska celebrates other cottonwoods among its Heritage Trees. Possibly as common as the "lone tree" on the western landscape is the "council tree" or "treaty tree." Many western states have one. The 1875 Allison Council Tree is located near Chadron, Nebraska. No treaty resulted in the meetings that took place under the auspices of a commission appointed by President Grant and led by Iowa's senator, William Boyd Allison. The purpose of the council was to persuade Sioux chiefs and elders to give up their rights to the Black Hills. Twenty-two feet in circumference and standing sixty feet tall, this tree still lives.

We have to travel to the western slope town of Delta, Colorado, to meet another old council tree. This cottonwood still stands at the center of the cultural life of the people who know it best. The Ute Council Cottonwood Tree, an award-winning survivor chosen as Colorado's Millennium Tree in 2000, is thought to be two hundred years old. The Ute Chief Ouray and his wife Chipeta sat beneath it in council with white settlers during the 1880s to try and settle problems between them. The tree stands in honor of Ouray and Chipeta. But even when the tree was young, the Utes had already been traveling along one of their nearby trails for a long time. This cottonwood witnessed many generations. The sounds of Ute voices have grown strong beneath it once again. In 1996, through the annual powwow, the Ute Nation began to share its history and culture with other tribes as well as with non-Natives. In 1999 the three Ute tribes (Northern, Southern, and Ute Mountain) united to strengthen and expand this cultural experience. The annual powwow continues, held in grounds just across the river from the old tree. Not only do the memories of Chief Ouray and Chipeta live on—so does the heritage, symbolized by this beautiful old tree. In May 2000 seven cuttings taken from the tree were planted in a special ceremony officiated by a Ute Mountain spiritual leader. Members of the Southern Ute Tribe participated, helping the vision of one of their own members come true. The seven cuttings were more than just little trees. Each one represents a band of the Ute Nation.

Cottonwood trees also symbolize states. Kansas chose the cottonwood as its state tree in 1937. The statute didn't specify which species, but the elaborate language of the statute reads like a prose poem:

WHEREAS, if the full truth were known, it might honestly be said that the successful growth of the cottonwood grove on the homestead was often the determining factor in the decision of the homesteader to "stick it out until he could prove up on his claim"; and

WHEREAS the cottonwood tree can rightfully be called "the pioneer tree of Kansas"; Now therefore . . .

That same year, 1937, Nebraska chose the American elm (*Ulmus americana L.*) as its state tree. Thirty-five years later, in 1972, legislators, at some citizen urging no doubt, had a change of heart and gave the Eastern Cottonwood its proper place as the state tree. Wyoming selected the Plains Cottonwood as its state tree on February 1, 1947.

Given the popularity of cottonwood trees throughout the western United States, I was surprised to learn that so few places bear "cottonwood" in their names. Now this list doesn't include all the Cottonwood valleys, passes, lakes, parks, avenues, roads, and other such local landmarks. But that official keeper of place names, the *Gazetteer of the World*, lists only one Cottonwood County (Minnesota), five towns (Alabama, Arizona, California, Idaho, and Minnesota), one village (South Dakota), and two creeks (Mexico and California). Kansas has its Cottonwood Falls, through which the Cottonwood River flows. At the mention of this location, it's worth pausing to laud the work of William Least Heat-Moon, whose microscopic and magnificent examination of Chase County, Kansas, has resulted in one of the finest chapters about cottonwood sensibility you'll ever have the pleasure of reading. But on we must go, to list two more Cottonwood rivers (Minnesota and California). And to this inventory we must add the county and town of Alamosa, Colorado in the San Luis Valley. Native Americans can call the valley an old home. Spanish conquistadors and explorers Zebulon Pike and John Fremont found it could be another word for bad luck. But in 1878 a group of settlers gave it the Spanish word for cottonwood, the trees that protected the area.

As for protection, most of us learn early not to seek shelter beneath a tree in a storm. But for Robert Michael Pyle and a childhood friend, the hollow bole of an old cottonwood was the only possible refuge during a terrible summer thunderstorm in Aurora, Colorado, one that made the papers back in 1954. Sure that the tree saved his life and that of his companion, Pyle, a PhD.-level ecologist, paid tribute to the tree and the canal along which it grew in one of the most evocative accounts of local natural history, titled *The Thunder Tree*.

Quirky Trees

One of the charming qualities we Americans are known for is our love of quirkiness. Whether it's a restaurant in the shape of a hat like the Brown Derby, or "Carhenge"—a western-Nebraska tribute to Stonehenge made from rusted old cars—we love the odd and unusual. And cottonwood trees, in the erratic way they grow, sometimes too fast to pay attention to straight lines, boast plenty of quirkiness. Two that show off a special quirkiness—and are friendly, too—are dubbed the "Hi Trees." They're part of the Nebraska Heritage Tree Collection, located in Florence, a historic part of Omaha dating to 1846. One tree extends a branch between two trunks in a way that makes it resemble the letter H. A tall cottonwood right next to it forms the I. Viewed at the just right angle (and this is essential), the trees offer a greeting to passers-by who hike or bike along a nearby trail.

How to Say Goodbye

In chapter 7, I will mention a couple of unfortunate events in the lives of cottonwoods and their communities. The "Oops! factor" caused the loss of hundreds of trees in one Montana county. Neighbors in Boulder, Colorado, felt left out when a grove of "century tree" cottonwoods were cut down for road widening. On their own, residents held a wake.

On Sunday, August 13, 2006, I attended another wake for a cottonwood tree at Vanover Park in Golden, Colorado. Golden knows how to say goodbye! The ceremony, organized by Jerry Hodgden and other members of the parks board, was months in the planning and included participation by local children, the

"Hi Trees" near Omaha, Nebraska. Photo by John Vaske, reprinted with permission.

Golden Landmarks Association (GLA), a cowboy barbershop quartet as well as soloist, historians, the city arborist, and a bagpiper.

The focus of all this love and affection was a 239-year-old Plains Cottonwood known as "the Vanover Tree." Readers dressed in nineteenth-century period costume related how the tree, occupying an ample slope of ground above Clear Creek, witnessed events since before Golden came into existence. Bands of Cheyenne, Arapahoe, and Ute Indians often camped nearby. As Golden transformed from territorial capital to mining town, citizens of every stripe walked beneath the tree. Beer brewer Adolph Coors got his first taste of "Rocky Mountain spring water" along the creek. The funeral procession of Buffalo Bill Cody trudged up the hill to nearby Lookout Mountain. Yet in spite of historical verification to the contrary, the nickname "Hanging Tree" held on. Troublemaker Edgar Vanover, whose name remains attached to both park and tree, was hanged nearby. That's true. And even though the cottonwood might have been part of his last look at earth, he was not hanged from this tree. As part of the service, fitting for a wake, the old tree was exonerated from its ill repute, given a plaque, and made a member of the GLA—as Golden's oldest living landmark.

The membership was short-lived, as the tree's September 2006 date with the chainsaw was inevitable. As city arborist Dave High explained to the crowd, in spite of attempts to restore the tree's health by drilling holes into the badly compacted soil and directly feeding the roots, the old tree continued to suffer. It had become a hazard. With half the canopy gone, decay kept spreading through the massive frame. In spite of the problems, on that sunny Sunday afternoon it stood to its full height of 85 feet. The leaves in the canopy chattered 100 feet above us (the canopy once extended to 150 feet). The tree measures 8 feet in diameter. Whether male or female, High wasn't sure, though some members of the GLA thought they remembered seeing cotton.

As part of the celebration, pieces of bark were sold, along with sculptures of the tree's imaginary wood spirits and souvenir bark medallions. And of course, there was a commemorative T-shirt. But the most important thing about this event was the way in which the community gathered before the fact, taking the time to teach, share, and celebrate the life of its longest-living resident. Through the life of the tree, the people of Golden got to tell and hear their own stories. Children wrote notes: "I love you, beautiful tree," one yellow streamer read, "I'm sorry you

---

Vanover Tree hung with streamers for its "wake." Golden, Colorado.
Photo by Kathleen Cain

have to leave." As the final event on the program, a lone bagpiper made his way across the bridge over Clear Creek and followed the path to the tree. He stopped. He finished his dirge. He bowed. There was "water in the eyes" all around. Communities everywhere can take a lesson from Golden in how to say goodbye to our sylvan neighbors with honor and respect.

There must be dozens of other cottonwood trees throughout our country that reflect our history. I hope to hear from readers about the trees I didn't include because I didn't know about them. That's exactly the kind of information an author needs for a second edition! And if you don't know about a historic cotton-wood in your town, county, or state, perhaps you can find one. City, community, county, and state foresters are eager to teach us about our local and native cottonwoods. Contact them. Or get online and visit the Web sites of American Forests, the Arbor Day Foundation, or any number of other groups dedicated to preserving and teaching us about trees (see the Resources section at the end of this book).

Yet even as we celebrate the history of these intrepid native trees, there is trouble stirring in the lands and waters that surround them—or, as the case may increasingly be, in the lands and waters that don't surround them. Let's turn our attention to some of the problems that cottonwoods face in their continued attempt to share space with us.

Circle of History

During November and December 2005, I took a tour of cottonwood trees in my home county of Lancaster in southeastern Nebraska. Guided by an enthusiastic lover of local history, I visited four trees, variously nicknamed Many Trunks, George (a.k.a. the West Spring Road Tree), the Guardian, and the Hanging Tree.

These trees survive on the southwest side of the county, near Denton. They live in places you'd expect to find them. Streams and creeks (or cricks, as I love to hear them called) lace this hilly landscape, a place where one resident claims he can stand on the peak of a certain hill and see the top of the barn near the Hanging Tree. Though most of the creeks suffer from severely reduced flow due to several years of drought, the old trees wait for the water to come back, as they have for thousands of years. ➤

"Many Trunks" Eastern Cottonwood Tree. Lincoln, Nebraska.
Photo by Kathleen Cain

MANY TRUNKS

Many Trunks, a healthy specimen of Eastern Cottonwood growing along a Burlington Northern & Santa Fe (BNSF) Railroad right-of-way, rises not far from such a creek. At the arborists' old standard measure of 4.5 feet—diameter at breast height, or d.b.h.—this well-balanced tree measures 22 ft.,11 in. (275 in.) in circumference. It appears to be about 85 feet tall. So does the crown spread. Sprawling limbs and branches still look healthy. Only a few show tell-tale signs of peeling bark, with gray cambium shining through. The neighborhood gang has claimed Many Trunks as its territory, skirting its base with leftover particle board and scrap lumber nailed together in typical kid fashion, with the nails pointing up. They've hammered spikes into the tree for footholds that take them ten feet off the ground into a splay of three trunks. One arches west, another east. A third aims for the Moon. The tree tries to keep its equilibrium, as evidenced by the rubble of twigs shed last fall—like a ship getting rid of ballast. Drought-stressed twigs are easy to identify by their round, swollen bottoms. In the economy of trees, Many Trunks sheds what it cannot support as the drought lingers. The water supply is invisible, but it's nearby. It doesn't have to lie more than about six feet below the surface for the wide-spreading roots to find it. Cottonwoods always know where the water runs. ➤

The road we drove in on leads to a cul-de-sac named Big Tree Circle in a new housing development. Just across the circle a fenced-in area resembles a commons that might be shared by the neighbors. But beneath a row of pine trees stretches a line of markers: headstones of concrete, each bearing a number. It's a pauper's field of sorts, containing the graves of people who were patients—or inmates—at "the State Hospital." Once upon a time, no other explanation was needed when you spoke that phrase. Everybody knew you meant the insane asylum. If we look beyond the entrance road, sighting through yet more trees, we can see what is now called the Lincoln Regional Center. Many Trunks has been here since the name changed more than twenty years ago. He has been here longer than the pine trees that whisper over the anonymous graves. And chances are good he has been here longer than the first grave was set beneath the pines.

As we follow the road west we eventually come close to the town of Denton. Like small towns throughout the Midwest and western U.S., Denton has a historical society supported by local people who want to preserve the memory of their town's past. Lorie Helvie, our tour guide for the day, is a member. She's a newcomer—having moved to town only six years ago—but what she may lack in knowledge she makes up for in enthusiasm and sheer good nature. New to the historical society as well, she calls on a longstanding member to help recall the stories that took place beneath the cottonwood trees. A few days later, we meet with Marilyn Giles, who can quote chapter and verse about Denton's history. She begins by telling the story of the Hanging Tree. The story made the front page of the *Lincoln Journal Star* in Nebraska's capital city, but Marilyn's known the story since long before it hit the paper.

HANGING TREE

In August 1884 a young girl who lived on one of the farms surrounding Denton went out to pick wild plums. When she didn't return, people went looking for her, only to discover she'd been raped, stabbed, and left for dead beneath a cottonwood tree. Her attacker was found hiding in a nearby barn and taken across the fields so the girl could identify him. In a terrifying second encounter with the man, the young girl screamed and clung to the doctor who'd been summoned to attend her. According to accounts written at the time, the girl was asked three times if this was the man. She answered yes and then described a mark the man bore on his arm. As the suspect was being transported to jail, he and the sheriff were overtaken by riders who redirected the prisoner to that tree behind the barn, the one whose peak is said to be visible from a certain hill, and lynched him from a branch of the cottonwood tree. Although scientific attempts to date the tree through coring have failed (the tree ➤

Graves of the Brown children protected by "the Guardian Tree."
Denton, Nebraska. Photo by Kathleen Cain

is rotten), a current deputy sheriff, also a member of the historical society, has used documentation to identify what he believes is the Hanging Tree.

We visited a tree knotted with burls from top to bottom. In the low angle of thin winter light the antler-headed old snag terrified me even before I knew it was the Hanging Tree. Dark gnarled limbs claw the air. An atmosphere of sustained melancholy lingers around the now-abandoned farmstead. Yet if the tree remains a witness to one cruel crime and unwilling participant in another, the story concludes with a happy ending. The young girl who was attacked survived, grew up and married, had children, and lived well into her eighties. Because of the young deputy's historical interest, the old sheriff who desperately tried to protect his prisoner has been inducted into the Nebraska Law Enforcement Hall of Fame. Though a local forester and the state's Big Tree Coordinator have doubts about this tree being *the* tree, whether this old cottonwood is the original Hanging Tree or not matters less than that it provides a symbol of bygone life and times in the midst of the community that still flourishes nearby.

THE GUARDIAN TREE
Another cottonwood of note near Denton stands along a verge of streamside woods at the far side of a cornfield where cattle have been let loose to graze the waste ➤

seed after harvest. The dignified old tree stands out at one end of the field. Slender for much of the way up, it branches in two, much higher than cottonwoods usually do (usually—yet who can tell with a cottonwood?). We stand too far away to see what it may have shed or lost to wind and storms; or to see how far down toward the creek bank its trunk extends. We can no longer see the road that once divided the field. But we can imagine a homestead here. We can imagine children at play, running through the fields as one of them did during a thunderstorm, only to be struck and killed by lightning, as the story goes. The parents in the Brown family buried their little girl beneath the tree. She was preceded by two brothers. This, too, is a part of the history of this vicinity, the loss of children at such early ages, to the hazards of the open prairie. It was common practice during the late 1800s to bury children on the homestead.

The parents must have thought the tree would keep them. And it has. The family moved to Kansas, but they returned to care for the graves, to outline the somber patch with native limestone, and to build a fence around the final resting place of their young ones. "A rose on earth . . . now a rose in heaven . . . something about roses. . . ." Marilyn Giles tries to remember the inscription on the little girl's grave. It's been a long time since she's been out there, but what she remembers is enough. When I return a month later with a friend who knows every road in the county, we walk across the corn field (sans cattle this time) to the tree and the graves. The stones reveal this family's bad luck:

Edmund Perry
Son of J.D. & M.A. Brown
Died Aug. 29, 1870
Aged 3 months, 18 days

James Burd Brown
Son of J.D. and M.A. Brown
Nov. 12, 1864
Nov. 21, 1864

And then there's the little girl:
Rosa Kezia
Daughter of J.D. & M.A. Brown
Died Jan. 20, 1875
Aged 9 yrs, 21 days ➤

She was lovely, she was fair
And for awhile was given
An angel came and claimed his own
And took her home to heaven

"Something about roses. . . ." Yes. Carved roses and tulips wind around the top of her
headstone. Hers is the only stone to be decorated, a sign perhaps of the family's
increasing prosperity, as well as a mark of their continued grief. Here they lie, the
three little sorrows of the Brown family. Nearby, the Guardian Tree (my nickname for
it), another Eastern Cottonwood, measures 21 ft. 7 in. in circumference. Never mind
that a lightning strike in January, though not impossible in Nebraska's reckless
weather, is improbable. But the particulars don't matter here as much as that the
family trusted that this tree would continue to stand steadily above the creek. Though
the children would never grow up, the tree *would*, they must have hoped. It has. It's
been struck by lightning, too. From a jagged explosion of bark about twenty feet up,
where the bolt hit, a rusty length of boiled sap weeps from the wood. Still keeping its
dignity as well as its duty, the old tree seems to have taken the electrical wallop in
stride. It's the tallest living thing out here for miles. It's bound to have called down,
however inadvertently, the powers of the summer—or the winter, for thunderstorms
in winter are not unknown—the area experienced such a storm last December. Who
knows how many more years the old tree will shelter the graves of Rosa and her
brothers? For now it's clear that the tree remains faithful.

If the Hanging Tree and the Guardian Tree mark solemn parts of history near
Denton, another one reigns over a favorite American pastime—baseball. Lorie
Helvie and her husband Scott walk us out through a path on their acreage near
Denton that leads to a low-lying field. The field is kept mowed and clear of the
rubble of limbs and branches that "George" (Scott's nickname for it)—more
formally known as the West Spring Road Tree—discards. George's circumference
equals 20 ft. 11 in. (251 in.) George is probably accurate, since nobody recalls any
cottoning, and they describe the tree as turning yellow before the leaves sprout, a
color that offers evidence of male flowers. George has a stout and easy-going way
about him, towering over the improvised baseball diamond, residing close to Cheese
Creek as he has since perhaps 1900. George is the kind of cottonwood that becomes
friendly and familiar; the one that, seen out a distant window, signals all the seasons;
the kind whose trunk you want to press your ear against, hoping to catch some faint
trace of a mammoth heartbeat or the flow of water. His roots are deep and wide
enough to shoulder on through the drought and gather any bit of moisture from ➤

the lowland soil. By now the root system easily covers the length and breadth of the baseball diamond. Summer games aren't just played beneath George's branches; they're also played atop his massive root system. Hit a home run and his roots will hear you rounding to third.

SOURCES:
The trip to "George" conducted by Lorie and Scott Helvie. A few days later, through the kind intervention of Lorie, additional information about the trees and their stories was provided through an interview with Denton Community Historical Society member Marilyn Giles. An article titled "On the Hunt for the Hanging Tree" appeared in the March 26, 2005, issue of the *Lincoln Journal Star*, pp. 1–2A. In December 2005, John Vaske volunteered for driver and guide duty to the Big Tree National Champion Eastern Cottonwood in Seward County, with a side visit to the Guardian Tree in Lancaster.

Sources

Aldo Leopold describes seeing this cottonwood in *A Sand County Almanac and Sketches Here and There*. American Museum of Natural History Special Member's Edition, published by Oxford University Press in 1968, p. 117.

Sources consulted for the section on Lewis and Clark include: David Lavender's classic, *The Way to the Western Sea/Lewis and Clark Across the Continent*. Harper and Row. New York. 1988; the excellent, thirteen–volume edition of *The Lewis and Clark Journals/The Abridgment of the Definitive Nebraska Edition*. Ed. Gary E. Moulton. University of Nebraska Press: Lincoln and London. 2003 (online version available at: http://lewisandclarkjournals.unl.edu; and the *Original Journals of the Lewis and Clark Expedition 1804–1806*. Ed. Reuben Gold Thwaites. Arno Press. New York. 1969. See also the Lewis & Clark Herbarium at: http://www.acnatsci.org/lewisclark/herbarium.html.

Visit the Web site at: http://lewisandclark.org for a Native American view of the Lewis and Clark expedition.

See "Lewis & Clark Cottonwoods" (educational booklet) for a discussion of the importance of cottonwoods to the Lewis and Clark expedition.
Compiled by Glenda E. Fauske. North Dakota Forest Service. 2002.

http://www. ndsu.nodak.edu/ndsu/lbakken/forest/infoed/doc/lewis_clark.pdf.
See also *Plants of the Lewis & Clark Expedition* by H. Wayne Phillips. Mountain
Press Publishing. Missoula, Mont. 2003. p. 20, and Paul Russell Cutright's
Lewis & Clark: Pioneering Naturalists. University of Nebraska Press:
Lincoln. 1969.

Accounts of the Balmville Tree are drawn from "Balmville Tree (celebrating its
300th birthday)." Lou Sebesta. *New York State Conservationist.* April 1999.
53:5, 201 and from the Newburgh, New York, Web site:
http://newburghrevealed.org/.

"Scythe Tree. Waterloo, New York."
http://roadsideamerica.com/attract/NYWATscythe.html

Information on the Kansas "Scythe Tree" comes from "The Scythe in the Tree."
Lincoln Beacon. July 30, 1896. Quoted in Blue Skyways.
http://skyways.lib.ks.us/genweb/lincoln/scythe.htm

Information on the use of cottonwoods for railroad ties comes from *Empire Express:
Building the First Transcontinental Railroad* by David Howard Bain. Viking Press.
New York. 1999. p. 242

Sources for *On the Bosque* include: *The Story of Bosque Redondo.* New Mexico
Department of Cultural Affairs. 2005; *Diné: A History of the Navajos.* Peter
Iverson. University of New Mexico Press: Albuquerque, 2002. Laurance D.
Linford. *Navajo Places: History, Legend, Landscape.* University of Utah Press:
Salt Lake City. 2000; *Arizona and New Mexico Tour Book.* AAA Publishing:
Heathrow, Fla. 2005. I attended the June 4, 2005, dedication ceremony for
the Bosque Redondo Memorial at Fort Sumner, New Mexico.

For the restoration of Bent's Fort, see *Bent's Old Fort* by George A. Thorson. The
State Historical Society of Colorado. Denver. 1979. "The Architectural
Challenge." pp. 132–133.

Custer's observations about cottonwood trees and their use on the plains appear in
My Life on the Plains. Sheldon and Company. New York. 1874.

Donald Culross Peattie quotes Fremont's description of cottonwood in *A Natural
History of Western Trees.* Bonanza Books. New York. 1953. p. 332.

Merrill J. Mattes discusses lone trees in. *The Great Platte River Road.* Nebraska State
Historical Society Publications. Volume XXV. Lincoln. 1969. p.152

Information about the Lone Tree can be found at Merrick County Area History & Attractions. "Lone Tree." http://www.cconline.net/community/attractions.htm and "Lone Tree." Nebraska Heritage Trees. Nebraska Forest Service. University of Nebraska. http://www.nfs.unl.edu/NHTrees.htm.

General information about the Alamo from brochure "The Daughters of the Republic of Texas present The Story of the Alamo/Thirteen Fateful Days in 1836." Daughters of the Republic of Texas. 1997.

Flora from the Gardens of the Alamo. Mark Nauschutz. p. 10.

The Buffalo Bill Cody Cottonwoods, the "Hi Trees," and other historic Nebraska cottonwoods are featured at Nebraska Forest Service. University of Nebraska. "Nebraska Heritage Trees." http://www.nfs.unl.edu/NHTrees.htm

See "In Kit Form: The Cottonwood Chapter" in *Prairyerth (a deep map)* by William Least Heat-Moon. Houghton Mifflin. Boston. 1991. pp. 325–334.

The Thunder Tree/Lessons from an Urban Wildland. Robert Michael Pyle. Houghton Mifflin. Boston and New York. 1993.

For information on the Ute Council Tree, visit the Council Tree Pow Wow & Cultural Festival Web site at: http://www.counciltreepowwow.org/tree-poem.htm.

Language from the March 23, 1937 bill considering the cottonwood as the Kansas State tree is quoted at http://www.netstate.com/states/symb/trees/ks_cotton-wood.htm.

Cottonwood place names can be found in the *Gazetteer of the World.* Ed. Saul B. Cohen. Columbia University Press. New York. 1998. Information on Alamosa, Colorado, comes from the county/town Web site, http://www.alamosa.org/.

Visit "Carhenge" online at http://www.carhenge.com/.

I attended the wake for the Vanover Tree on August 13, 2006, in Golden, Colorado, where I talked with Jerry Hodgden and Dave High. The Vanover Tree was also featured in a *Denver Post* article, "Ancient Tree's Tale Rings with Drama of the West." August 11, 2006.

7

TROUBLE IN COTTONWOOD COUNTRY

When I took part in a cottonwood "walk and talk" sponsored by Boulder County, Colorado, Parks and Open Space in the spring of 2005, I asked a question that still troubles me: Since landscape nurseries sell only male cottonwood trees— either cottonless or sterile hybrids—are cottonwoods in danger of declining?

I understand why female trees have been banished from back yards, gardens, and parkways. They're erratic. They're messy. They cause problems that cost money. "Cotton" that clogs a home air conditioner creates a nuisance. Caught in the filtering system of a large office building or a hospital, the stuff becomes a line item in the budget—and a potential health hazard. I get it. But still, if cottonwoods are restricted to a single species and sterile or male clones are primarily used in riparian restoration, isn't there a long-term problem in the making here (not to mention the increasing amount of pollen in the air from the males)?

I grew up in a town like many across the United States that experienced the ravages of Dutch elm disease. As beetles carried the deadly fungus from one tree to the next, we learned too late the consequences of planting a single species. Creating a monoculture left the elms defenseless. The disease spread, uninterrupted by natural barriers that planting diverse species would have created. While not an exact comparison—selling only male, sterile, or cloned cottonwood trees to the exclusion of females—planting only one gender still creates a monoculture. Could such a practice create an imbalance potentially dangerous to cottonwoods— as well as many other species that depend on them—in the future? My question assumes that Nature always strikes a balance. Probably closer to the truth is that Nature constantly tries to restore balance from its own extremes, as well as our own, since humans wield the same power to change the landscape as erosion, an avalanche, or an earthquake does. Nevertheless, why contribute to imbalance? And, back to the question: Are the cottonwoods in danger?

"Ghost Cottonwood." Photo by Gregory McNamee, reprinted with permission.

Although the "walk and talk" was excellent in every other respect (the volunteer naturalists opened the trunk of a station wagon to reveal a full display of Plains Cottonwood leaves, stems, and seeds that they could talk about for half an hour without notes, and didn't even *consider* canceling in spite of the cold spring rain), the answer I got did not satisfy me: that we have larger environmental issues to worry about. I wouldn't challenge that reality, but it dismissed my question. It took nearly a year to find the answer—part of the pilgrim's path. I asked every forester, horticulturist, and nursery owner I met. All agreed to one extent or another that a monoculture of male cottonwoods limits biological diversity, in either residential settings or in the wild. Yet even in riparian restoration efforts, the tendency for many years has been to plant cottonwood poles—vegetative cuttings, essentially clones, often taken from one area and sometimes from only one individual. It's a bit surreal to consider, but in some restored areas you can walk through a riparian community that's technically one tree. In many cases, restoration by this method has been the best and only choice possible, given the limit of human and financial resources. And some species of cottonwoods reproduce this way by themselves, as Ray Daugherty taught me as we walked through a grove of Narrowleaf Cottonwoods. But one group of researchers has taken seriously the issue of ensuring gender diversity in riparian restoration with cottonwoods. Yes! they have answered. The sex of cottonwoods (willows, too) is critical to restoring the diversity of a riparian habitat and ensuring the habitat's ability to sustain itself. And yes, there is a danger of creating a monoculture by planting only male or sterile hybrid pole cuttings. The team has developed a way to create and enhance the health and diversity of restored areas. They determine the sex of cottonwood trees in the winter dormant season by cutting open and examining the flower buds (these buds always appear in the same place on new twigs, below the terminal bud). Trees can be marked (using blue and pink ribbons, of course!) and cuttings taken from each. Seeds can also be planted in special nurseries and the saplings transferred to the restoration site. It may take time to change longstanding habits and paradigms, but those on the front lines involved with riparian restoration pay close attention to what's happening with research. The 2003 research results by Thomas Landis and his colleagues should gain an even wider reading than they have already.

Still, cottonwoods face plenty of other problems.

In addition to restricting the sale of female cottonwoods in garden shops and nurseries, many municipalities ban the planting of cottonwoods altogether. The cities of Denver and Westminster, Colorado, for example, prohibit the planting of cottonwood trees in public rights of way. Some cities and towns allow the planting of hybrids and cultivars and, like the forestry department of Fort Collins,

Colorado, make an effort to plant native species. This makes practical and economic sense. Cottonwood roots have a tendency to sucker, in a ranking that goes from moderate (Plains and Eastern) to aggressive (Narrowleaf). Roots damage underground pipes, power and sewer lines, and building foundations. Cottonwoods planted too close to a house can cause problems, too, as writer Kathleen Norris and her husband discovered when theirs started shouldering up against the foundation of their house in the upper Dakotas, where trees are not taken for granted, and where the old joke still holds (a native told me) that the state tree of North Dakota is a telephone pole. Norris and her husband mourned the loss of their cottonwood, joined by a neighbor in his seventies who had been a youngster when the tree was planted.

It's one thing to take down a cottonwood that's trying to move your basement wall or invade your sewer lines. Cottonwoods are "wild" trees. Their roots relentlessly search for water. The seeds are messy when the cotton whips up a summer blizzard. They shed twigs like crazy in response to drought stress. They drop limbs at random. They're "erratic" in the way they grow, a challenge to suburban symmetry. They really need to be in the wild where they can live without disturbing others and without being disturbed. But that's harder than it sounds. When you consider the rate of development in many areas of the country, the danger for cottonwoods increases exponentially. One example is the corridor along Interstate 25 (part of the old Santa Fe Trail, incidentally) through New Mexico, Colorado, and Wyoming. In Colorado alone, during the last thirty years this corridor has become one long string of expanding cities and towns, including Douglas County, the fastest-growing county in the nation between 1990 and 2000. With its attendant shopping malls, and commercial and residential development, urban sprawl extends from Pueblo to Cheyenne. As more land is developed, less remains in a natural condition, a situation that repeats itself throughout the West. Of course, what's a natural condition you may ask? If we follow the natural history of that idea, it could lead us back to the Ice Age. For the sake of discussion, let's consider the time period from one hundred years in the past to one hundred years in the future. Both historic and scientific sources claim that more cottonwood trees grow now than they did a hundred years ago. Pictures I examined at Buffalo Bill Cody's Scouts Rest Ranch in North Platte, Nebraska, for example, offer just one simple proof of that. In a photograph taken in 1886, the year Cody built his western Nebraska retreat, bare ground surrounds the Victorian-style house. The only trees to be seen, most of them cottonwoods, silhouette the background, growing along the North Platte River, which is still visible from the ranch today. Similar historical photographs of riparian areas in the Black Hills and at the Bosque Redondo in New

Mexico show bare and open plains, even along the waterways. Of course, the thing to remember is that during the time of the western migration, all the riparian areas, the waterways, served as major highways. They had provided a major form of shelter for Native Americans, who used the trees in the riparian habitat as a natural resource. Later they were stripped of their forests and vegetative cover to provide firewood, building material, and shelter for European settlers. In the last two centuries development has also meant planting and replanting.

Loss of Cottonwood Habitat

With the pace of development throughout the West, are we recreating that treeless plain the European settlers described in their letters and diaries? Even a trend by contemporary builders to try and keep development areas more natural—often by keeping the trees—does not always include maintaining existing water sources for trees. Streams and waterways are trenched, piped, dammed, or otherwise diverted. Without enough water, or water at the right times of the year, even the hardy native cottonwoods eventually die. Water loss also threatens their natural means of reproduction. Remember, in the wild cottonwood seeds often float downstream a long way from the mother tree before they find the right soil conditions—where seedlings can stay moist long enough for the root and shoot to get established. When land gets used for residential or commercial development, it often means destruction of riparian habitat, the place cottonwoods call home. In the course of his research, Dr. Gary Whitham, director of the Merriam-Powell Center for Environmental Research at Northern Arizona University, estimates that only about 3 percent of riparian habitats remain throughout the west. A USDA Forest Service report quotes a source that's even less optimistic: only 1 percent.

Habitat loss can occur little by little. The destruction doesn't always affect hundreds of acres or miles of streamsides. One such example comes from Boulder, Colorado, a city whose restrictions on growth have added to the expansion of smaller towns nearby. To widen a state highway, a stand of thirty "century trees"—one-hundred-year-old cottonwoods—was cut down by state crews. Though the cutting had been approved by state and county officials more than two years beforehand, the sudden loss of the familiar landmarks was a shock to neighbors and residents who were unaware of the plan. And let's face it; public notices announcing hearings for tree removal (set in type that often requires a magnifying glass to read) aren't always the first things we turn to in the local paper. In a heartfelt gesture that signals a different kind of awareness of the presence and importance of trees, though, one woman held an Irish-style "wake" for the small grove. Mulch from the trees was made available for use, though there's no indication anyone had the foresight to take or save cuttings from these long-time residents of an old crossroads—one that without them will become just another paved-over intersection.

Author Sharman Russell has written about extensive loss of riparian habitat from her perspective as a resident of southwestern New Mexico. She describes how the overgrazing of cattle leads to the ruin of riparian habitat. Her article pointed out that grazing was allowed in 70 percent of the west under about 25,000 permits. Current figures from the Bureau of Land Management (BLM) indicate that 160 million acres—more than half the land the agency manages—is being grazed through permits issued to 15,000 livestock operators. Livestock use riparian areas for water, shelter, and shade. Cottonwoods and their companion trees, shrubs, and grasses in this habitat require a certain groundwater level to exist. Too many cattle competing with trees threaten the trees' ability to regenerate. Browsing destroys seedlings and saplings. Trampling compacts the open ground young trees need to thrive and harms the root systems of mature trees.

Jay W. Street, another western advocate of cottonwood trees, especially Rio Grande Cottonwoods that inhabit the river valleys of New Mexico, lists several more problems that human intervention causes: polluting water and soil, building roads and mines, introducing invasive species, and reducing habitat which in turn reduces the presence of insects, birds, and other animals. The story of a Rio Grande Cottonwood named Naomi brings his concerns to life.

I first heard about Naomi from Suzanne Probart, executive director of Tree New Mexico, and Matt Schmader, superintendent for the City of Albuquerque Open Space Division. In describing how Rio Grande Cottonwoods represent the culture of New Mexico, they used Naomi as an example. Newspaper coverage at the time tells the same story. In 1995 a decades-long battle between residents of Albuquerque who lived on different sides of the Rio Grande came to a head. The fight was over whether a bridge—the Montano Bridge—should be built across the river to accommodate some twenty thousand daily commuters traveling from the west side of town to the city. Residents on the north side, an area of affluent horse property and small ranches, opposed the bridge. In spite of lawsuits and counter-suits, the city won out and moved ahead with plans to build. Several cottonwoods stood in the way, but one in particular occupied center position.

Thought to be perhaps one hundred years old, Naomi became the pivot point around which both sides fought, protested, and rallied. She was even vandalized and set on fire. Where travelers from every culture that ever lived in New Mexico had once used a tree like Naomi to find their way along the river trails, their descendants fought in her shadow; some to protect her, some to destroy her. The

"Dewitt Tree." Photo by Kelly Cain, reprinted with permission.

destroyers won. They got their bridge and their road. In what can only be inter-preted as a final show of power, city crews, led by the mayor, moved in just after midnight—the time they could legally begin cutting—and took Naomi down with a bulldozer. In another strange irony that has the twist of legend in it, a few years later forest fires swept through the bosque in Albuquerque, destroying yet more cottonwood trees. In a state that can claim only 5 percent of its area as riparian, the people of Albuquerque and New Mexico have not let such indignities stop them when it comes to cottonwoods, though, as we'll see in chapter 8, "Good News."

With stories like Naomi's pulled from the headlines, Russell and Street are not just lone environmentalists crying out in the wilderness. Their claims are also supported by studies of riparian areas. Here are two examples.

Scientists have long known that riparian areas provide critical breeding grounds for high numbers of bird species—almost 50 percent in the western United States. The study that quoted only 1 percent of the western landscape as riparian habitat also emphasizes the importance of such areas for migrating birds (considered as an investment, where else can you find such a good return on 1 percent?). Yet problems arise when these areas are overgrazed. Livestock "simplify" a riparian area. Trampling and grazing lessen the availability of food and shelter for migratory species. Livestock pollute soil and water. Migrating birds need a more elaborate (diverse) environment in order to thrive, even on stopovers. The study doesn't suggest getting rid of the cattle. It does suggest better manage-ment: Moving livestock even a short distance away from a riparian corridor helps create a habitat that can be shared, to the benefit of several species. And in this context, remember that if birds are involved, so are cottonwoods. And if the cottonwoods are involved, so is everything else.

Jenifer Morrissey, a member of the Colorado Riparian Association, provides an important overview of interactions in riparian habitats. In a paper entitled "Awed by Cottonwoods," she describes the benefits of cottonwoods to their water-side locale. They stabilize stream banks by preventing erosion and slowing water flow. They shade and shelter companion trees and plants in the habitat, as well as birds, mammals, insects—and humans. Ironically, as Morrissey describes, cattle benefit from cottonwoods, too. So does the water nearby. But again, too many animals endanger and even destroy the trees whose tasty seedlings and saplings they find irresistible.

Looking at the bigger picture, Morrissey reports that riparian forests aren't renewing themselves in Colorado. Human intervention through damming and diversion has changed the course of waterways that once provided natural nurseries for cottonwoods. The trees have depended upon the rhythms of the seasons for most of their long existence. Spring flooding performs the yeoman's work of scouring the banks and preparing the soil to receive seeds. Once a waterway is dammed or diverted, the release of water follows a human—and artificial—timetable rather than a seasonal one. Such a reworking of the waterways provides plenty of benefits to humans. Morrissey is not shy about naming those benefits, even for herself: they range from drinking water to hamburgers and paper products. But a reduced spring runoff disrupts the life cycle for cottonwoods. Higher flows at the wrong time flood out seeds and seedlings; lesser flows deprive them of enough water to survive. Morrissey does discuss the positive effect that irrigation ditches have on cotton-wood success, about which we'll learn more in the final chapter.

The Zion Cottonwoods

A Web page for Zion National Park describes that natural wonder of the Colorado Plateau as a refuge for, among so many other living things, Fremont Cottonwoods. The Virgin River winds through Zion's 229 square miles, a force of nature that defines the park. Accounts of flash floods describe how the river can toss boulders and cottonwoods around as if they were stones and twigs. Yet the future of the Zion cottonwoods is threatened by not having enough water at the right time. As part of a government flood control effort in the 1930s, revetments—levees made by wrap-ping stones in wire mesh—were built to contain the banks of the north fork of the Virgin. The levees keep the river in bounds, but they channelize it so deeply that it cannot reach its natural floodplain. On the practical side, the levees keep roads inside the park from flooding and protect Zion Lodge, but when the river is restrained this way, so is the ability of cottonwoods to regenerate naturally. The tufted seeds can no longer ride the flood waters out to their margins. Nor do they benefit from the rich mix of ingredients the flooding river brings to the soil—that "just right" mix for cottonwood seedlings to become saplings and eventually healthy trees.

In 2002, Zion National Park and the Grand Canyon Trust issued a joint report indicating that the cottonwoods will need another human intervention in order to survive. The report offered six ways to solve the problem. One of two methods, each of which involves removing the levees, seems most likely to succeed. Either way, the price tag is high—between $4 and $6 million. Jim McMahon, an ecologist and former writer for the *Rocky Mountain News* who supervised the study, describes the cottonwoods in Zion as a "retirement community." They have become "same-age stands"—all about seventy years old—evidence that the trees are not regenerating. By comparison, McMahon has observed along another fork of the Virgin that:

*The cottonwood trees and their response to flooding is really most
interesting. As you walk a river you can see the age classes from
the years that were successful . . . of course you have to know how to look.
There's clear evidence on the South Fork in Zion NP.*

McMahon has described the same geriatric condition Jenifer Morrissey
discusses, where water has been similarly diverted in Colorado.

In 2002, Zion park officials expected to spend at least a year talking to water
users downstream who will also be affected by any change in the river's return to
more normal flood patterns. It's always a tough call where humans and nature
intersect, both competing for the same resources. Here's the current status of the
effort, according to Zion's resource manager, Jeff Bradybaugh:

*We continue to work on other critical pieces of the puzzle we will need: we're
beginning a research project on riparian re-vegetation methods for the area
constrained by river revetments, sediment studies, small mammal studies and
other information that will be needed to finalize the plan for how the
revetments are removed, river banks managed or "stabilized," and re-estab-
lishment of natural floodplain process to the extent possible.*

Bradybaugh estimates that without intervention, the cottonwoods will be part
of Zion's history within thirty to sixty years. At that point, other questions will need
to be answered: What happens to the river without trees to stabilize the banks, to
prevent erosion, and provide habitat for birds and mammals? What of the sheer
value of wildness they represent, and natural beauty, as the western artist Maynard
Dixon discovered? In later years Dixon so identified with their solitary sturdiness
that the cottonwood tree became his personal symbol. He moved temporarily to
Zion Canyon to paint, and in late 1939 he and his wife purchased land near Mt.
Carmel, so he could be close to the land that inspired him. It would be tragically
ironic if Dixon's paintings become a historic rather than an artistic footprint of
Zion's cottonwoods.

The Same Old Story

This story of loss and destruction repeats itself throughout the West and along the
Great Plains, both in the United States and in Canada. A natural history of the
Canadian prairie tells the fate of declining cottonwood communities along the
north country's rivers, including the Missouri, the Bighorn, the Milk, and the South

Saskatchewan—where damming has interrupted the natural rhythm between water and trees. More precisely, after twenty years of damming, 23 percent fewer cottonwoods grow along the Waterton River and 48 percent fewer along the St. Mary. Trees along the Belly River, which has not been dammed, are doing fine. Though Jim McMahon's concentrated effort has been farther to the south in Utah, his words and knowledge have general application, that "the fate of Cottonwoods is tied inextricably to the condition of our rivers." And though his close attention has allowed him to observe that the trees have "learned" to drop their seeds later in order to adjust to an artificial flooding season, even this effort to adjust will not be enough.

The Oops! Factor

In continuing the discussion about human manipulation of waterways, there's another story of cottonwoods, humans, levees, flooding—and eagles—that really does start with Oops! It provides a perfect example of what not to do in managing or reacting to problems within an intricate natural setting where everything is connected to everything else (Barry Commoner was right). Even basic mistakes set complex problems in motion.

According to published accounts, this story took place in 1997 in St. Maries, a town in Benewah County, Idaho. The setting lies along a stretch of the St. Joe River where worn-out levees failed to prevent flooding in 1996. County officials hoped to obtain a sizable federal grant to restore the levees, and in order to meet some of the application requirements they cut down hundreds of cottonwood trees. In doing so they violated decades-old environmental legislation at both state and federal levels. The resulting entanglement between agencies and the dispute over laws and regulations left no one happy—least of all the residents who actually owned the levees and some of the trees. Had they been asked, the residents could have provided information that might have prevented the county from making such a mistake in the first place. Residents knew firsthand that the cottonwood trees served as perches for bald eagles—as well as protective habitat for other raptors, songbirds, and water birds. But no one asked ahead of time. The county found itself facing violations of the Idaho Forest Practices Act, the federal Clean Water Act, and the Endangered Species Act—which the Audubon Society and the U.S. Fish and Wildlife Service eventually used to bring the cutting to a halt.

By that time, however, the damage was done. One photo shows cottonwood trunks tumbled like giants cut down without warning, as one resident discovered when she came home from work to find her trees gone. In a terrible irony, one logger was killed by a falling tree shortly before officials arrived to stop the cutting.

The aftermath proved equally devastating, as county, state, and federal officials, as well as wildlife biologists and residents, tried to sort through the mess. As the biologists pointed out (and what may one day be common knowledge), cottonwood roots serve to stabilize, not destabilize the banks of riparian waterways—but that's if the trees are alive. Dead roots only last so long before they become dislodged by flooding, causing even more problems. And there's no shortage of floodwater along the St. Joe. At last report, there was enough blame to go around for everybody. And yet, in spite of the blame and anger, there's a lesson in the trees. And though nothing is ever as easy as it looks from the outside, quite likely this unfortunate situation could have been prevented if one basic ground rule had been in place: communicate. Let's hope that some future community—of cottonwood trees, eagles, and people—will benefit from Benewah County's hard lesson.

The Best Intentions

When it comes to restoration efforts, even the best intentions don't guarantee success. That's what Brent Vinger and others at the Ft. Peck Community College in Poplar, Montana, discovered when they planted more than four hundred cottonwoods along a stretch of the Missouri River. Cottonwood saplings, successfully grown from seed at the nursery, did not survive. Natural conditions along the river were against them. Dry weather decreased river levels. Spring runoff lessened. Water release policies applied by the U.S. Army Corps of Engineers further reduced the water flow, to a level that could not sustain the cottonwoods. But the college's agriculture department will try again, starting all over from seed. If at first you don't succeed. . . .

Natural Threats

Threats caused by human activity would seem to be enough to contend with, but cottonwood trees face plenty of danger in the course of their ordinary lives. For a seed delicate enough to be dislodged by a raindrop, it's a wonder they survive at all. Yet they often thrive in spite of the odds. And it's no exaggeration to say that a cottonwood faces a life of struggle from beginning to end. This life of adversity is especially true for the Plains, Fremont, Rio Grande, Narrowleaf, and Lanceleaf cottonwoods—all native to the western United States. Adapting to the changes in geological time has become a way of life for these trees. When the *Populus* genus first appeared on Earth more than 50 million years ago, the question of nourishment from water was not a problem as it is today; quite the opposite. This genus had already made its way into the world, as the fossil remnants reveal in detail, in the warm, lush Eocene summer, securely flowering and releasing its seed along the banks of streams and rivers. Such has always been its path, from those eons ago until now, with *deltoides* and its other subspecies, the actual cottonwoods, arriving slightly later, around 24 mya. The reason we know these fossil dates reflects the life of adversity: The leaves have been discovered in volcanic ash fall.

In the paradoxical ways of nature, changes in the watery habitat in which cottonwoods thrive also threaten their survival. Particularly west of the Mississippi (though east of it, too, as these last many years have shown), cottonwoods face the life-threatening danger of long-lasting drought. For the Plains Cottonwood, drought is a major force that causes other problems. Though cottonwoods tolerate dry conditions better than non-native species, long periods without sufficient moisture weaken them physically and lessen their ability to resist damage from insects and disease. Yet they do resist.

Out of sheer stubbornness it seems, some remain standing long after their centers have been hollowed out by heart rot, refusing to fall even though they are prone to doing so. Drought can come before or after withering heat. Temperatures can get too hot even for trees to work. Thermometer readings much above 62–68°F inhibit photosynthesis, and 122°F is the equivalent to the human temperature of 107°F, the point at which death often occurs. High temperatures within the Plains Cottonwood's territory can range from 100–115°F (by contrast, 100°F is the average maximum in the Eastern Cottonwood's range). Drought conditions make cottonwoods more susceptible to fire, and they do not tolerate fire at all. Forest fires throughout the western United States are often ignited by lightning. According to my local meteorologist, 20 million lightning strikes occur every year in the United States. When timber is dangerously dry—enough so that camp and cooking fires are prohibited in state and national parks, as well as on private land (a frequent ban during the last several years here in Colorado)—one big hit with its billion volts of electricity is all it takes. A single lightning strike can tear a cottonwood open from crown to trunk, set the tree ablaze, and boil the sap of the inner bark within seconds. Some tree species like the Douglas fir rely on fires to heat their seed-sheltering cones at temperatures high enough to burst the cones open and scatter the seed. Not so with cottonwoods. Though some species develop a little resistance as they age, old and young cottonwoods alike suffer from even a light burn. And when fires burn down to the water's edge of a stream, a creek, or a river, that's where the flames will devour the cottonwoods.

If a lightning strike isn't severe enough to start a fire, it can harm or even kill, a cottonwood tree. I have seen the aftereffects of such a strike. During one thun-

"Scar Struck" Plains Cottonwood, Crown Hill Open Space, Lakewood Colorado.
Photo by Kathleen Cain

derstorm that didn't seem any more severe than those that regularly pass through on summer afternoons, the entire 320-foot-long campus building where I worked shuddered once before the lights went out. Word came to evacuate. We stumbled out into daylight to see a crowd gathered near the east end of the building, where a venerable old cottonwood stood, a relic from days when the land was farmed. The tallest structure around, the tree took a direct hit. A wave of electricity tore through the crown, ripped bark off one side of the trunk to ground level, and laid open the delicate white inner cambium. Shredded bark smoldered like wood from a camp-fire. The boiled water and nutrients inside the tree smelled like a mix of mildew and dirty, wet socks. Glistening green leaves lay in tatters on the ground, surrounded by splinters of wood. A mother robin keened beside her dead nestling and refused to leave, in spite of the crowd. Lifeless blackbirds and finches lay everywhere. We gathered around the tree in shocked silence. The lightning bolt had killed the tree's roots, the facilities manager told us. By the next spring our beautiful relic was gone, leaving only a dark circle in the grass. Even that has vanished over time.

I've also made the acquaintance of a tree I call "Scar Struck," a female Plains Cottonwood that lives in a nearby open space. She was probably hit by lightning about twenty years ago. Half of her frame was blasted away. The skeletal remains of her branches and limbs lie decomposing in the grass, stretching nearly fifty feet from her trunk and now providing a perfect home for ants, fungus, and mushrooms. She wears a scar shaped like a winding river, visible from a distance by its grayish–white glint in the sunlight. The scar stretches from the top of her crown down the south side of her trunk. She has worked hard for many years to seal off the damage. On either side, the scar looks as if her bark has been rolled in an attempt to tuck it under any healthy tissue, like a big callus or scar tissue. The strike has put her off balance. She tips to the north. And yet even this spring she put out healthy new foliage and abundant seeds, having probably caught the pollen from any number of male trees nearby. And even though a late spring freeze caught her off guard, the seeds that are left were still grow-ing, almost ready to release in the wind by the end of May. In spite of her troubles, Scar Struck loves life. She does not give it up easily. Yet on a warm day, in the wind, she moans. From the ground to about two feet up the trunk, her constantly stressed wood stretches and tears. She creaks like an old house.

The western United States is notorious for the violent thunderstorms that destroyed the first tree and scarred the second. These storms also cause flash floods or tornado-force winds that can upend tree trunks and send the roots skyward. And while cottonwood trees rely on the wind for pollination and seed sowing, wind remains a major threat to their survival. "Windthrow" describes this danger at its extreme, and cottonwood trees suffer from it more than many other species of trees. Cottonwood roots tend to be shallower than those of other trees. They spread side-ways. Most cottonwoods live in regions where fierce winds prevail. According to a current U.S. government geography reference, spring and summer wind speeds within the Great Plains rank among the highest in the country's interior.

Biologist and natural historian Peter Thomas describes the effect of wind on trees like that of an arm moving a lever. When worked at certain places consis-

Leyden Tree ("Twisted Sister"). Photo by Craig Hillegass, reprinted with permission.

tently, the constant motion weakens the tree to the breaking point; wind fatigue, we might call it. Trees can sense the power of the wind. The cambium responds by growing thicker at the place where force is being exerted. Next time you're near cottonwoods, keep Thomas's comparison in mind. Notice which way the trunks lean compared with the direction of the prevailing winds. Notice how the trunks thicken at the places where they bend, stretch, or lean as far as they can in one direction before they straighten up, trying to keep their balance. It's a constant effort, and one that, to my mind, makes cottonwoods (Plains Cottonwoods, anyway) the Martha Graham dancers among trees.

   Windthrow, however, causes far more serious problems for the tree than having limbs and branches sculpted by an invisible chisel. You've seen the results of windthrow if you've ever seen a cottonwood slightly tipped, or maybe upended, with its roots exposed. Again, as Peter Thomas explains, the action is like that of a loose tooth: as a cottonwood moves back and forth in the wind, the soil encircling the shallow roots is disturbed. The far-spreading roots don't reach deep down into the soil, preferring places where the groundwater is only two to six feet deep, so they have a shallow foothold. Constant swaying loosens the soil and roots until one or both cracks and breaks and the tree tips over. Still, in spite of all these natural forces, a cottonwood tree can endure. Craig Hillegass, city forester for Arvada, Colorado, sent me to visit a tree I have nicknamed "Twisted Sister," a female Plains Cottonwood growing along the banks of Leyden Creek. Craig thinks the tree might have been injured when young. Yet in spite of the injury, she has continued to twist her way through life.

When rivers and streams freeze in winter, ice can harm the trees, even though temperature extremes within the Plains Cottonwood range reach $-50°F$ in northern areas and $0°F$ in the southern. In the winter of 1804, during the long, cold nights at Fort Mandan on the upper Missouri, Lewis and Clark listened to the cottonwood timbers, from which their fort was built, pop and crack as the wood froze. Late freezes and early frosts also harm cottonwoods. Water allows rot to set in and opens the way for harmful pathogens to get into the tree.

If cottonwood trees are lucky enough to survive all these health hazards, there's always a hungry beaver or two waiting to feast on the leaves and bark. Beavers enjoy a beneficial relationship with cottonwoods. The trees supply both building material and food. Younger trees make perfect logs for a cozy lodge. Leaves and bark are loaded with sugar, as the beavers well know. But too much of a good thing for one creature can cause problems for another. If the beavers cut down too many cottonwoods, the resulting ponds can flood out young, new trees. Without trees, the banks of creeks and streams erode. With weakened banks, waterways are more susceptible to harmful flooding which can endanger other species, including our own. Riparian systems demonstrate exquisite connections.

Another such connection to cottonwoods observed by wildlife biologists in Yellowstone Park involves elk and wolves. Once the wolves were gone from Yellowstone, elk populations increased. Like so many animals, elk enjoy cottonwood bark. In such large numbers their browsing habits led to "girdling" the trees, eating away rings of bark and causing the trees to die. Bring back the wolves, and the elk decrease and move into higher terrain. With their bark intact, the cottonwoods come back, too.

Cottonwoods have lived so long on earth that they have developed ways to counteract many natural threats to their survival—one of the several reasons Jenifer Morrissey stands in awe of them. If they make it through that tender first year, seedlings grow several feet and become saplings. The woody stem that began as a shoot thickens into bark. Bark on a mature cottonwood serves the same purpose as armor plating on a tank. It grows several inches thick and is designed to protect the inner parts of the tree, to keep invaders out.

Even young cottonwoods show resilience to the natural forces that threaten them. They can send out new shoots from a trunk that's been damaged—even decapitated. If a limb gets hit by lightning, like Scar Struck the tree works toward the common good, sacrificing a limb to save the whole and persisting over many years to seal off the damaged area. A cottonwood will do the same thing in a drought—shed leaves and twigs it can no longer sustain. "Drop a branch, save a tree" could be the cottonwood's motto during hard times. And if flood, fire, lightning, and drought do not pose enough threats, cottonwood trees face plenty of others. They may not suffer from plague, exactly, but pestilence and locusts (of a sort) do cause problems.

Many trees have developed clever defense systems: thorns, spines, stickers, and even chemicals that poison their enemies. This is true particularly in places where vegetation (and thus nourishment for animals and insects) is sparse; in the deserts, for example, or in landscapes where large open spaces exist between plants, shrubs, trees, and other vegetation. And though cottonwoods are a pioneer species, hardy organisms that go forward into new and open land—they have not developed the sword-and-prickle defense methods that cactus, holly, and roses have perfected. Consequently, cottonwoods suffer the effects of browsing by both domestic and wild animals. Without daggers, their first line of defense is to grow. They get out of the way by growing as fast as they can.

As another line of defense, every living tree creates its own chemistry lab. We've heard about the chemical compounds and substances that continue to be discovered in the world's rainforests, where, scientists tell us, less than three acres of forest can contain nearly eight hundred plants. Taxol is one such substance acclaimed for fight- ing cancer. Others are so familiar that we may not think of them as part of a tree's defense system—caffeine, strychnine, and morphine, for instance. Trees also produce tannins and resins to keep away animal (including human) and insect pred- ators. Who wants to eat a leaf, a fruit or a nut that's bitter, causes indigestion—or even worse, paralysis and death? Trees also communicate with each other and their surrounding environment through chemicals, sometimes through the root systems and sometimes by sending chemical signals through the air. Tannin is one such protective chemical. An astringent, tannin helps cottonwoods repel insects, fight disease, and survive a harsh environment. A research team from Northern Arizona University has discovered some interesting relationships between the amount of tannin in different species of cottonwoods, the rate of decomposition of fallen leaves, and the amount of nitrogen returned to the soil through decomposition. Tannin levels also affect the flavor factor for beavers—more tannin, less good taste.

Trees also produce gums and resins. If you've ever been around pine trees, you know that inevitably you end up with some sticky goo on your hands or clothes. One function of the resin is to provide a trap for harmful insects. Imagine trying to swim through that stuff if you're less than a millimeter long! Of course, in the ongoing game of adaptation, some insects have learned to swim through even the most viscous fluids that plants and trees can produce. Cottonwood leaves also contain resins and a waxy substance that helps keep moisture in and harmful insects out. But gauging by the list of insects and diseases that assail the cottonwoods, these defenses do not always succeed.

One disadvantage of being rooted to a single spot is that cottonwood trees, while playing host to birds and animals that do not harm them, can also become home to little beasties that browse, bore, chew, and suck the life out of them. In the course of their lives, insects lay eggs and enjoy different stages that prolong both the residence and the damage. Not all insects cause problems for cottonwoods. Mites, aphids, and box elder bugs frequent Plains Cottonwoods, but they don't cause problems the way other insects do and can actually keep harmful insects away. Ants are meticulous housekeepers and their "clean" colonies do not cause infections or problems for cottonwoods. But the formal names of insects that do cause trouble sound like a Who's Who of the Middle Ages. The common names describe the kind of damage each one causes.

The Plains Cottonwood attracts *Chrysomela scripta*, the cottonwood leaf beetle. The tree has its own moth—the cottonwood dagger moth—*Acronicta lepusculina* in the elaborate language of science. *Malacosoma disstria* (sounds like a curse, doesn't it?), the forest tent caterpillar, sets up camp within the leaves. *Phyllocolpa bozemani* (and you thought the only Bozeman was in Montana), the poplar leaffolding sawfly, is not the only creature flying or crawling through Plains Cottonwood leaves. It's joined by *Alsophilia pometaria*, the cankerworm, and *Hyphantria cunea*, the fall webworm. It's unlikely that all these insects would be present in one tree at the same time—or is it? Either way, maybe you want to wear a hat the next time you're walking beneath cottonwoods!

The Eastern Cottonwood's list of insect invaders resembles an army of 10 distinct battalions. Reflecting the intricate ways of nature, one borer, *Paranthrene dollii dollii*, prefers the lower stem. Another, *Paranthrene tabaniformis*, seeks out terminal stems and small branches. *Saperda calcarata*, commonly known as the poplar borer, is very particular. Like a connoisseur, it selects trunks at least three years old, and leaves behind a tell-tale pattern of tunnels as it works. Its damage lessens the commercial value of the wood and can cause trees to break.

Named specifically for the tree, the cottonwood borer, *Plectrodera scalator*, would have no life without its sylvan host. Equipped with mighty mandibles, the female chews into the base of the tree and deposits her eggs. After the eggs hatch, the young burrow into the tree and can take up to two years to mature. These borers have long antennae and elaborate bodies that make them look like they're dressed for a black-and-white ball. They're big enough to perch on your index finger—see http://www.gpnc.org/cwoodborer.htm for a portrait. In various stages they eat the roots of the tree and burrow into and around the base of the cottonwood. Older trees may be hardy enough to resist the invasion, but these beetles can damage the roots and root collar of all sizes of trees. Root damage causes the tree to lose its balance and tip over. Even more specifically named for the damage it does, the cottonwood twig borer *Gypsonoma haimbachiana* causes abnormal shapes to develop, as does *Chrysomela scripta*, the cottonwood leaf beetle, which feeds on both terminal buds and leaves. If the poplar tentmaker, *Ichthyura inclusa*, builds its tents often and long enough, eventually it strips the limbs bare; in midsummer the tree can wear the stark look of autumn. I saw this look on a few of Buffalo Bill's Cottonwoods at North Platte, Nebraska, last summer. High up in the outer branches, limbs full of webby tents swayed in the afternoon breeze.

The Eastern Cottonwood suffers from damage caused by a dozen diseases. Like its western counterpart it is subject to cankers: *Septoria musiva* opens the way for other cankers to invade and causes leaf spots. *Cytospora chrysosperma*, a canker shared by both Eastern and Plains species, like many organisms, attacks when and where the tree is already weak. *Fusarium solani* waits for wetter conditions, such as those after a flood, to make its assault.

The Plains Cottonwood also has specific diseases to contend with. Leaf rusts cause a tree to lose its leaves early, weakening the whole structure and making it more susceptible to other troubles. Of these, *Malampsora medusae* cause some of the most serious problems (and bear within it the name of the powerful, many-headed Medusa). Plains Cottonwoods also suffer from cankers. The worst of these is *Cytospora chrysosperma*, commonly called Cytospora. Plains Cottonwoods also endure two most unpleasant-sounding conditions, root and butt rot.

If we consider each tree a fortress, it is easy to imagine the great battles for life waged within. An insect develops a taste for leaves in a certain stage of development or a certain part of the tree. Over time—and consider how many generations of insects come and go in a single summer—the tree develops a chemical reaction or some other resistance to this invasion. Using the advantage of such short-lived (relatively speaking) progeny, the insect develops a counter-reaction. And so it goes. Trees under cultivation or management receive human help by way of insecticides or companion plantings. Those in the wild must do as they have always done in the constant interplay of action and reaction known as evolution. And as we'll see in the last chapter, "Good News," cottonwoods may have more powerful positive effects on other members of their communities than anyone suspected.

Invasive Species

If cottonwoods reach their average age of seventy years, the ailments that afflict them begin to sound like human complaints: a generally weakened physical condition; susceptible to falling; and easy prey to infections and disease. A threat earlier in their lives often comes from invasive species. Botanists define invasive species as plants that grow aggressively enough to threaten the existence of others around them. According to the USDA, even though it's a native tree, *Populus deltoides*, the Eastern Cottonwood, is considered invasive in some parts of the northeastern United States. In the West, however, two non-native invasive species pose a major threat to cottonwoods in riparian areas: the Russian olive (*Elaeagnus angustifolia* L.) and the tamarisk, also known as salt cedar (*Tamarix* L). Russian olive is listed as a noxious weed in Colorado and New Mexico. As a potentially invasive species it's banned in Connecticut.

The shade from Russian olive trees means certain death for cottonwood saplings. This non-native was introduced by immigrants from Russia in the nineteenth century, part of the inevitable human tendency to bring along something from an old home to a new one. Along with cottonwoods, Russian olives were planted as welcome windbreaks, but they quickly moved out of bounds. Members of the Department of Geography at the University of Western Ontario reported on a fifty-year study that determined how quickly Russian olive trees moved downstream along a particular stretch of the Milk River from Canada into northern Montana. Different measures, including size, distribution, and the death of both species of trees, showed that the Russian olives moved north and south. By the end of the study Russian olives were growing on sixty-nine of seventy-four different places along the river. Like cottonwoods, they follow the water. They're also subject to some of the same threats, including harm to the saplings when winter ice breaks up on the river. But they have some advantages over the native trees. They don't have to rely on the wind as cottonwoods do for pollination and seed dispersal. Birds and animals help spread Russian olive seeds. Whereas cottonwood seed viability is measured in days, Russian olive seeds can remain viable for up to three years. Their seeds can sprout on either clear, bare ground or land that's covered with vegetation. Cottonwoods are more particular, needing open ground that's been scoured and prepared by flooding. Unfortunately Russian olives aren't as tasty to cattle and other livestock as cottonwood leaves and bark. The university's study suggests that Russian olives could be the dominant tree along this area of the Milk River in a decade, and that they could replace the cottonwoods there before the end of the twenty-first century.

The tamarisk, an Asian and Mediterranean adventurer brought to the United States in the 1800s, can gulp water from a stream at a rate of two hundred gallons a day—an acre of the stuff can consume almost 3 million gallons annually, depriving the native cottonwoods and other riparian species of their fair share. Cottonwoods consume water, too, but they give back to the habitat in return. Tamarisks ravage it. They leave behind a salty trail in areas they invade. Salts come up through the roots and spread out into the leaves. When the leaves drop, salt enters the soil around the tamarisk and other trees nearby. Cottonwoods can tolerate a certain level of salinity, but not to the extent that tamarisks create. Major rivers in the West are under invasion from the tamarisk and the Russian olive, much to the detriment of healthy riparian areas. Like many places across the country, we have a local group called the Russian Olive Terminators (ROT) that systematically works to remove Russian olives from riparian areas. Tree by tree, it took about five years to clear a couple of miles along nearby Walnut Creek.

If you've gotten close to cottonwoods in the wild—or even at a local park, perhaps, you might have noticed that some are shorn of their limbs, either by trimming or simply by self-pruning—the result of sacrificing a branch or limb that's weak or diseased. At an open space reservoir near my house, I can see examples of both methods of pruning, as well as the way the tree has worked to recover from its wounds—as Ray Daugherty instructs, trees do not really heal, they seal off the damage. On one tree, a huge limb hanging over the walking path was trimmed two years ago. Even last spring, it still "wept" with sap and water as the tree began to quicken in the spring. The limb has finally developed a dark, dry callus over the wound and formed a spindle-shaped scar in the middle. Beneath the scar new wood can grow, but the open wound still creates an entryway for pathogens and insects. Cottonwoods work to form calluses over other parts of the tree that have suffered damage—from places where squirrels have chewed branches and twigs, or even places where cankers have formed.

Trees work hard to protect their innermost chamber: the heartwood. Heartwood forms the core of the tree, much as the backbone functions in the human body. It's the center from which the tree extends itself into the world. Heartwood is always described as "dead wood," yet it serves as a storehouse for waste material and substances that can repel even the most intrepid invaders, whether insects or pathogens. If you've ever opened a cedar chest and smelled the pungent tang of the wood, you've smelled heartwood. By and large, we consider the aroma of cedar pleasant; insects react in just the opposite way. The scent repels them. And yes, you've never heard of cottonwood chests. The wood of most cottonwoods—with the exception of *P. balsamifera*—is noted for a generally

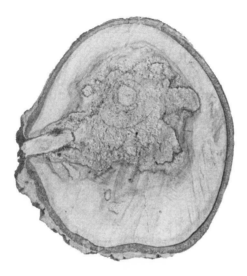

*Cottonwood heart rot, reprinted with permission from
North Dakota State University Extension Service.*

unpleasant odor. Most people who burn cottonwood logs describe the smell as pungent, sour, stale, or rotten—take your pick! The aroma of that wounded cottonwood limb I mentioned above, the one that "wept" in the springtime, reminded me of a combination of mildew and pickle juice—with a faint hint of burning rubber quenched with lemonade! However you describe it, the odor proves the cottonwood's attempt to use scent to keep invaders away.

Cottonwood trees are particularly susceptible to heart rot. Heart rot occurs when fungi get inside the wood and cause decay. Such invasion happens easily in the wild when limbs break or snap in the wind, providing the perfect entry point for a tree that's already moist inside because of its high water content. Planted trees suffer the same way, too, as well as from pruning or any wounding of the wood. The appearance of "mushrooms" or "conks" on trees proves the presence of fungi. Arborists estimate that every conk indicates about a cubic foot of decay.

Succession

All of these challenges in the life of a single cottonwood tree are natural. As part of the mortal world, cottonwoods die. A drama known as "succession" plays itself out in every normally functioning riparian area—or in those that approach normality. It is the rule of a cottonwood's life that it goes first, a lone traveler onto open ground, to lead the way for other species. Cottonwoods are the dominant species in these areas, the keystone on which all others will come to depend, from tiny lichens to a stalwart companion tree like the elm. Then in their turn, the other trees, shrubs, and grasses that eventually become neighbors to cottonwoods: box elder, elm, hackberry, hickory, maple, willow—the litany can continue for several lines—will "succeed" to the riparian kingdom. They will take over. In the tipping of life scales, the neighbors will thrive and the cottonwoods will falter, for any number of the reasons I have mentioned in this chapter—perhaps a tree may even succumb to all the misfortunes of its kind. Part of a cottonwood's life is death. Yet even in death it persists. One day at Crown Hill Open Space Park, Ray Daugherty and I marveled at the number of species that were quite at home in the living quarters provided by a "snag," a cottonwood that had died probably twenty years ago, by Ray's estimate. A raccoon, skunk, possum, or some other small mammal, found a cozy apartment in a hollow section of the lower trunk. Woodpeckers—"downies" (pileated) and flickers are common—had carved out quarters on the upper floors. At least one owl had taken over when they moved out. Swainson's hawks frequent the park, and surely claim this tree as a lookout point for hunting. Ants traveled a highway from ground level to the upper dormitories of the trunk, which serves as a natural sculpture in its own right, resembling the photograph at the beginning of this chapter. Spiders relaxed in several dark nooks and crannies. The tree offered its fallen branches back to the soil. The years-long process of decomposition, of unbecoming a tree, was underway. Termites had moved in. Lichens and moss did their bit. Even slime mold played its part. And the native grasses already covered the fading limbs with both shroud and the veil of new life. In the energies of nature, it is sometimes impossible to say where one life ends and another begins. That's the dynamic of succession. When it works, the cottonwoods are gone and the companions rule the kingdom. In a healthy riparian habitat, we should be able to look around and see new cottonwood saplings beginning life in open ground. But these days, they all need a little help.

Current Environmental Dangers

These natural hazards in a cottonwood tree's life endanger its very existence—fire, flood, wind, animal browsing, disease, and insect damage. But there's more, I'm afraid (though "Good News" arrives eventually), problems created by our still-industrial lifestyle. Acid rain harms leaves as well as tree roots and soil conditions. More carbon dioxide than the atmosphere can manage gets released when fossil fuels are burned. An additional problem caused by overgrazing is that livestock release harmful levels of ammonia into the soil near riparian areas. Soil pollution from heavy metals increases the level of contamination. In urban areas especially, add to this list the substances used to de-ice winter roads, and roads built through new developments pack down the soil and cover root systems. Rover doing his business at the foot of the tree in the park or open space overloads the soil with potassium. Ozone interferes with photosynthesis and causes problems for trees as well as people. Recent studies with cottonwoods and ozone reveal some ironic results—and just when we thought the country air might be better for us all. In 2003, Jillian Gregg, a Cornell graduate student, planted identical cottonwood clones (*P. deltoides*) in urban areas around New York City as well as in rural areas fifty miles away, to test the effects of air pollution—mainly ozone—on growth. Even she was surprised to learn that the city trees grew twice as fast as their rural counterparts. The reason? Nitric oxide also forms in the mucky urban air, but . . . it removes ozone. Fifty miles away in the country, nitric oxide concentrations are less, yet ozone drifts in, hampering the growth of the cottonwoods and raising a further question: What effect does the ozone exposure have on other living things?

It often seems that we have forgotten the lesson taught to us in elementary school science class—that trees are the lungs of the earth. And in that context, we should pay special attention to the health and well-being of all trees, but especially to the messages cottonwoods relay. As the fastest-growing hardwood trees in North America, by their very nature they return the most oxygen to the air. Now that we know some of the problems these trees face, let's find out what some of the solutions to those problems might be.

Sources

Thomas D. Landis, et al. discuss the importance of sexual diversity among cottonwoods in riparian restoration in "Sex and the Single Salix: Considerations for Riparian Restoration." *Native Plants*. Fall 2003. pp. 111–117.

Ray Daugherty's handout to students on *Populus* species mentions the municipal ban on cottonwoods in Denver and Westminster, Colorado.

Kathleen Norris describes this cottonwood tree in an essay, "Dreaming of Trees," from *The Place Within: Portraits of the American Landscape by Contemporary Writers*. Ed. Jodi Daynard. W. W. Norton. New York and London. 1997. pp. 159–168.

Dr. Gary Whitham's estimate appears in "Life under one tree's rule?" Peter Spotts. *Christian Science Monitor*. October 14, 2004.
http://www.csmonitor.com/2004/1014/p.13s01.html

The 1 percent figure for riparian habitat in the West was quoted from Knopf, F.L.,
et al., "Conservation of riparian ecosystems in the United States." *Wilson
Bulletin* 100: 272–284 in "The Importance and Future Condition of Western
Riparian Ecosystems as Migratory Bird Habitat" by Susan K. Skagen, Rob
Hazlewood, and Michael L. Scott. *USDA Forest Service General Technical Report,*
PSW-GTR-191. 2005. p. 525.

Columnist Clint Talbott reported on the loss of a favorite cottonwood grove in "The
clueless tree-killers." *Boulder Daily Camera*. January 29, 2006.
http://www.dailycamera.com/bdc/opinion_columnists/article/0,1713,BDC_2
490_4421806,00.html

Russell, Sharman. "Home on the range." 3 pp. http://www.zianet.com/snm/range.htm

Grazing statistics appear in "BLM Publishes New Grazing Regulations to Improve
Management of Public Lands Grazing." BLM (Bureau of Land Management).
http://www.blm.gov/nhp/news/releases/pages/2006/pr060712_grazing.htm

Jay W. Street discusses the dangers to Rio Grande Cottonwoods in "Rio Grande
Cottonwood Tree." http://www.desertusa.com/mag01/jan/papr/cwood.html

Suzanne Probart and Matt Schmader shared the story of Naomi during a personal
interview on May 8, 2006, in Albuquerque, New Mexico. Though he does not
name her, Tony Davis tells Naomi's story in "Traffic flow 1, trees 0" in *High
Country News*, Vol. 27 No. 22 November 27, 1995. http://wwwhcn.org/servlets/
hcn.PrintableArticle?article_id1484 The percentage of riparian habitat in New
Mexico comes from the Tree New Mexico web site at: http://treenm.com.

Research on the importance of western riparian habitats to migratory birds was
published by Susan K. Skagen, et al. "The Importance and Future Condition
of Western Riparian Ecosystems as Migratory Bird Habitat." *USDA Forest
Service General Technical Report*, PSW-GTR-191. 2005.

Morrissey, Jenifer. "Awed by Cottonwoods." *green line ONLINE*. 11(1): 1–6. Spring
1999. Colorado Riparian Association.
http://www.coloradoriparian.org/GreenLine/V11-1/Cottonwoods.html

McMahon, James P., et al. "The Potential for Restoration Along the Virgin River in
Zion National Park." Grand Canyon Trust. 2001.

"Utah/Zion's geriatric cottonwoods." Hotline (column) in *High Country News*. April
29, 2002. p. 2

Additional quotations from Jim McMahon are from e-mail correspondence dated October 31, 2005.

Additional quotations from Jeff Bradybaugh are from e-mail correspondence dated October 31, 2005.

Burnside, Wesley. *Maynard Dixon, Artist of the West.* Brigham Young University Press. Provo, Utah. 1974. p. 136

Candace Savage discusses the condition of cottonwood communities along Canadian rivers in *Prairie: A Natural History.* Greystone Books. Douglas & McIntyre Publishing Group. Vancouver/Toronto/Berkeley. 2004. pp. 212–217.

Peter Chilson reported the Benewah County, Idaho, story. "County caught in cottonwood quagmire." *High Country News.* Western Roundup. May 12, 1997. pp.1–3. http://www.hcn.org/hcn.Article?article_id=3219.

David F. Van Haverbeke describes natural threats to the Plains Cottonwood in "*P. deltoides* var. *occidentalis* Rydb." http://forestry.about.com/library/silvics/blsilpopdel.htm p.14

Information on the Ft. Peck restoration effort comes from: "Ft. Peck Community College cottonwood plantings." *Tribal College Journal.* http://www.tribalcollege-journal.org/themag/backissues/winter2005/winter2005oc.htm

D. T. Cooper describes natural threats to the Eastern Cottonwood in "*Populus deltoides* Bartr. ex. Marsh/Eastern Cottonwood." http://forestry.about.com/library/silvics/blsilpopdel.htm p.6

Lightning statistics obtained from KMGH–TV, Channel 7 (Denver) Web site: http://www.thedenverchannel.com/weather/index.html.

Information on wind speeds on the Great Plains comes from *An Outline of American Geography*, by Stephen S. Birdsall and John Florin. Chapter 11. "The Great Plains and Prairies." http://usinfo.state.gov/products/pubs/geography/geog11.htm

Peter Thomas discusses the effect of wind on trees in *Trees: Their Natural History.* Cambridge University Press. Cambridge. 2000.

Robert L. Beschta describes the interactions between cottonwoods, elk, and wolves in "Reduced Cottonwood Recruitment Following Extirpation of Wolves in Yellowstone's Northern Range." *Ecology.* February 2005. Vol. 86, Issue 2, pp. 391–403.

Statistics on the rainforests can be found at
http://www.rainforestweb.org/Rainforest_Information/Plants/.

Jim Mason's online article "Cottonwood Borer" appears at
http://www.gpnc.org/cwoodborer.htm.

Results of the study along the Milk River were reported by C.M. Pearce and D.G.
Smith in *Environmental Management* 28(5): 623–637. November 2001.

Information on the activity of ROT along Walnut Creek was provided by Patti
Wright, Volunteer Coordinator for the City of Westminster (Colorado) Open
Space Program.

The extension service of North Dakota State University provides information about
heart rot on the Web page: "Deciduous Tree Diseases" at
http://www.ext.nodak.edu/extpubs/plantsci/hortcrop/pp697-1.htm#Heart.

In a speech titled "Water Doesn't Have to be for Fighting," Forest Service Chief
Dale Bosworth mentioned the daily intake of saltcedar (tamarisk).
http://www.fs.fed.us/news/2004/speeches/09/water.shtml

Invasive species information for Russian olive trees comes from the USDA
PLANTS database. http://plants.usda.gov/java/nameSearch?keywordquery=
russian+olive&mode=comname

Information about the tamarisk comes from the Colorado Forestry Association
online. "Tamarisk Awareness Day."
http://www.coloradoforestry.org/our_forest/tamarisk_awareness.html

A brief article about the Cornell study was published in Cornell News, "City-grown
air pollution is tougher on country trees" at
http://www.news.cornell.edu/releases/July03/ozone_trees.html.

The study itself, "Urbanization effects of tree growth in the vicinity of New York
City" was published in *Nature*, July 10, 2003, by Jennifer Gregg, et al.

8

GOOD NEWS

As reports of the dangers to cottonwoods through loss of riparian habitat, particularly in the western United States, continue to filter in—while drought
conditions worsen and water becomes ever more precious—the news can make
you start wringing your hands. But there is good news, too. And while restoration
efforts may not fully counterbalance some of the damage that's been done to
cottonwood trees in the last century, each new project that helps restore or
preserve habitat offers hope. Additionally, cottonwoods are making a new contri-
bution to how we clean up toxic messes. One species of cottonwood has even
become a model for long-term scientific research. And, one thing to keep in mind,
where cottonwood destruction or restoration is at work, is how fast these trees
grow. Cut 'em down, they come right back!

The Swamp Cottonwood (*Populus heterophylla*) has had a tough time of it the last
fifty years or so. According to natural historian Donald Culross Peattie, it was once
the source of 50 percent of the excelsior manufactured in the United States and
enjoyed a wide growing range throughout the South and Northeast. It is currently
considered a rare species and is on the endangered list in Connecticut,
Massachusetts, and Michigan. In New York it has threatened status. In Pennsylvania,
it is now "extirpated"—no trees have been found in the wild for twenty years. If this
all sounds as if it's the last gasp for the Swamp Cottonwood, there's good news, too.

The Cleveland Museum of Natural History tells of a welcome find by Jim
Bissell, a curator of botany. In 1990, Bissell responded to the request of a property
owner in Lake County, Ohio, to investigate a stand of trees. Bissell was thrilled to
discover nearly twenty swamp cottonwoods. He knew about the possibility of their
existence from the museum's herbarium records, which dated to 1893. A museum
botanist had documented such a stand more than one hundred years earlier, but
had described it only as being "close to Painesville, Ohio (Lake County)." Swamp

Sunlight through Eastern Cottonwood leaves. Seward, Nebraska.
Photo by Kathleen Cain

cottonwoods have not been located in any of the surrounding counties, and only in a couple of places in Michigan. The trees prefer the marshy, swampy areas of the southeastern river deltas.

But the Ohio find is not the only treasure of Swamp Cottonwoods to be uncovered. In late 2002 members of Nature Conservancy Canada, while conduct-ing a site inventory at Bickford Oak Woods, also made a unique find: a stand of more than sixty Swamp Cottonwoods. Bickford lies along the St. Clair River, near Sarnia, and is part of Canada's Carolinian Zone, an area whose forest cover has experienced severe reduction, from 80 percent to 11 percent over many years. True to their nature, the Swamp Cottonwoods were found growing in the heavy clay soils they favor, lying in a low area of rising and falling landscape. Swamp Cottonwoods have never been found in Canada before, so the discovery also means that a new tree has joined the species list for the country.

In chapter 6, I mentioned the restoration project underway at Bosque Redondo near the site of old Fort Sumner, New Mexico, from a historical point of view, but it belongs in this chapter, too. Undertaken by the state park system, this project has resulted in the planting of more than 10,000 cottonwood saplings in a riparian setting near the Rio Grande. The area was deforested in the 1800s by that disastrous U.S. Army project led by Major James Carleton. In the summer of 2005, as part of a dedication ceremony for the new Bosque Redondo Memorial, dedicated to the memory of Navajo and Apache people imprisoned near the fort after the Long Walk, saplings were sold to help raise money for the Friends of the Bosque Redondo. Some of the trees were created by cloning from remnants of the original cottonwoods on site at the fort. At the bosque, a hard but necessary lesson has been learned about compassion for others and stewardship of the land. But, like the Navajo and Apache people who have not only survived the effects of the Long Walk but lived to prosper as nations, the cottonwoods of the bosque flourish once again, too.

With only 5 percent of riparian habitat left in the "Land of Enchantment," Tree New Mexico (TNM) is clear about its mission. The organization works to ensure "sustainable forests in urban and rural communities and natural areas through restoration, public education, and advocacy." Suzanne Probart, executive director of TNM, has a special fondness for the Rio Grande Cottonwoods native to her state. I quoted her earlier when she described the "graciousness" that this species of cottonwood brings to the desert environment. She also emphasizes their impor-tance to the culture of New Mexico. As archeological digs have revealed, the trees have been part of the riparian communities far longer than any of New Mexico's many populations; long before the Native Americans, the Spanish conquistadors, or the European immigrants arrived, finding their way down the Santa Fe Trail from one cottonwood grove to the next. Though some people still have a view that trees are expendable, TNM works to counter that view by providing educational programs and actually restoring riparian habitats. The group's River Rescue proj-ect has planted trees in more than forty areas in New Mexico since 1990. A pole planting technique that's been discussed in other chapters is part of the effort. Through partnerships with the City of Albuquerque Open Space Division, TNM is able to get riparian forests started in just a few years, resulting in trees that stand from six to twelve feet tall, with an 85 percent success rate. TNM distributes and helps plant thousands of trees each year and offers programs for all ages and to communities in every part of the state. One exchange that took place between Fort Sumner and Albuquerque, for example, centered around Navajo culture.

TNM partners with many local and national organizations, including American Forests. A local collaborator, the City of Albuquerque Open Space Division under the supervision of Matt Schmader, whom we met earlier, along with "Our Lady of the Ditch," reports that since 1984 the Open Space Division has planted more than 21,000 cottonwood hybrids—a Fremont crossed with a Narrowleaf.

In chapter 7, I mentioned Jenifer Morrissey's concern about loss of riparian forests in Colorado. Morrissey sees irrigation ditches as an advantage that human change brings to cottonwood survival. The ditches create a narrow channel bed. In turn, a "bench" develops on either side of the channel—just the right place for cottonwood "recruitment." Since the water flow and physical setting of an irrigation ditch matches the trees' needs for growth, protection, and survival, cottonwoods flourish along these ditches. Dams along the South Platte and Arkansas rivers have boosted the chances of cottonwood survival along their banks. Here the irrigation ditch example works on a larger scale: narrow channels develop, and so do the benches on which cottonwoods have a better chance of growing.

Farther west, in Utah's Zion National Park, officials and interested others continue to prepare sedimentation and small mammal studies in an effort to go forward with a second-step proposal to restore the North Fork of the Virgin River. The project would allow the natural healing of the river to take place and restore the ability of the Fremont Cottonwoods along its banks to regenerate in rhythm with the river's natural flow. Though time-line estimates extend to several years before funding can take place, and several years more to complete the project, those responsible for the natural resources of the park show persistence—an essential quality in a place whose history is measured not in years but in periods of geological time.

In Arizona, volunteers for the U.S. Fish and Wildlife Service have been busy at the Imperial Wildlife Refuge. The agency's 2001 volunteer report noted that 14,000 trees—including cottonwoods—have been planted on refuge lands as part of a habitat restoration project. Tree-planting efforts are underway by many organizations all over North America. Something unique to remember about cottonwood planting is how sustainable these trees are. They regenerate easily, so once given a chance in an area that can support them, they usually thrive.

One of the most touching stories I found about cottonwoods comes from a joint venture, a phrase we used to hear only in connection with business and corporate activities. It's a process that now often includes public and private efforts, and from my reading I believe it's a trend in restoration efforts. This example involves cottonwood trees, eagles, the Fort McDowell Yavapai Nation, the U.S. Bureau of Indian Affairs, and the Flood Control District of Maricopa County in Arizona. At the request of the Yavapai Nation, the Sonoran Joint Venture brought these groups together to protect bald eagle habitat on the Yavapai Reservation. Just four miles wide and ten miles long, the reservation lies near the confluence of the Salt and Verde rivers. Bald eagles hold a sacred place in Yavapai culture, and nesting sites in cottonwood trees are essential. But, similar to the situation in Zion National Park

Looking up into a Fremont Cottonwood.
Photo by Gregory McNamee, reprinted with permission.

where flood control efforts have prevented the trees from regenerating naturally, the cottonwoods on the reservation are all the same age—like the Zion trees, about seventy years old. Flood controls upstream prevent the trees from regenerating. In 2000, four nesting pairs of bald eagles used the trees. Six fledglings survived and left the nests. Through the joint venture, the groups worked together to plant cottonwood saplings, using a special pole-planting technique. Cut from healthy trees, the poles measured about eight inches in diameter and twelve feet long and were planted deep enough to reach groundwater. Dimension and depth proved vital—at groundwater level the sturdy poles found enough moisture to survive and could resist further scouring from the river or browsing from animals. Good work spreads as fast as good news. Plans were made for the winter of 2002 to sponsor pole-planting technique workshops on other reservations in Arizona.

Such a pole-planting technique, by the way, was the result of another joint venture between the USDA's Los Lunas, New Mexico, Plant Materials Center, the U.S. Army Corps of Engineers, the U.S. Bureau of Reclamation, and the U.S. Fish and Wildlife Service. Three-to-four-year-old Fremont Cottonwood saplings, grown commercially (or "farm-raised" as the fact sheet describes them), were first planted on the kind of sites they like best—not only moist, but places with a permanent water source. The survival rate was 80 percent—similar to that achieved by Tree New Mexico's River Rescue project. Of course, with the use and diversion of natural water sources all over the west, a permanent water source is not always available, even to the Fremont Cottonwoods.

The pole-planting technique, developed at the Los Lunas Center of the National Resources Conservation Service (NRCS), has been used throughout New Mexico and the Southwest to help restore riparian habitats. In these habitats, as the examples above illustrate, natural flooding no longer occurs because the water has been diverted. Without flooding, the natural action of the entire ecosystem is disturbed. As the dominant tree species in these habitats, cottonwoods benefit the understory of trees, shrubs, and grasses. When cottonwoods cannot regenerate naturally, other vegetation suffers—animals do, too. Without a little human help (the cause of the water diversion in the first place), instead of "succeeding" on their own, these habitats will develop into "xeriscape"-type environments.

Directions for the pole-planting technique are detailed, consisting of several basic steps. The "poles" are branches removed from young, healthy cottonwood trees (Rio Grande, Plains, Fremont, Lanceleaf, and Narrowleaf), harvested and planted when the donor trees are dormant, in late winter or early spring. A few branches are left toward the top, but otherwise the poles are stripped bare. Before they're ever planted, plenty of work has gone into studying a restoration site. The depth of the groundwater has been measured to make sure it will be within reach of the poles—about 4 to 6 feet. The water's been tested for salinity—cottonwoods can only tolerate a certain level of salt. Varying soil quality affects the successful outcome of the planting: Clay soil has to be approached differently than soil full of cobble or that containing sand or gravel. The elevation of a site has to be considered, as well as the amount of moisture present or a tendency toward flooding. Cottonwoods need to be planted about 3 ft./1 m. of aerated soil above the water table.

Poles have to be kept moist between cutting and planting time. Using what's called "clonal stock" limits diversity. Poles taken from a male cottonwood are not unique trees from different parents pollinated by the wind but clones of a single parent. It's like planting the same tree over and over again, a limit to both gender and genetic variety. To compensate, the use of seedlings in such restoration plantings is also encouraged. And, as we've seen in chapter 7, new research is challenging the exclusive use of clones and encouraging that more attention be paid to careful collection of diverse planting stock to begin with. Another challenge is one cottonwoods face everywhere in the wild: browsing by wild and domestic animals. Five-foot fences of chicken wire are nestled around the poles to keep the browsers away. But there's always a tribe of cottonwood leaf beetles or other insects waiting to indulge in their favorite food, so insect control is also needed to help keep the poles healthy and growing. Once planted, these cottonwoods will be subject to the diseases and other hazards common to their genus and species. And the water supply has to be kept regular, and boosted in places where that feature is lacking. The good news is that this technique has an 80–90 percent success rate.

The Plant Materials Center has more research under way, trying to test the effectiveness of a sprinkler irrigation system across the Rio Grande floodplains, to find out whether such a system would help cottonwood seeds that have dispersed naturally and whether or not the process would help the trees continue to establish themselves. The timing has to be right, to mimic natural floods and water flows. Preliminary results appear positive.

More recently, the Nature Conservancy announced good news from along the banks of the Yampa River in northwestern Colorado. In June 2005, Great Outdoors Colorado (GOCO) awarded $750,000 (funds directed from the state's lottery system) to further protect almost 1,300 acres of ranchland along the river. The Yampa is important in its own right, as one of the last nearly free-flowing rivers in the Colorado River Basin. A more free-flowing river allows for the perpetuation and health of the riparian habitat and its dominant cottonwood species. The Yampa property, part of the Wolf Mountain Ranch, includes important wildlife habitat and what has been described as a "globally rare forest of narrow-leaf cottonwood, box elder, and red-osier dogwood. . . ." The habitat is home to nesting bald eagles, river otters, and between ninety and one hundred bird species, including Sandhills cranes and the last of the Columbian sharp-tailed grouse in Colorado. The second-largest elk herd in the state also frequents this area, so it's easy to understand why it's such a natural treasure. It's an environment that's completely connected, as are the efforts to protect it. By means of a conservation easement, this latest parcel of land has been added to the 3,100 acres along the Yampa that the Conservancy has worked to protect since 1985. A conservation easement is a practical way to protect lands and habitats. Though binding, it's a voluntary agreement between a land owner and others interested in protecting habitat and keeping rural lands (a working ranch in this case) safe from the kind of development that makes use of such areas in ways that are not always in the best interests of plants, animals, land, or people. As was true for the Yavapai Nation restoration of Fremont Cottonwoods, the Yampa River project has succeeded because of the collaboration of many groups: the Nature Conservancy, GOCO, the Routt County Purchase of Development Rights Program, the Colorado Conservation Trust, and, of course, residents of the valley. It's interesting to note that in some of these joint ventures or consortium-style efforts, groups that formerly have been adversaries are now allies.

Closer to metro Denver, another smaller but no less important example of a conservation easement has emerged as part of the South Platte River Heritage Corridor Plan. Under terms of the agreement, forged between the Trust for Public Land (TPL), a national nonprofit land conservation organization and owners of the McIntosh Dairy (the oldest and largest working dairy in Colorado's largest metropolitan county—Adams), 245 acres will be kept from development while the owners, the McIntosh family, will be able to keep the land and continue their business. The easement includes bottomlands where hundred-year-old cottonwoods still preside over the landscape.

Farther north, the North Dakota Forest Service has developed a remarkably complete educational booklet, one created for the bicentennial celebration of the Lewis and Clark expedition. Titled "Lewis & Clark Cottonwoods," the booklet pays special tribute to the tree that served the expedition more than any other species the Corps of Discovery encountered. The booklet also tells the story of the natural history of the cottonwood in North Dakota, a context inevitably tied to that of the Missouri River and other waterways essential to riparian forests. And as the rivers have changed and been changed, so has the sustainability of the cottonwood. One section of the booklet assesses the current status of cottonwoods in the state. The Forest Service presents and faces the difficulties that natural conditions impose for the trees, as well as those created by urban sprawl, continuous development, agricultural practices, browsing and overgrazing by wild and domestic animals, and competition from invasive trees and grasses. To reinstate the health of the riparian forests will require focused, consistent effort by a consortium of public and private groups working to restore not only the cottonwood, but the riparian habitat of which the tree is such an integral part.

In the long term, it's true to say that as goes the cottonwood so will go the Missouri—and hundreds of other American rivers and waterways. To this end, the North Dakota Forest Service has developed a many-pronged approach to education and action. The booklet offers a well-rounded source for both efforts. Basic information about the life and history of the trees in North Dakota, as they relate to the Lewis and Clark expedition, expands to include a range of suggested activities for adults as well as K–12 schoolchildren. During the bicentennial the Forest Service offered free cottonwood seedlings to schools and, in cooperation with the Arbor Day Foundation, provided guidelines (with all the pesky logistics addressed) on how to promote special tree-planting activities. A video and a list of activities for home and school use offer easy access to useful information. Even though the Lewis and Clark bicentennial celebration ended in 2006, the need to educate all our generations about the intrinsic value of cottonwood trees remains. Most importantly, the North Dakota Forest Service is, as it declares, "committed to wisely managing the remaining cottonwood forests for future generations to enjoy." This booklet provides a proactive model for other communities and states wishing to learn and act on behalf of their cottonwood—and riparian—forests.

Another North Dakota cottonwood treasure is a Web page called "Questions on: Cottonwood" run by Ron Smith, a horticulturist with the North Dakota State University Extension Service. If you're a North Dakota resident, you can e-mail Smith and expect an answer within a reasonable amount of time (summer is always busy). But the beauty of this Web site is that Smith has probably already answered any question you might have about cottonwoods. All you have to do is read it. If you're not a North Dakota resident, expect to receive robo-mail, an automatic response to your request, saying you'll have to get in line behind those who are. Residents, please identify yourselves as such in the initial e-mail.

Like North Dakota, the state of Wyoming has been disparagingly described, both in the past and the present, as "treeless." According to a woman who lived there at the time, the town of Cheyenne could only claim twelve trees in 1876. Planting trees was an important effort for early Cheyenne residents, and cottonwoods gained a special place of prominence. The first cottonwoods came from Nebraska. Successive plantings took place up through the middle of the twentieth century. The

Plains Cottonwood officially became the Wyoming state tree on February 1, 1947. But lately residents have gotten worried about trees again—namely, cottonwoods. Those trees planted mid-century have just about reached the end of their life spans. So a new group has taken root in Cheyenne to help out: The Cheyenne Cottonwood Society. The goal of its thirty or so members is to plant cottonwood trees along the historic streets in Cheyenne, to keep the heritage of those earlier trees alive. The group has gotten support from the city council as well as the Cheyenne Urban Forestry department, although with the caution to plant wisely and incorporate biological diversity in their efforts. The urban forester suggests planting the trees widely apart (cottonwood roots love to roam in their search for water), and to include elms and other companion species. It's good advice.

Cheyenne is not the only place to have a newly formed cottonwood society (could this also be a trend?). *Way* up north, north to Alaska, as a matter of fact, Sally Koppenberg, one of the "Dirt Divas" who maintains a gardening blog of the same name, invites readers to join the "Save the Cottonwood Society." She's taken up the cause of the native cottonwood species—*Populus balsamifera* subsp. *trichocarpa*—better known as the Black Cottonwood. Her descriptions of the way these trees are generally viewed echo the disregard for cottonwoods in many places: considered more weed than wood, and cut down as developers move in to make way for houses. In the East, the Swamp Cottonwood suffered a similar fate when it continued to be cut down for commercial use in midcentury, when Donald Culross Peattie hoped that it would be replanted so the species could survive. Today, it is considered a "rare" tree, as the examples from Cincinnati and Canada described above reveal, though people seem to have forgotten the cause of its rarity. Is there an object lesson here?

According to Koppenberg, in her part of the state—south-central Alaska— development has greatly increased during the last fifteen years. She estimates that 5–10 acres are cut down daily. While the general perception of the Black Cottonwood is "that old thing," Koppenberg sings the praises of these trees, with both fierceness and facts. "If you start a voice, it will pick up," she says, the determination in her own voice palpable. Describing a quality that sounds as if it could be one way to counter the effects of global warming, she relates the unique ability of these trees to gather carbon both above and below ground, at a rate faster than other trees do. Cottonwoods are good for the soil they inhabit, she points out. They enrich it and increase its ability to retain water. And, we've already talked about the ability of all species of cottonwood to slow or contain erosion. The Black Cottonwood benefits many other species. Bees use the resin, which acts like a repellent, to plug their hives and keep out intruders. Koppenberg notes that the chemical in the resin is being used to create special protective paint that can keep harmful animals and insects away from other trees—her mother even makes a Cottonwood Balm soap from the early buds. Poplar hybrids (and the Black Cottonwood is, after all, a poplar, cousin to the better regarded quaking aspen) are the subject of much research at the moment, according to the NRCS. *P. trichocarpa* × *deltoides* (a cross between the Black Cottonwood and the Eastern) is quick to grow, quick to resprout, and noted for its value in both ornamental and conservation plantings, as well as its use for paper, lumber, and plywood. Scientists note how similar the hybrid is to the native. In addition to the many other species we've noted that cottonwoods provide habitat for, add butterflies and brown bats for the Black Cottonwood. Koppenberg adds to the list of praises the fact that two species of butterflies winter over in Alaska. One prefers the exclusive quarters of the Black Cottonwood. Edible parts of the tree provide food for tiny shrews and voles. Koppenberg's father, a well-known log home builder in Alaska, has proved the exception to the don't-build-with-cottonwood rule. He's built two cottonwood log homes and has bragging rights on size, shape, and the two-for-several ratio of cottonwood to spruce logs it would otherwise have taken. Added benefits include insulation quality and endurance. His descriptions, based on real-life experience working with cottonwood, echo the industry uses for cottonwood described by no less an authority than the NRCS mentioned above, a unit of the USDA (not that government approval would necessarily mean anything in Alaska). Koppenberg encourages her readers to plant cottonwoods, and answers in advance the age-old issue of inconvenience. In addition to the troublesome "cottoning" of the females, the Black Cottonwoods drop long, messy catkins that tend to decompose in an unpleasant heap if not attended to. But rather than discourage their planting, this Dirt Diva advises readers to plant them out there at the edge of the woods—a good idea, as long as the woods are still there. That way, the trees can continue to reproduce in the wild naturally, and the plantings will not be limited, as they are already in so many places, to the dangers of monoculture from either having all clones or all males. As a designer of landscape space, Koppenberg always begins with the trees, in spite of the often puzzled looks on her clients' faces. Such plantings will help reduce another fear about which Koppenberg, formally trained in environmental science and a nursery owner, worries. The valley where she lives is subject to high winds. Cottonwoods, the tallest trees in her part of Alaska—90 feet is common and 120 feet is not unheard of— provide shelter from the wind (remember that windbreak formula? A tree can provide shelter three feet out from itself for every foot of growth). If the Black Cottonwoods continue to be cut at their current rate, though, Koppenberg fears the result will be a "wind tunnel" through the valley. The economic damage alone from such a result would certainly be more severe than the cost of cleaning up cotton and sticky catkins every summer.

Efforts like those of the Cheyenne Cottonwood Society and the Save the Cottonwood Society of Palmer, Alaska, have all the earmarks of successful restoration efforts. They're local. They're focused on native species. The proponents have practical working knowledge of their own environments. And yet, both efforts take the longer view—to create, sustain, and protect their part of the world for the generations that are coming.

Recovery from the Oops! Factor

In chapter 7, I mentioned the story of how cottonwoods were cut down along a stretch of the St. Joe River in St. Maries, Idaho, in which several hundred cottonwood trees were cut down before officials realized they were in violation of state and federal law, and actually increased the dangers from flooding by their actions.

Oops! stories about cottonwoods appear in local news accounts all over the country. But one in Iowa had a happy ending. When an Osceola County family wasn't looking, the county engineer cut down almost thirty cottonwoods that had been planted by Barbara Berkenpas's great-grandfather. Though Barbara's family had offered several options to cutting down what was known as "Cottonwood Mile," the county engineer moved in with the cutting crews anyway. A lawsuit followed, with the Berkenpas family winning about $7,000. A further appeal resulted in an award of nearly $23,000 and took into consideration the "sentimental, historic, and environmental value" of the cottonwoods. While we're on the topic of legal approaches to trees, let's consider it from the trees' point of view.

Legal Standing

Though not posited in legal terms, Native American philosophical, spiritual, and scientific beliefs have long held the view of equality toward natural objects. The cottonwood still holds the place of sacred personhood at the center of the Omaha tribe. It still stands at the sacred center of the Sun Dance ceremony, as it has since the beginning of that practice. The philosophy contained in the three words "all my relations" reveals a Native American view toward nature that grants all living beings certain inalienable rights.

When first Martin Buber (1878–1965) and then Joseph Campbell (1904–87)—long after native people put the concept into practice worldwide—

spoke of objects in nature as "thou" rather than "it," I wonder whether they hoped that perhaps some day the notion would find its way into other realms beside those of philosophy and mythology.

In 1972, Christopher Stone, a lawyer with an extensive philosophical background himself, after tossing out an idea for his students to mull over between classes, wrote an essay that eventually became reading material for a case before the Supreme Court: "Should Trees Have Legal Standing?" *Sierra Club v. Morton* pitched Disney World against a wilderness area in the Sequoia National Forest. Stone's essay asked: Why not grant legal status to rivers, mountains, stones, or trees—and yes, even cottonwoods? After all, he pointed out, such inclusion is in keeping with American legal history, of granting rights to ever more members of the community—to slaves, women, aliens, even the unborn. Why not let nature stand as an entity before the law? Not in an unfettered status, mind you; not a status necessarily or exclusively equal to that of humans. But Stone argued for status nevertheless: the right of a forest to be represented, to legally resist harmful or injurious activities. If a corporation could have legal status before the court, then why not a forest, a river, or a mountain—as more than mere property?

Part of Stone's legal argument rests on the pillar of legal representation being granted to those that cannot speak for themselves: human beings, incapable for any number of reasons (mental incompetence, for example), as well as corporations and government entities. Stone argues for guardianship or trusteeship so that natural objects can be represented in a way that gives them their own legal standing; not just because harm to them causes injury to the humans associated with them, but because the damage is suffered by the river (water pollution), the mountain (strip mining), or the trees (clear cutting) in question.

In a retrospective essay written for the twenty-fifth anniversary of "Should Trees Have Standing?" and published in 1996, Stone identifies trends in environmental law judgments that echo arguments in his initial work. Those arguments once found their way into Supreme Court Justice William O. Douglas's reading material for the Disney case (Disney won, by the way, but withdrew from the project). They just might continue to reverberate in positive findings for the environment in legal cases. I contacted Professor Stone to ask whether he had updated the essay since 1996 (he hasn't) and whether he thought that the legal concepts he outlined will eventually be incorporated into American law. His metaphorical answer:

I don't know. . . . Ideas, like trees (and here I'm judging from my own hedges) can take years to seriously bud and branch until the roots have established, and then they can just take off on you when they're ready.

Cottonwoods and Global Warming

Whether you believe it's a purely natural phenomenon or one brought about by human activity, the most serious environmental danger facing the world right now is global warming. One dangerous result, known as the "greenhouse effect" refers to the increased amount of carbon dioxide trapped in our atmosphere. One small way that several conservation organizations suggest to counter the effects of rising CO_2 levels is to plant trees. These "lungs of the earth" take in carbon dioxide and return oxygen to the air as part of their natural life cycle. Cottonwoods should rank high on the list of planting choices. By the simple fact of their quick growth they return more oxygen to the atmosphere. Like all trees, they sequester carbon, from their roots to their leaves. Just how much carbon became a question of interest to scientists at the Biosphere 2 Laboratory (B2L) in Arizona. Even though short-term experiments previously indicated that cottonwoods might sequester more carbon in the soil than other trees, a four-year study at B2L didn't show such results. Using Eastern Cottonwoods, scientists grew the trees under varying levels of carbon dioxide. Trees "inspire," or breathe in carbon dioxide and ultimately return oxygen to the air. While the biomass of the trees increased and higher levels of carbon dioxide in the soil boosted the level of respiration in the soil, eventually the soils became depleted of nutrients and the trees did not sequester additional carbon. But planting trees—and planting cottonwoods—is still a good idea as a way to return oxygen to the atmosphere.

Cottonwoods, along with trees in general, enhance life on Earth in more ways than we might know. All conservation organizations discuss the importance of trees in one way or another. A local group in my state does a great job of educating us all to the absolute necessity of trees. The Colorado Tree Coalition (CTC) devotes a whole section on its Web page to "Tree Benefits." The first sentence on the page sets the tone: "Trees are major capital assets in cities across the U.S." From carbon sequestration to outlining what a big tree can do for you (reduce greenhouse gas, save energy), CTC provides free tree information at your fingertips.

Cottonwood Genome

As part of a major scientific breakthrough, the Black Cottonwood (*P. trichocarpa*) will go down in history as the first cottonwood—and the first tree—to have its DNA completely sequenced. In September 2004 the U.S. Department of Energy (DOE) announced results of a two-year international effort to complete the sequencing. Partners included Genome Canada, Sweden's Umeå Plant Science Centre, Stanford University, and Ghent University in Belgium.

Why the Black Cottonwood—the tree Sally Koppenberg tells us so many Alaskans view with indifference, if not disdain? This tree is "one member of the most ecologically and commercially valuable group of trees in North America," says the DOE (so much for the stereotype of "that old thing"). Yet its commonality, as Dr. Gary Whitham points out in his research on the effect of cottonwood genetics on riparian habitats, is exactly why such research is important, since for so long the focus has been on rare or exotic species.

You might also ask why such research has taken place under the auspices of the DOE. In the hope that scientists can learn more about the amount of carbon that cottonwoods (poplars) sequester, the DOE looks toward expanding the use of these trees to help with cleanup at waste sites. The effort, known as phytoremediation, is discussed in following paragraphs. The new genome sequencing information will help science, forestry, and industry produce faster growing trees as well as trees with more biomass. Using cottonwoods as a biomass source is not new. Such research dates back at least two decades. It's just that we're learning more about the research and its applications, especially since the pressure is on to develop more and cleaner alternative energy sources.

Why did scientists choose to sequence the Black Cottonwood instead of, say, the oak, which an Arbor Day Foundation vote in 2001 proved to be America's favorite tree (now the National Tree in fact)? Why not the pine, or the redwood? Remember economist E. F. Schumacher's "small is beautiful" philosophy? The Black Cottonwood's genetic package is more compact, forty to fifty times smaller than the pine genome and easier to work with—although 500 million or so letters of genetic code seems like a lot to the lay cottonwood-lover's eye. More than 40,000 genes have been found in the Black Cottonwood. Scientists from many different areas are comparing these genes to those of other plants, to find out what common contents plants have carried—and which ones they have changed or discarded—during their long existence on Earth.

So is the cottonwood genome sequencing just intended to build a bigger, better tree? Are only economic considerations important? The use of alternative fuels certainly counts as a social consideration. But I like what David L. Emerson, Canada's minister of industry, said—that the sequencing information can be used to protect forests from insects and diseases, that it can help to develop ways to detect, diagnose and control problems, which could translate to better conservation and management of forests. In my opinion he makes the same argument for applying cottonwood genetic sequencing information that Nancy Reagan and Michael J. Fox have made for applying information about the human genome to medical science.

Another reason that genome sequencing of the Black Cottonwood is so important concerns forest biology. Surprisingly, not as much is known about the biological
interactions in forests as we might assume. Much past research has focused on
individuals—a tree or a plant—rather than a group of trees or a group of plants.
Perhaps this shift to study plant communities in a genetic context reflects our times,
like the global change in consciousness to consider the world as a village and not just
individual countries taking up space next to one another. After all, unless we refused
to look, our view of ourselves could never be the same once we saw that Apollo shot
of Earth taken from the moon, of our little blue marble turning in space.

Yet, even the good news about the sequencing of the Black Poplar gene comes with
warnings. (I debated whether to include this section in chapter 7 or chapter 8. It probably belongs in both.) Judging from the use of the word "Frankentree" in regard to the
genetic engineering of trees, the general public remains unconvinced about the long-
term safety of genetically modified plants—even though corn, for example, has been
modified for more years than most of us have been aware of (my grandfather, a county
agricultural extension agent, sang the praises of such modification in the 1940s and
1950s). Frankentree appears often in literature leery or critical of some of the intended
applications of manipulating tree genetics. With its genetics now completely revealed,
the Black Cottonwood has become the "model tree" for research. How do we balance
the potential for danger with that of the good this knowledge brings?

Via e-mail, I asked fifteen people you've met previously in this book what they
thought the potential would be for positive results for forestry (science and industry) of the genome sequencing project—as well as any drawbacks, specifically the
fears of Frankentree. Three responded. Keith Wood, urban and community
forester with Colorado State University (and former city forester for Westminster,
Colorado) answered this way:

> There is probably cause for some concern when manipulating tree
> species/crops/humans/etc. genetics. But if kept to proper uses and regulated
> as such, I see benefits to this research and development. As foresters we need
> to be aware of this development and ensure that good forestry is a part of all
> this. Species diversity, management and/or disturbance in many ecosystems
> are important for their sustainability over time. If we start developing mono-
> cultures of fabricated species and using them widely we might have some
> negative issues.
>
> On a related note, timber harvesting on public forests brings out the best and
> worst in everybody . . . so in many cases it has ceased or goes through a

tediously slow process of public review/appeals. So where do we get the wood fiber we all demand on a daily basis? This puts more pressure on our privately owned forests and thus they turn to genetic manipulation to achieve fast fiber production, relatively quick rotations, etc. So we do need this research and development. . . .

Martin Flanagan, a Big Tree hunter from Montana and the Western Director for the Champion Tree Project International, had this to say:

I believe that the sequencing project is a good thing. What we choose to do with it remains a mystery. There may be drawbacks; however, the positive will no doubt outweigh them. I don't believe that the "Frankentree" fears are unwarranted. Only in the hands of the wrong people, however, and mistakes can happen.

David Gilbert, Public Affairs Manager for the DOE Joint Genome Institute, said, "We have not had to respond to the 'Frankentree' issue . . . simply because we don't (and aren't contemplating) doing any genetic engineering of the tree, but our colleagues may." He added that the genome research is due to be published soon in the journal *Science.*

I mentioned phytoremediation briefly above. This is a method that uses plants to absorb heavy metals or soil and water contaminants. Not all that new, it was part of the Supreme Court case in 1980 that granted the "patenting of life." In 1997 phytoremediation was used as part of the cleanup of nitrates that leaked into the soil and groundwater at Rocky Flats, the site of a former plutonium trigger manufacturing plant in Colorado. Cottonwoods were the plant of choice. They were hybrids, the 'Jeronimus' cultivar of the native Plains Cottonwood developed by Colorado nurseryman Ken Jeronimus and his son Mike. A more current use is in Danbury, Connecticut, at old hat manufacturing sites heavily polluted with mercury. Richard Meagher, a plant geneticist from the University of Georgia, led a team of graduate students working with fewer than fifty cottonwood trees to help with the cleanup. But the trees aren't ordinary cottonwoods. They've been genetically programmed to take in the mercury as a nutrient. By the nature of the process they become "sacrifice" trees. By absorbing the toxins they become toxic themselves and are disposed of accordingly. As Meagher explained to a newspaper reporter, the trees are eventually cut down and incinerated.

As you might expect, controversy surrounds the use of genetic modification, even in as necessary an effort as phytoremediation. Questions arise on all sides of the many issues. Even a practitioner like Meagher acknowledges that his may not be the best approach, but he counters with the consequences of even more dangerous methods of digging up contaminated soil and moving it. Critics, from the Sierra Club to scientists who are plant geneticists themselves, worry about the escape of genetically altered species into the wild; and wind, of course, carries cottonwood pollen. Accidents happen. Scientists and researchers stress the use of sterile or "cottonless" males (although cottonless does not necessarily mean sterile). It's a complex set of issues that can boast as many wonders as it conjures horrors. Nothing is ever all good or bad, all black or white. The best we can do is to become informed, to study all the sides, to ask questions, to work with whom and what we know in figuring out solutions and approaches to the complex times we live in. These are not issues that can be resolved in sound bites or simplistic thinking. Yet, what a wonder, that we can now look so deeply into the book of the Black Cottonwood and begin to read all its chapters.

Sources

For information on the Swamp Cottonwood find, see "Cottonwood Hollow. Concord Township, Lake County. 77.65 acres." The Cleveland Museum of Natural History. http://www.cmnh.org/naturalareas/cottonwood-hollow.html

Aynsley Morris reported on the Swamp Cottonwood find in Canada in "New Tree for Carolinian Canada." *Carolinian Canada Newsletter.* Winter 2003–2004. p. 1.

Suzanne Probart and Matt Schmader provided information on Tree New Mexico and riparian restoration efforts in New Mexico during a personal interview on May 7, 2006. *See also* the Tree New Mexico Web site at: http://www.treenm.com/index.htm and the City of Albuquerque Open Space Division at: http://www.cabq.gov/openspace.

Mesta, Robert. Joint Venture Coordinator, Sonoran Joint Venture, U.S. Fish and Wildlife Service. "Fort McDowell Yavapai Nation Rejuvenates Bald Eagle Habitat." Birdscapes: News from International Habitat Conservation Partnerships. http://library.fws.gov/Birdscapes/fall01/Ppus.html

U.S. Fish and Wildlife Service. 2001 Volunteer Report. http://library.fws.gov/Pubs/Volunteer2001.pdf

The Yampa agreement is discussed in a news release, "Agreement Protects Wildlife, Ranchlands and Views Along Yampa River," available at http://nature.org/

wherewework/northamerica/states/colorado/press/press1988.html, as well as in a brief article in the "United States" column of *Nature Conservancy,* Winter 2005, pp. 53–54.

As part of habitat restoration at Imperial Wildlife Refuge in Arizona, volunteers for the U.S. Fish and Wildlife Service helped plant more than 14,000 trees—including cottonwoods.

James Henson, plant physiologist and species coordinator, describes the research on establishing Fremont Cottonwoods in "Fremont's Cottonwood/*Populus fremontii* S. Wats." USDA. National Resources Conservation Center. 2002. http://Plant-Materials.nrcs.usda.gov

Directions for planning riparian restoration using the pole–planting technique are published in "Guidelines for Planning Riparian Restoration in the Southwest" and "The Pole Cutting Solution/based on two decades of technology development at the Los Lunas Plant Materials Center/Guidelines for Planting Dormant Pole Cuttings in Riparian Areas of the Southwest." Both published by the Plant Materials Program. Los Lunas Plant Materials Center. Natural Resources Conservation Service. USDA. n.d.

"Lewis & Clark Cottonwoods" (educational booklet). Compiled by Glenda E. Fauske. North Dakota Forest Service. 2002. http://www.ndsu.nodak.edu/ndsu/lbakken/forest/infoed/doc/lewis_clark.pdf.

"As trees are lost to age and wind, locals seek to restore canopy." AP. *Star-Herald News.* 5/212006. http://www.starherald.com/

Koppenberg, Sally. "In Defense of the Cottonwood." Dirt Divas Gardening blog. April 20, 2006. http://dirdivasgardening.blogspot.com/2006/04/in-defense-of-cottonwood.html

Phone interview with Sally Koppenberg. May 30, 2006.

Professor Christopher D. Stone's arguments for legal standing to natural objects appear in *Should Trees Have Standing: and Other Essays on Law, Morals and the Environment.* Oceana Publications. Dobbs Ferry, New York. 1996. His statement on the future of this argument comes from e-mail correspondence dated May 25, 2006.

Neesom, Guy. "Black Cottonwood *Populus balsamifera* ssp. *trichocarpa* (Torr. & Gray ex. Hook.) Brayshaw." Plant Guide. National Resources Conservation Center. USDA. 2003.

See the "Tree Benefits" portion of the Colorado Tree Coalition's Web site at
http://www.coloradotrees.org.

For information on the genome sequencing of the Black Cottonwood, see, "The
Book Opens on the First Tree Genome." DOE Joint Genome Institute. U.S.
Department of Energy. Office of Science. Press release. September 21, 2004.
http://www.jgi.doe.gove/News/news_9_21_04.html

For information on the Arbor Day vote that resulted in the oak becoming America's
National Tree, see "Oak Becomes America's National Tree."

http://www.arborday.org/media/pressreleases/pressrelease.cfm?id=95

Responses to the Poplar Genome Project and "Frankentree" issues from Keith
Wood, Martin Flanagan, and David Gilbert were from e-mail correspondence.

Information on the use of cottonwoods at the Rocky Flats site comes from "Rocky
Flats may turn to trees for cleanup." Paula Aven. *Denver Business Journal.* March
21, 1997. 48 (28): 13A and an interview with Mike Jeronimus on March 6,
2006.

Dr. Richard Meagher was interviewed about the Danbury project by AP reporter
Paul Elias for an article entitled "Pollution solution lovely as a tree," which
appeared in the *Rocky Mountain News* on July 4, 1005. p. 11B.

EPILOGUE

In considering the good news along with the bad, I am heartened by what I see throughout our country and our continent when it comes to the number of people working to restore cottonwood trees and riparian habitat. Though often they don't seem aware of it—they're too busy "doing"—those who lead local, state, national and international efforts, teaching the rest of us about the value and importance of cottonwoods, are doing a tremendous job. It's a job that never ends. Working to restore riparian habitat in the western United States alone could be—is—a life-time's work. We are fortunate to have so many competent, dedicated professionals out on the front lines serving as city foresters, county extension agents, community foresters, Big Tree Coordinators, naturalists, state and federal foresters, leaders of citizen conservation groups, horticulturists, nursery operators, concerned landowners, and thousands of volunteers who support these programs every year. I believe the tide is turning in preservation and restoration efforts. Consortiums exist all over the country, formed by groups that were formerly adversaries (and still are, in some instances). But in many more cases, Native American tribes and the Bureau of Land Management, for instance, or local water boards and conser-

Fremont Cottonwood at Horseshoe Canyon, Canyonlands National Park, Utah.
Scratchboard illustration by Evan Cantor, reprinted with permission.

vancy groups are working together. Joint ventures and creative partnerships are springing up everywhere in the name of cottonwoods.

I can't claim to impart any great or final wisdom on the life and times of cottonwood trees. I'm a pilgrim on this path myself. The best I can do is what I have done and will continue to do: report what I have learned, and share it. There is always more to learn. But I had to close the book at last and tell the most important stories. Perhaps you will write and tell me what I missed. I offer what I have learned in the hope that next time you see the cottonwood star you will feel some connection between earth and sky, some connection between yourself and nature that you didn't feel before. In parting, let me tell you one more story.

Changing the Game

What I know about golf could be written on the head of a pin. My last attempt at the game was more than thirty years ago. I tallied up so many "points" that my friends wondered whether I'd confused the game on the green with bowling. One (the same one who asked, "Who's going to read a book about cottonwood trees?!") suggested I go to the clubhouse. Tell the man behind the counter your score, he said . . . the club gives a prize to each person who has the highest one at the end of a game. Basking in my naiveté, I did as I was told, only to discover that I provided the staff entertainment that day. Ah, well.

During the course of a routine checkup last year, my dentist, Dr. Mike Golinvaux, asked what I'd been up to lately. I told him about my book. His eyes lit up as he began to tell a story—about golf and cottonwood trees. He ended by inviting me to visit the trees. One perfect Colorado summer evening a few months later, I met Mike at his golf course. We scooted out to the lower nine on a golf cart. I didn't learn to play golf, but I did gain an important perspective about cottonwood trees and the game.

Valley Country Club was established in 1956. It's located in what was once, like so much of the Denver metropolitan area, rural farmland. Cherry Creek runs through the course. In addition to willows and cattails, all three species of cottonwood native to Colorado flourish along the creek and on the course: Plains, Lanceleaf, and Narrowleaf. Eastern cottonwoods have also been planted here, along with one or two that look suspiciously like Black Cottonwoods (the balsam poplar species native to the northwest). The trees are well cared for, pruned and shaped to a special perfection. Branch litter barely hits the ground before it's picked up, though a few wild and fertile females have been allowed to grow. Several other species share the undulating greens, including pine, honey locust, and elm.

Cottonwood tree "player" at Valley Country Club, Aurora, Colorado.
Photo by Kathleen Cain

But the cottonwoods lend an unmistakable character to the course: graceful, solid, and . . . stubborn.

We wheel out to the eleventh hole for my first lesson in cottonwood-and-golf logistics. It's par 4, Mike explains, arrowing a hand down the fairway, then signaling left and sighting the flag, up an incline at the far distant hole. But before a golfer can even think about the hole or the par, he or she had better give serious consideration to "that darn tree." A mature cottonwood stands its ground, just to the left about 200 yards down the fairway, in front of a "dead zone" opposite a pond. The tree's location rules out any chance of cutting the corner, a move that can shorten a long hole and lessen the number of strokes. Forget aesthetics or cool shade. The tree has become part of the game. And in spite of the golfer's quip that "trees are 80 percent air," this *Populus deltoides* Bart. ex Marsh. subsp. *monilifera* (Ait.) Eckenwalder—Plains Cottonwood—has to be reckoned with to gain a final score of 4 or under on the hole.

Like the eleventh, the fourteenth hole also has its *Populus deltoides* Nemesis, another cottonwood. Again because of location, the major hazard is hitting the tree and ruining the shot. To get over the tree requires a lot of oomph. Yet too much oomph sends the ball sailing through the fairway. Hitting the tree makes a bad shot worse. Such a hit results in "pinball action"—as the ball pings off the 20 percent of tree that isn't air! The ball can spin off bark, limbs, or leaves at any angle—with 360 to choose from! Sometimes golfers don't even bother looking for a ball when that happens. The tree forces the shot.

The trees, here long before people or golf courses, bring their own set of hazards. Several serve as nesting sites for raptors—harrier hawks, perhaps, based on Mike's description of the way the birds fold their wings and drop onto their victims. To a hawk, a golf ball scooting along the ground looks a lot like a mouse running through a field, and hawks can be especially testy during nesting season. Several unprotected scalps have felt the sting of talons, and golfers watch out for each other when the game moves beneath the "falcon trees."

The cottonwoods on the course get special attention. We stop to examine the copper wire laced up along the trunks and carefully netted around the upper branches: lightning rods. Since they are part of the course's treasure, great care is taken to protect the trees. Even the lower branches are pruned to increase the challenge. The cottonwoods here are not just another bunch of pretty trees. They're part of the game. If anything were to happen to even one of them, the whole game would change, Mike tells me. The parallel in nature is hard to miss. Whether we're talking about the challenge of golf or the challenge of letting cottonwoods live in their natural settings, if we lose the trees, the whole game changes. . . .

EDUCATIONAL RESOURCES

American Forests—http://www.americanforests.org
Created in 1875, before state or national forests were created, for "the protection of the existing forests of the country from unnecessary waste." Today American Forests "works to protect, restore, and enhance the natural capital of trees." Supports national and international conservation efforts. Home of the National Big Tree Register.

Arbor Day Foundation—http://www.arborday.org/index.cfm
Continuing the tradition established by founder J. Sterling Morton in 1872, the foundation inspires people to plant, nurture, and celebrate trees—and offers all the resources necessary to do just that.

Cooperative/County Extension Services—To find your local cooperative/county extension office, go to: http://www.csrees.usda.gov/Extension/index.html

Cottonwood Photo Page—These elegant photographs by nature writer and photographer Gregory McNamee are among my favorites. http://www.flickr.com/photos/gregorymcnamee

Cottonwood Questions/Questions on: Cottonwoods
http://www.ext.nodak.edu/extnews/hortiscope/tree/cttnwood.htm
North Dakota horticulturist Ron Smith has probably answered any question you might have about cottonwoods. Designed for North Dakota residents (please identify yourselves as such if you e-mail), this online source can help homeowners, gardeners, and others. One of the best cottonwood resources.

Cottonwood Tree Lesson Plan—
http://www.kshs.org/teachers/trunks/pdfs/symb_jtree.pdf
Part of a "history trunk" lesson on state symbols created by the Kansas State Historical Society. Can be adapted for various levels to teach K–12 students about cottonwoods. Though designed specifically for Kansas, can also be adapted for other locales.

Donald Shobe Woodwork
This woodworking artist sees and releases the intrinsic natural beauty of cottonwoods by creating one-of-a-kind bowls. Though they can be used for food storage and serving, you may want to find a special place to display such

a unique work of art. Google Don/Donald Shobe Bowls. Or, contact Donald
Shobe at 8884 S. Brentwood Street/Littleon, CO 80128. 303-933-0847.

Lewis and Clark 200.gov—Educational Resources
The Cottonwood Tree. http://www.lewisandclark200.gov/edu/cottonwood.cfm
This entire Web site is an educator's gold mine. Even though the bicentennial
of the expedition has come and gone, cottonwood trees are becoming more
important all the time in scientific discovery and research.

Moonwise Herbs —http://www.moonwiseherbs.com/main.htm
Moonwise Herbs is "designed to cultivate earth wisdom through herbal
education, wild and whole foods meals, compassionate communication,
handcrafted herbal wares and more!!" I highly recommend the cottonwood
soap— deliciously fragrant and softens your skin. The cottonwood body spray
was too strong for me, but it works great as an air freshener! There's no other
scent like it!

Nature Conservancy—http://www.nature.org
The Conservancy works "to preserve the plants, animals, and natural
communities that represent the diversity of life on Earth by protecting the
lands and waters they need to survive."

PLANTS Database—http://plants.usda.gov
The PLANTS Database "provides standardized information about the vascular
plants, mosses, liverworts, hornworts, and lichens of the United States and its
territories." A standard reference source for botanists, horticulturists,
foresters and others involved with plants. Searchable by common name.
Distribution maps available for all species.

Sierra Club—http://www.stateforesters.org/sflist.html

Spirit of Trees—http://www.spiritoftrees.org/trees/trees.html
A resource for therapists, educators, environmentalists, storytellers, and tree
lovers! You will find here an abundance of resources, in particular a varied
collection of multicultural folktales and myths. Also provides links to major
tree organizations worldwide. *See also* "Curricular Resources" link.

State Foresters—See the National Association of State Foresters at:
http://www.stateforesters.org/sflist.html

USDA Forest Service—http://www.fs.fed.us/
Most of your questions about our national forests can be answered here.

GLOSSARY OF TERMS

Bole—Tree trunk

Cambium—Paper-thin layer of "inner bark" where new wood is made

Chimaera or Chimaera graft—Grafted plant with stock (bottom) from one plant and scion (top) of another

Cottonwood star—Shape of a five-pointed star made by pith inside branches of cottonwood trees

Cultivars—Abbreviation for "cultivated varieties"

Flower buds—Buds that grow below the terminal bud, containing the flowers

Genus—Member of a species with additionally distinct characteristics

Leaf scar—Scar left at the place where last year's leaf fell off the tree

Lenticel—From the Latin word for "little mouth"; features that look like dots on twigs and help trees breathe

Micropropagation—Another word for cloning, a way to create an identical genetic replica from plant tissue

Petiole—Leaf stalk

Phloem—Tissue that carries food (sugar) down through the trunk to the roots and other parts of the tree

Scion—Top of a tree (used in grafting)

Species—Group of (in this case) plants with similar characteristics that can reproduce sexually among themselves

Stock—Bottom of a tree (used in grafting)

Stomata—Millions of tiny cells on the under surface of leaves that open and close to release oxygen and moisture

Terminal bud—Bud that grows at the very tip of the branch on each year's new growth

Vegetative propagation—Ability of plants to reproduce in ways other than by seed

Xylem—Tissue that carries water and nutrients up through the trunk to the leaves and other parts of the tree

BIBLIOGRAPHY

Adams, Robert. *Cottonwoods*. Smithsonian Institution Press. Washington, D.C. 1994.

"Agreement Protects Wildlife, Ranchlands and Views Along Yampa River." http://nature.org/wherewework/northamerica/states/colorado/press/press1988.html.

Aldrich, Bess Streeter. *The Rim of the Prairie*. University of Nebraska Press. Lincoln. 1960.

Arbor Day Foundation Web site: http://www.arborday.org/programs/NationalTree/cottonwood.cfm.

"As trees are lost to age and wind, locals seek to restore canopy." AP. *Star-Herald News.* 5/21/2006. http://www.starherald.com.

Aven, Paula. "Rocky Flats may turn to trees for cleanup." *Denver Business Journal.* March 21, 1997. 48 (28):13A.

Balog, James. *Tree: A New Vision of the American Forest.* Barnes & Noble Publications. New York. 2004.

Black Elk, Nicholas. *The Sacred Pipe: Black Elk's Account of the Seven Rites of the Oglala Sioux.* Recorded by Joseph Epes Brown. University of Oklahoma Press. Norman. 1953.

"The Book Opens on the First Tree Genome." DOE Joint Genome Institute. U.S. Department of Energy. Office of Science. Press release. September 21, 2004. http://www.jgi.doe.gove/News/news_9_21_04.html.

Bosworth, Dale. "Water Doesn't Have to be for Fighting." Speech to Workshop: Western Water Supply Challenges. September 29, 2004. Salt Lake City, Utah. http://www.fs.fed.us/news/2004/speeches/09/water.shtml.

Bureau of Land Management. "BLM Publishes New Grazing Regulations to Improve Management of Public Lands Grazing." http://www.blm.gov/nhp/news/releases/pages/2006/pro60712_grazing.htm.

Burnside, Wesley. *Maynard Dixon, Artist of the West.* Brigham Young University Press. Provo, Utah. 1974.

Cain, Jerome A. Calculations of circumference of cottonwood tree at Dewitt, Nebraska.

Caldecott, Moyra. *Myths of the Sacred Tree*. Destiny Book. Rochester, Vt. 1993.

Chilson, Peter. "County caught in cottonwood quagmire." *High Country News*. Western Roundup. May 12, 1997. http://www.hcn.org/hcn.Article?article_id=3219.

Cirlot, J. E. "Tree." *A Dictionary of Symbols*. Philosophical Library. New York. 1962.

"City-grown air pollution is tougher on country trees." Cornell News http://www.news.cornell.edu/releases/July03/ozone_trees.html.

Colette. *Earthly Paradise/An Autobiography*. Drawn from her lifetime writings by Robert Phelps. Farrar, Straus & Giroux. New York. 1966.

Colorado Tree Coalition. http://www.coloradotrees.org.

"Colorado. United States" (column). *Nature Conservancy*. Winter 2005.

Colton, Harold S. *Hopi Kachina Dolls*. University of New Mexico Press. Albuquerque. 1959 (rev. ed).

Community College Park. City of Westminster, Colorado. Department of Parks & Recreation. n.d.

Cooper, D. T. "*Populus deltoides* Bartr. ex. Marsh/Eastern Cottonwood." http://forestry.about.com/library/silvics/blsilpopdel.htm.

Custer, George A. *My Life on the Plains*. Sheldon and Company. New York. 1874.

Cutright, Paul Russell. *Lewis & Clark: Pioneering Naturalists*. University of Nebraska Press. Lincoln. 1969.

Daugherty, Ray. "*Populus sargentii* Dode/Plains Cottonwood." Handout to students. 2002–2005.

Daughters of the Republic of Texas. "The Daughters of the Republic of Texas present The Story of the Alamo/Thirteen fateful days in 1836." 1997.

Davis, Tony. "Traffic flow 1, trees 0." *High Country News*, Vol. 27, No. 22. November 27, 1995. http://wwwhcn.org/servlets/hcn.PrintableArticle? article_id1484.

"Deaths Preliminary Data for 2004." Centers for Disease Control. National Center for Health Statistics. http://www.cdc.gov/nchs/products/pubs/pubd/ hestats/prelimdeaths04/preliminarydeaths04.htm.

Dickey, Roland F. *New Mexico Village Arts*. University of New Mexico Press. Albuquerque. 1990 (first printed in 1949).

"Earth." *The World Book Encyclopedia*. World Book, Inc. Chicago. 2004. pp. 26–31.

Eiseley, Loren. "How Flowers Changed the World." *The Immense Journey*. Vintage Books (Random). New York. 1957.

Elias, Paul. "Pollution solution lovely as a tree." *Rocky Mountain News*. July 4, 2005. p. 11B.

Encyclopedia of North American Trees. Ed. Sam Benvie. Firefly Books. Buffalo, N.Y. 2000.

The Encyclopedia of Religion. 2d edition. Ed. Lindsay Jones. Macmillan Reference USA (Thomson Gale). Detroit. 2005.

Fergus, Charles. *Trees of New England: A Natural History*. FalconGuide. Guildford, Conn., and Helena, Mont. 2005.

Fire Effects Information System (FEIS). USDA Forest Service. Index of Species Information. "Populus balsamifera ssp. balsamifera." http://www.fs.fed.us/database/feis/plants/tree/popbalb/index.html.

Flanagan, Martin. Western director, Champion Tree Project International (CTP). Comments on CTP activities and *Populus* genome sequencing. E-mail correspondence during 2005.

"Ft. Peck Community College cottonwood plantings." *Tribal College Journal*. http://www.tribalcollegejournal.org/themag/backissues/winter2005/winter2005oc.htm.

Geological Time Scale. Web Geological Time Machine. University of California, Museum of Paleontology. http://www.ucmp.berkeley.edu/help/timeform.html.

George, Kristine O'Connell. *Old Elm Speaks: Tree Poems*. Il. by Kate Kiesler. Clarion Books. New York. 1998.

Gilbert, David. Comments on *Populus* genome sequencing. E-mail correspondence during August 2006.

Gypsy Moth Management in the United States: A Cooperative Approach Environmental Impact Statement. United States Department of Agriculture, Forest Service, Animal and Plant Health Inspection Service. November 1995.

Reported as "Gypsy Moth Tree Preference page." Ohio State University
Extension Service. http://lucas.osu.edu/gm/fulltree.htm.

Gilmore, Melvin R. *Uses of Plants by the Indians of the Missouri River Region.*
University of Nebraska Press. Lincoln and London. 1977. From the *Thirty-third
Annual Report of the Bureau of American Ethnology.* Washington: Government
Printing Office. 1919.

Gregg, Josiah. *Commerce of the Prairies.* J. W. Moore. Philadelphia. 1881.

Grinnell, George Bird. *Pawnee Hero Stories and Folk-Tales.* University of Nebraska
Press. Lincoln. 1961.

Guinness Book of World Records 2006. Guinness World Records Limited. London.
2005.

Haley, J. Evetts. *Charles Goodnight, Cowman and Plainsman.* University of Oklahoma
Press. 1949.

Hay, John. "A Tree and a Star," in *A Beginner's Faith in Things Unseen.* Beacon Press.
Boston. 1995.

Heat-Moon, William Least. *Prairyerth (a deep map).* Houghton Mifflin. Boston.
1991.

Henson, James, "Fremont's Cottonwood/*Populus fremontii* S. Wats." USDA.
National Resources Conservation Center. 2002. http://Plant-
Materials.nrcs.usda.gov

Hillerman, Tony. *Tony Hillerman's Navajoland.* University of Utah Press. Salt Lake
City, Utah. 2001.

Hogan, Linda. "All My Relations," in *Dwellings.* W. W. Norton. New York and
London. 1995.

Holler, Clyde, ed. *The Black Elk Reader.* Syracuse University Press. Syracuse, N.Y.
2000.

Holling, Holling Clancy. *Tree in the Trail.* Houghton Mifflin. Boston. 1942, 1970.

Hopi Stories of Witchcraft, Shamanism, and Magic. Ekkehart Malotki and Ken Gary.
University of Nebraska Press. Lincoln and London. 2001.

Hopi Tribe Web page. http://www.nau.edu/~hcpo-p/arts/kachina.htm.

Horgan, Paul. *Great River: The Rio Grande in North American History.* Wesleyan
    University Press/University Press of New England. Hanover. 1984.

Iverson, Peter. *Diné: A History of the Navajos.* University of New Mexico Press.
    Albuquerque. 2002.

Jacobs, Warren David, and Karen I. Shragg. *Tree Stories: A Collection of Extraordinary
    Encounters.* SunShine Press Publications. Hygiene, Colo. 2002.

Jacobson, Arthur Lee. *North American Landscape Trees.* Ten Speed Press. Berkeley,
    Cal. 1996.

Jean, George. *Writing: The Story of Alphabets and Scripts.* Discoveries. Harry N.
    Abrams. New York. 1992.

Jeronimus, Mike, owner of Box Elder Creek Nursery, Lochbuie, Colorado.
    Personal interview on March 6, 2006.

Johnson, Kirk. Chief curator chair, Department of Earth Sciences, Denver
    Museum of Nature & Science. E-mail correspondence concerning fossil
    record of *Populus* species.

Johnson, Kirk, and Robert G. Raynolds. *Ancient Denvers.* Denver Museum of
    Nature & Science. 2003.

"Kansas. Kansas State Tree." Netstate.com.
    http://www.netstate.com/states/symb/trees/ks_cottonwood.htm

Kaza, Stephanie. *The Attentive Heart: Conversations with Trees.* Fawcett Columbine.
    New York. 1993.

Kloefkorn, William, and Ted Kooser. *Cottonwood County.* Windflower Press.
    Lincoln, Neb. 1979.

Knight, Paul J., Spencer G. Lucas, and Anne Cully. "Early Pleistocene
    (Irvingtonian) Plants from the Albuquerque Area, New Mexico." *Southwestern
    Naturalist.* September 1996. 41(3): 207–217.

Knopf, F. L., et al. "Conservation of riparian ecosystems in the United States."
    Wilson Bulletin 100: 272–284.

Koppenberg, Sally. "In Defense of the Cottonwood." Dirt Divas Gardening blog.
    April 20, 2006. http://dirtdivasgardening.blogspot.com/2006/04/in-
    defense-of-cottonwood.html.

Kroeber, Alfred L. *The Arapaho*. University of Nebraska Press. Lincoln and London. 1983.

Landis, Thomas D., et al. "Sex and the Single Salix: Considerations for Riparian Restoration." *Native Plants*. Fall 2003. pp. 111–117.

Lavender, David. *The Way to the Western Sea: Lewis and Clark Across the Continent*. Harper & Row. New York. 1988.

Lenz, Mary Jane. *Small Spirits: Native American Dolls from the National Museum of the American Indian*. Smithsonian Museum of the American Indian (in association with University of Washington Press). Washington and New York. 2004.

Leopold, Aldo. *A Sand County Almanac*. Oxford University Press. New York. 1948.

Lewington, Richard and David Streeter. *The Natural History of the Oak Tree*. Dorling Kindersley. London/New York/Stuttgart. 2003 (1st American ed.).

Lewis and Clark Trail Heritage Foundation, Inc. http://lewisandclark.org.

"Lewis & Clark Cottonwoods" (educational booklet). Compiled by Glenda E. Fauske. North Dakota Forest Service. 2002. http://www.ndsu.nodak.edu/ndsu/lbakken/forest/infoed/doc/lewis_clark.pdf.

The Lewis and Clark Journals: The Abridgment of the Definitive Nebraska Edition. Ed. Gary E. Moulton. University of Nebraska Press. Lincoln and London. 2003.

Linford, Laurance D. *Navajo Places: History, Legend, Landscape*. University of Utah Press. Salt Lake City. 2000.

"Lone Tree." Merrick County Area History & Attractions. http://www.cconline.net/community/attractions.htm.

"Lone Tree." Nebraska Heritage Trees. Nebraska Forest Service. University of Nebraska. http://www.nfs.unl.edu/NHTrees.htm.

Man, Myth & Magic: The Illustrated Encyclopedia of Mythology, Religion and the Unknown. Ed. Richard Cavendish. Marshall Cavendish. New York. 1995.

Manchester, Steven R., et al. "Foliage and Fruits of Early Poplars (Salicaceae: *Populus*) from the Eocene of Utah, Colorado, and Wyoming" (manuscript). Florida Museum of Natural History. University of Florida. Gainesville. 2003.

Mason, Jim. "Cottonwood Borer." Great Plains Nature Center (Wichita, Kansas) Web site. http://www.gpnc.org/cowoodborer.htm.

Mattes, Merrill J. *The Great Platte River Road.* Nebraska State Historical Society Publications. Volume XXV. Lincoln, Neb. 1969.

McGaa, Ed (Eagle Man). *Mother Earth Spirituality: Native American Paths to Healing Ourselves and Our World.* Harper. San Francisco. 1990.

McGraw-Hill Encyclopedia of Science and Technology. Vol. 18. 9th ed. New York. 2002.

McMahon, James P., et. al. "The Potential for Restoration Along the Virgin River in Zion National Park." Grand Canyon Trust. 2001.

Medicine Man Gallery presents MaynardDixon.org http://www.maynarddixon.org/articles/mdixon3.html.

Morris, Aynsley. "New Tree for Carolinian Canada." *Carolinian Canada Newsletter.* Winter 2003-2004. p. 1. http://www.carolinian.org/Publications/ newslet_dec2003.pdf.

Morrissey, Jenifer. "Awed by Cottonwoods." *green line ONLINE.* 11(1): 16. Spring 1999. Colorado Riparian Association. http://www.coloradoriparian.org/GreenLine/V11-1/Cottonwoods.html.

eNature. National Wildlife Federation. http://ww.eNature.com.

Naughton, Gary. *"The Cottonwood: Prairie Pioneer." Wildlife and Parks.* 53 (3): 3–7. May–June 1996.

Nauschutz, Mark. *Flora from the Gardens of the Alamo.* n.d.

"Nebraska Heritage Trees." Nebraska Forest Service. University of Nebraska. http://www.nfs.unl.edu/NHTrees.htm.

Nesom, Guy, and James Henson. "Black Cottonwood/*Populus balsamifera* ssp. *trichocarpa* (Torr. & Gray ex Hook.) Brayshaw." USDA. National Resource Conservation Plant Guide. 2003.

Norris, Kathleen. "Dreaming of Trees." *The Place Within: Portraits of the American Landscape by Contemporary Writers.* Ed. Jodi Daynard. W. W. Norton. New York and London. 1997.

Ogren, Thomas Leo. *Allergy-Free Gardening: The Revolutionary Guide to Healthy Landscaping.* Ten Speed Press. Berkeley and Toronto. 2000.

The Omaha Tribe of Nebraska. http://www.omahatribeofnebraska.com/index.html.

Original Journals of the Lewis and Clark Expedition 1804–1806. Ed. Reuben Gold
  Thwaites. Arno Press. New York. 1969.

Patent, Dorothy Hinshaw. *Plants on the Trail with Lewis and Clark.* Clarion Books.
  New York. 2003.

Pearce, C. M., and D. G. Smith. "Plains cottonwood's last stand: Can it survive
  invasion of Russian olive onto the Milk River, Montana floodplain?"
  Environmental Management. 28(5): 623–637. November 2001.

Peattie, Donald Culross. *A Natural History of Trees of Eastern and Central North
  America.* Houghton Mifflin. Boston. 1950.

Peattie, Donald Culross. *A Natural History of Western Trees.* Bonanza Books. New
  York. 1950.

Phillips, H. Wayne. *Plants of the Lewis & Clark Expedition.* Mountain Press
  Publishing. Missoula, Mont. 2003.

"Populus spp. Family: Salicaceae. Cottonwood." Technology Transfer Sheet. Center
  for Wood Anatomy Research. USDA Forest Service. Madison, Wis. http://
  www2.fpl.fs.fed.us/TechSheets/HardwoodNA/htmlDocs/populussp.html.

"*Populus × acuminata* Rydb. (pro sp.) [*angustifolia × deltoides*] Lanceleaf
  Cottonwood. PLANTS Profile. Natural Resources Conservation Service.
  USDA. http://plants.usda.gov.

"Porcupine–Cheyenne." Digital image from the Northwestern University Digital
  Library Collections. The North American Indian (1907–1930) v. 06, The
  Piegan. The Cheyenne. The Arapaho. ([Seattle]: E. S. Curtis; [Cambridge,
  Mass.: The University Press], 1911), plate no. 216.

Probart, Suzanne, executive director of Tree New Mexico. Personal interview on May
  7, 2006, in Albuquerque, New Mexico, and subsequent e-mail correspondence.

Pyle, Robert Michael. *The Thunder Tree.* Houghton Mifflin. New York. 1993.

Ridington, Robin and Dennis Hastings (In'aska). *Blessing for a Long Time: The
  Sacred Pole of the Omaha Tribe.* University of Nebraska Press. Lincoln and
  London. 1997.

Robinson, Roxana. *Georgia O'Keeffe: A Life.* Harper & Row. New York. 1989.

Rogers, Walter E. *Tree Flowers of Forest, Park, and Street.* Dover. New York. 1965.

Ronda, James P. *Finding the West: Explorations with Lewis and Clark.* University of New Mexico Press. Albuquerque. 2001.

Russell, Sharman. "Home on the range." http://www.zianet.com/snm/range.htm.

Sabini, Meredith, ed. *The Nature Writings of C. G. Jung.* North Atlantic Books. Berkeley, Cal. 2002.

Savage, Candace. *Prairie: A Natural History.* Greystone Books. Douglas & McIntryre. Vancouver/Toronto/Berkeley. 2004.

Schmader, Matthew, supervisor for the City of Albuquerque Open Space Division. Personal interview and tour of "Our Lady of the Ditch" on May 7, 2006, and subsequent e-mail correspondence.

Schweinfurth, Kay Parker. *Prayer on Top of the Earth: The Spiritual Universe of the Plains Apaches.* University Press of Colorado. Boulder. 2002.

"The Scythe in the Tree." Lincoln Beacon. July 30, 1896. Quoted in Blue Skyways. http://skyways.lib.ks.us/genweb/lincoln/scythe.htm.

"Scythe Tree. Waterloo, New York." http://roadsideamerica.com/attract/NYWATscythe.html.

Sheldon, Addison. *History and Stories of Nebraska.* Lincoln. University Publishing Co. 1926.

Shigo, Alex. *100 Tree Myths.* Shigo and Trees. Durham, N.H. 1993.

Silvics of North America. Volume 2. Hardwoods. USDA. Forest Service. Agriculture Handbook 654. http://www.na.fs.fed.us/spfo/pubs/silvics_manual/table_of_contents.htm.

Skagen, Susan K., et al. "The Importance and Future Condition of Western Riparian Ecosystems as Migratory Bird Habitat" *USDA Forest Service General Technical Report*, PSW-GTR-191. 2005.

Smith, Ron. Hortiscope. "Questions on: Cottonwood." NDSU Extension Service.http://www.ext.nodak.edu/extnews/hortiscope/tree/cttnwood.htm.

Spotts, Peter N. "Life under one tree's rule?" *Christian Science Monitor.* October 14, 2004. http://www.csmonitor.com/2004/1013/p13s01.html.

Stack, R. W. and H. A. Lamey. "Deciduous Tree Diseases." PP-697 (Revised), November 1995. North Dakota State University. NDSU Extension Service. http://www.ext.nodak.edu/extpubs/plantsci/hortcrop/pp697-1.htm#Heart.

Steele, Thomas J., S. J. *Santos and Saints: The Religious Folk Art of Hispanic New Mexico.* Ancient City Press. Santa Fe, N.M. 1994 (First printed in 1974).

Sternberg, Guy, and Jim Wilson. *Native Trees for North American Landscapes from the Atlantic to the Rockies.* Timber Press. Portland and Cambridge. 2004.

Stone, Christopher D. *Should Trees Have Standing and Other Essays on Law, Morals and the Environment.* Oceana Publications. Dobbs Ferry, N.Y. 1996.

Stone, Christopher D. E-mail correspondence. May 25, 2006.

Street, Jay W. "Rio Grande Cottonwood Tree." Desert USA. http://www.desertusa.com/mag01/jan/papr/cwood.html.

Talbott, Clint. "The clueless tree-killers." *Boulder Daily Camera.* January 29, 2006. http://www.dailycamera.com/bdc/opinion_columnists/article/0,1713,BDC_2490_4421806,00.html.

Thomas, Peter. *Trees: Their Natural History.* Cambridge University Press.Cambridge. 2000.

Thorson, George A. *Bent's Old Fort.* The State Historical Society of Colorado. Denver. 1979. "The Architectural Challenge." pp. 132–133.

Tree New Mexico Web site. http://treenm.com.

Trenbolm, Virginia Cole. *The Arapahoes, Our People.* University of Oklahoma Press. Norman. 1970.

USDA, NRCS. 2005. *The PLANTS Database*, Version 3.5 (http://plants.usda.gov). Data compiled from various sources by Mark W. Skinner. National Plant Data Center, Baton Rouge, La.

"Utah/Zion's geriatric cottonwoods." Hotline (column) in *High Country News.* April 29, 2002.

Van Haverbeke, David F. "*P. deltoides* var. occidentalis Rydb. Plains Cottonwood." http://forestry.about.com/library/silvics/blsilpopdel.htm.

Vickerman, Larry. Director, Denver Botanic Gardens at Chatfield. E-mail corre-
    spondence concerning the growth of Colorado native species of cottonwood at
    the Chatfield Arboretum. June 2006.

Weir, Stuart. *The Native Trees of the Southern Rocky Mountains from Yellowstone to
    Santa Fe.* http://home.earthlink.net/~swier/rkymtntrees.html.

Wood, Keith. Assistant Staff Forester. Urban and Community Forestry. Denver-
    Metro Office. Colorado State University. Communication about all aspects of
    cottonwoods/Populus. E-mail correspondence during 2005–2006.

Wright, Barton. *Hopi Kachinas: The Complete Guide to Collecting Kachina Dolls.*
    Northland Press. Flagstaff. 1977.

INDEX

H

Hackbart: Daryl, 98–101; Susan, ix,
  98–101
Hagerty, Donald, 134
"Hanging Trees," 162, 164, 166ff.
Hartley, Marsden, 134
Hastings, Dennis, 122
Heat-Moon, William Least, 160
Heaton, P. S., 156
Helvie: Lorie, x, 166, 169; Scott, x,
  166, 169
Henry Ford Museum, 109
Heye Foundation, 123
"Hi Trees" (Omaha, Nebr.), x, 160,
  161(illus.)
High, Dave, 162
Hidatsa People, 115, 142, 143, 144
Hillegass, Craig, x, 95–97.
  187(illus.), 189
Hodges, John, ix
Hodgden, Jerry, 161
Hogan, Linda, ix
Holocene epoch, 85
Holling, Holling Clancy, 156
Hopi People: 43, 122, 125, 150;
  katsintithu and, 124, 125, 127
"Hweeldi," 149ff.
Hybridization, natural: 13–14;
  Lanceleaf Cottonwood, 14, 29, 32;
  Narrowleaf Cottonwood, 27, 29, 32;
  Plains Cottonwood and Aspen, 14;
  Plains Cottonwood and Balsam
  Poplar, 14; Plains Cottonwood and
  Narrowleaf Cottonwood, 14, 29, 32.
  See also Cultivars.

I

Ice Age, 68, 84, 85, 65, 176
Idaho, 13, 16, 32, 183–84, 212
Illinois: 139; Swamp Cottonwood
  and, 46

Imagination. See Cottonwoods;
  imagination and.
In'aska. See Hastings, Dennis.
Indiana: Swamp Cottonwood and, 46
Insects. See Cottonwoods; insects and
  pests.
Intergradation, 11–13, 22,
International Poplar Commission, 72
Invasive species, 43, 62, 193, 209. See
  also Russian olive trees; Tamarisk.
Iowa, 212
Ireland, 82
Irving, Washington, 146

J

Jefferson, Thomas 141, 143
Jeronimus, Ken, 70ff., 217; Mike, xi,
  63, 70ff., 217
'Jeronimus' cultivar, xi, 20, 70ff.,
  71(illus.), 217. See also Cultivars.
Jiminy Cricket, 133
"John Wayne: A Love Song,"
  (essay) 135
Johnson, James Wyman, 148
Johnson, Kirk, x, 84, 88
Jung, Carl, 126
Junipers, 40
Jurassic period, 57, 81

K

Kablaya (Spread), 116, 119
Kachina dolls: 36, 124ff.; Blue Corn
  Woman, 125(illus.), 125–127;
  carvers of, 36, 43, 122ff.; definition
  of, 123–26; Santos and, 130, 131;
  symbols, use of, commercial, 123,
  124, 127, 129. See also Katsina;
  Katsintithu; Tithu.
Kansas: 12, 16, 17, 22, 28, 168; Chase
  County, 62, 160; cottonwood as
  state tree, 159; cottonwood lesson

ABOUT THE AUTHOR

A native Nebraskan, Kathleen Cain has always loved cottonwood trees. Her father took her to all the places his family had lived and once showed her a stand of cottonwood trees planted by her great-grandfather in the late 1800s. She decided to write this book when her father showed her the hidden "cotton-wood star."

The Cottonwood Tree: An American Champion is her second nonfiction book. The first, Luna: Myth and Mystery was published by Johnson Books in 1991. An early recipient of a literary fellowship from the Colorado Council on the Arts, she has written and published poetry, essays, and feature articles in both literary and popular magazines. She has been a contributing editor for The Bloomsbury Review since 1982. She retired from Front Range Community College in Westminster, Colorado, in 2003 and has devoted full time to writing since then. She has worked as a volunteer naturalist with Jefferson County (Colorado) Open Space, and plans to pursue her abiding interest in natural history.

Kathleen Cain, Taos, New Mexico.
Photo by Eileen Niehouse, used with permission.